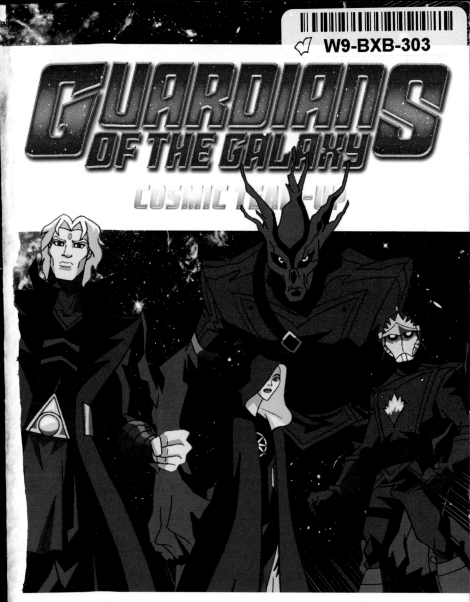

MARVEL UNIVERSE GUARDIANS OF THE GALAXY: COSMIC TEAM-UP. Contains material originally published in magazine form as MARVEL UNIVERSE AVENGERS EARTH'S MIGHTIEST HEROES #18, MARVEL UNIVERSE ULTIMATE SPIDER-MAN #22, MARVEL UNIVERSE HULK: AGENTS OF S.M.A.S.H. #4 and INCREDIBLE HULK #271. First printing 2014. ISBN# 978-0-7851-9031-8. Published by MARVEL WORLDWIDE, INC., a subsidiary of MARVEL ENTERTAINMENT, LLC. OFFICE OF PUBLICATION: 135 West 50th Street, New York, NY 10020. Copyright © 1982, 2013 and 2014 Marvel Characters, Inc. All rights reserved. All characters featured in this issue and the distinctive names and likenesses thereof, and all related indicia are trademarks of Marvel Characters, Inc. No similarity between any of the names, characters, persons, and/or institutions in this magazine with those of any living or dead person or institution is intended, and any such similarity which may exist is purely coincidental. **Printed in the U.S.A.** ALAN FINE, EVP - Office of the President, Marvel Worldwide, Inc. and EVP & CMO Marvel Characters B.V.; DAN BUCKLEY, Publisher & President - Print, Animation & Digital Divisions; JOE QUESADA, Chief Creative Officer; TOM BREVOORT, SVP of Publishing; DAVID BOGART, SVP of Operations & Procurement, Publishing; C.B. CEBULSKI, SVP of Creator & Content Development; DAVID GABRIEL, SVP Print, Sales & Marketing; JIM O'KEEFE, VP of Operations & Logistics; DAN CARR, Executive Director of Publishing Technology; SUSAN CRESPI, Editorial Operations Manager; ALEX MORALES, Publishing Operations Manager; STAN LEE, Chairman Emeritus. For information regarding advertising in Marvel Comics or on Marvel.com, please contact Niza Disla, Director of Marvel Partnerships, at ndisla@marvel.com. For Marvel subscription inquiries, please call 800-217-9158. **Manufactured between 5/16/2014 and 6/23/2014 by SHERIDAN BOOKS, INC., CHELSEA, MI, USA.**

10 9 8 7 6 5 4 3 2 1

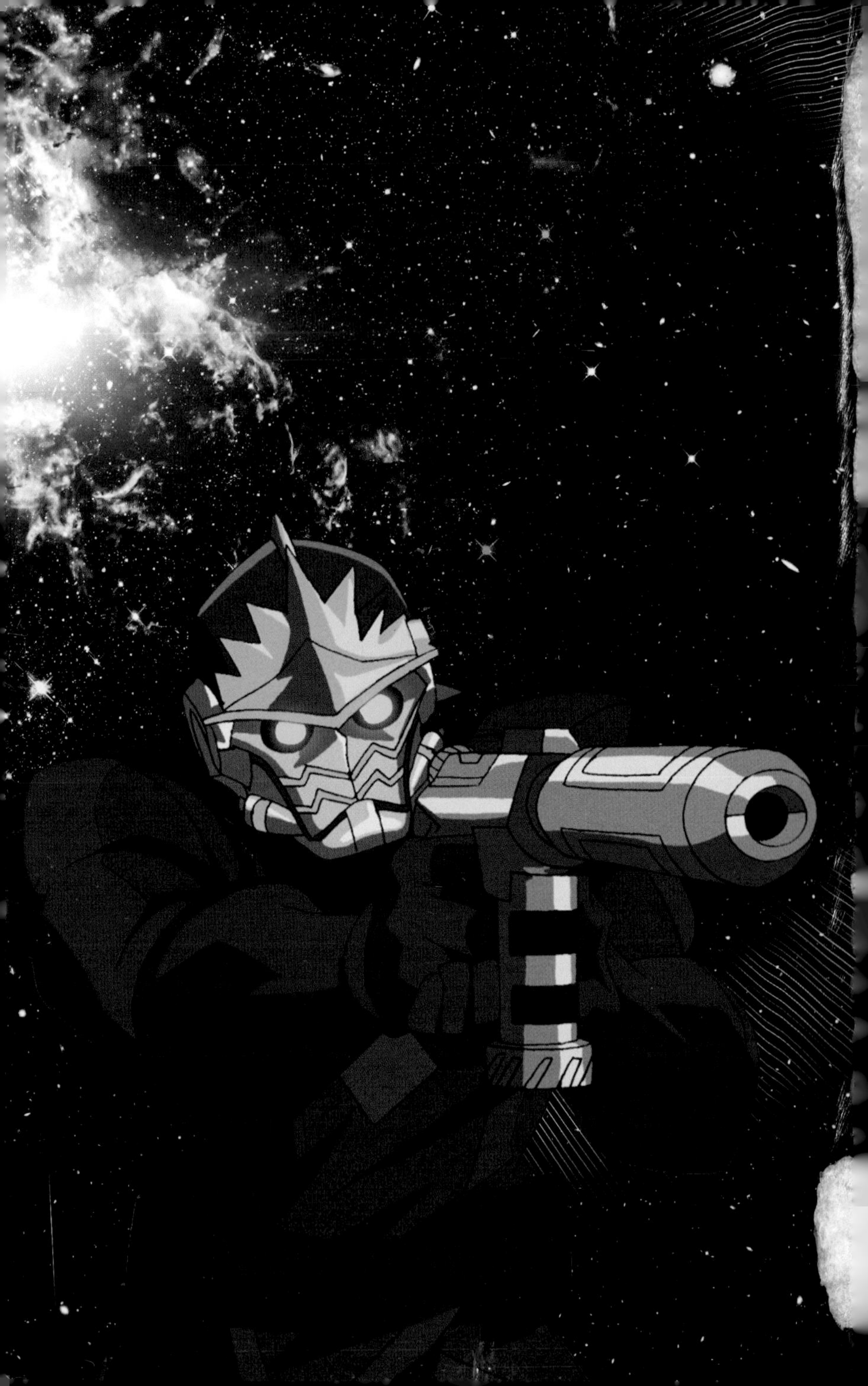

GUARDIANS OF THE GALAXY

COSMIC TEAM-UP

"MICHAEL KORVAC"
WRITERS: **DAN ABNETT** & **ANDY LANNING**
ADAPTED BY **JOSH FINE**
LAYOUT & LETTERING: **JOE CARAMAGNA**
EDITOR: **SEBASTIAN GIRNER**   SENIOR EDITOR: **MARK PANICCIA**

"GUARDIANS OF THE GALAXY"
WRITER: **BRIAN MICHAEL BENDIS**
ADAPTED BY **JOE CARAMAGNA**
EDITOR: **SEBASTIAN GIRNER**
CONSULTING EDITOR: **JON MOISAN**
SENIOR EDITOR: **MARK PANICCIA**

"IT'S A WONDERFUL SMASH"
WRITER: **STEVEN MELCHING**
ADAPTED BY **JOE CARAMAGNA**
EDITOR: **SEBASTIAN GIRNER**
CONSULTING EDITOR: **JON MOISAN**
SENIOR EDITOR: **MARK PANICCIA**

"ROCKET RACCOON!"
WRITER: **BILL MANTLO**   ARTIST: **SAL BUSCEMA**
COLORIST: **BOB SHAREN**   LETTERER: **JIM NOVAK**
EDITOR & COVER ARTIST: **AL MILGROM**
SPECIAL THANKS TO **NELSON RIBEIRO**

COLLECTION EDITOR: **ALEX STARBUCK**
ASSISTANT EDITOR: **SARAH BRUNSTAD**
EDITORS, SPECIAL PROJECTS: **JENNIFER GRÜNWALD** & **MARK D. BEAZLEY**
SENIOR EDITOR, SPECIAL PROJECTS: **JEFF YOUNGQUIST**
SVP PRINT, SALES & MARKETING: **DAVID GABRIEL**
BOOK DESIGNER: **RODOLFO MURAGUCHI**
COVER DESIGNER: **NELSON RIBEIRO**

EDITOR IN CHIEF: **AXEL ALONSO**   CHIEF CREATIVE OFFICER: **JOE QUESADA**
PUBLISHER: **DAN BUCKLEY**   EXECUTIVE PRODUCER: **ALAN FINE**

AND THERE CAME A DAY...A DAY UNLIKE ANY OTHER, WHEN EARTH'S MIGHTIEST HEROES FOUND THEMSELVES UNITED AGAINST A COMMON THREAT...TO FIGHT THE FOES NO SINGLE SUPER HERO COULD WITHSTAND... ON THAT DAY WERE BORN...

EARTH'S MIGHTIEST HEROES! THE AVENGERS

GUEST-STARRING

THE GUARDIANS OF THE GALAXY!

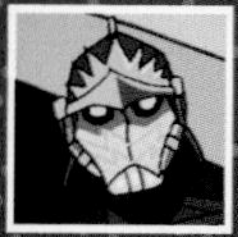

STAR-LORD

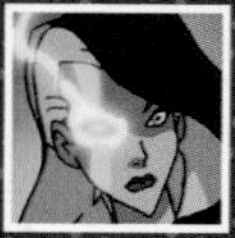

QUASAR

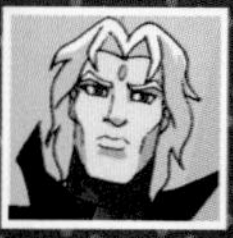

ADAM WARLOCK

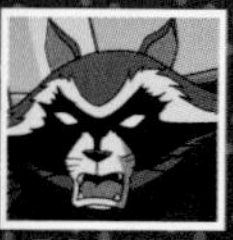

ROCKET RACCOON

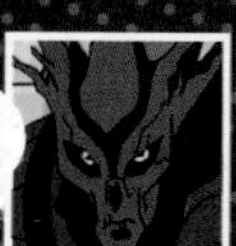

GROOT

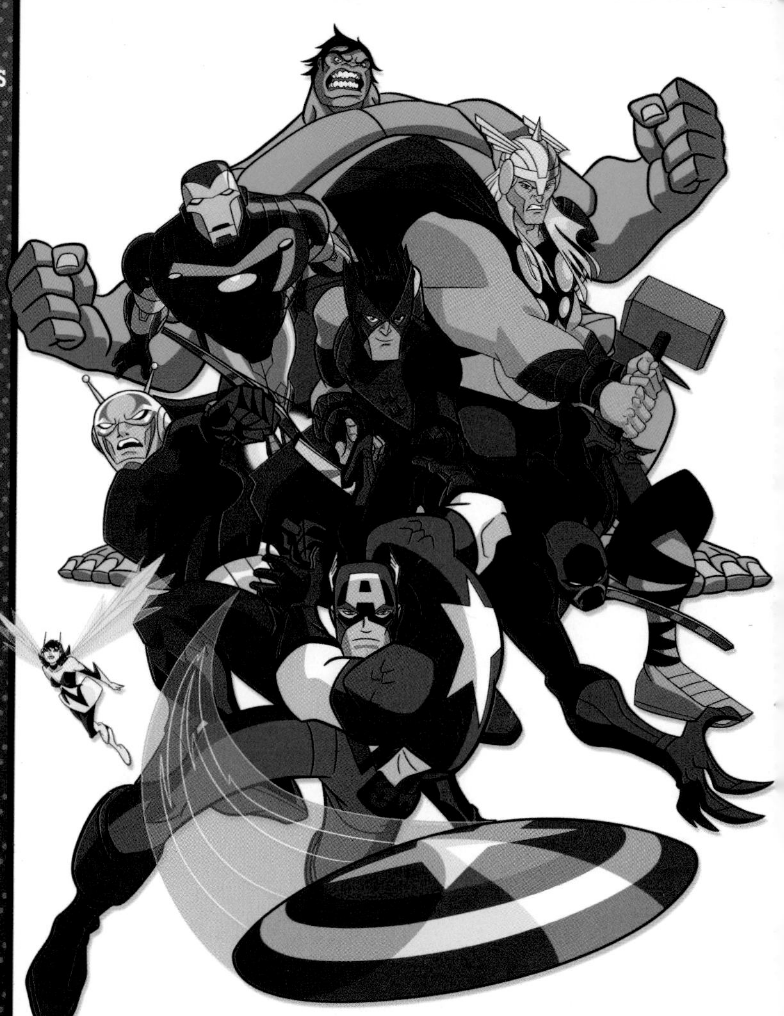

BASED ON
"MICHAEL KORVAC"
BY DAN ABNETT & ANDY LANNING

ADAPTED BY **JOSH FINE**

layouts and lettering by JOE CARAMAGNA

SEBASTIAN GIRNER editor MARK PANICCIA senior editor

AXEL ALONSO editor in chief JOE QUESADA chief creative officer
DAN BUCKLEY publisher ALAN FINE executive producer

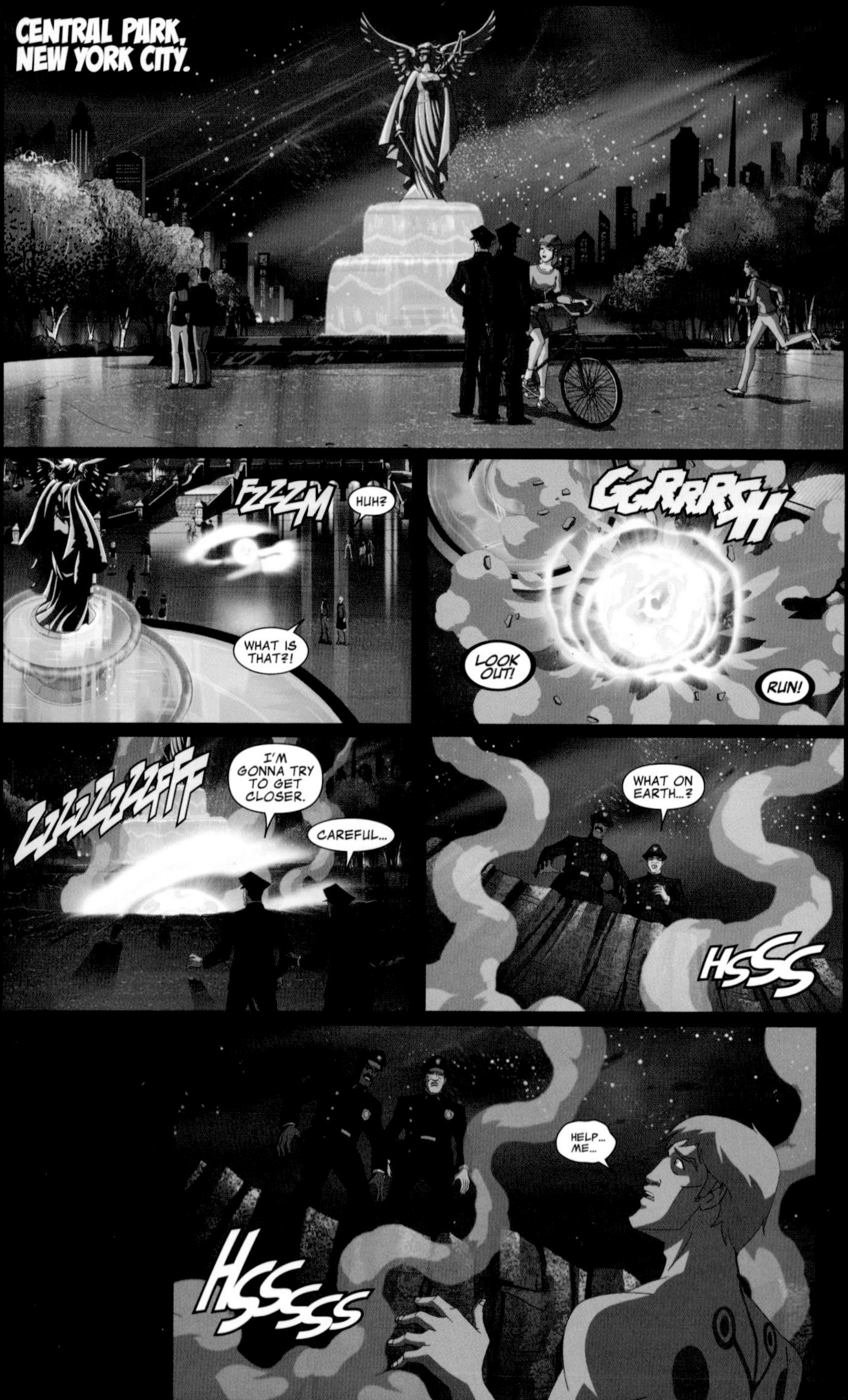
CENTRAL PARK, NEW YORK CITY.
FZZZM
HUH?
WHAT IS THAT?!
GGRRRRCH
LOOK OUT!
RUN!
ZZZZZZZZZFFF
I'M GONNA TRY TO GET CLOSER.
CAREFUL...
WHAT ON EARTH...?
HSSS
HELP... ME...
HSSSSS

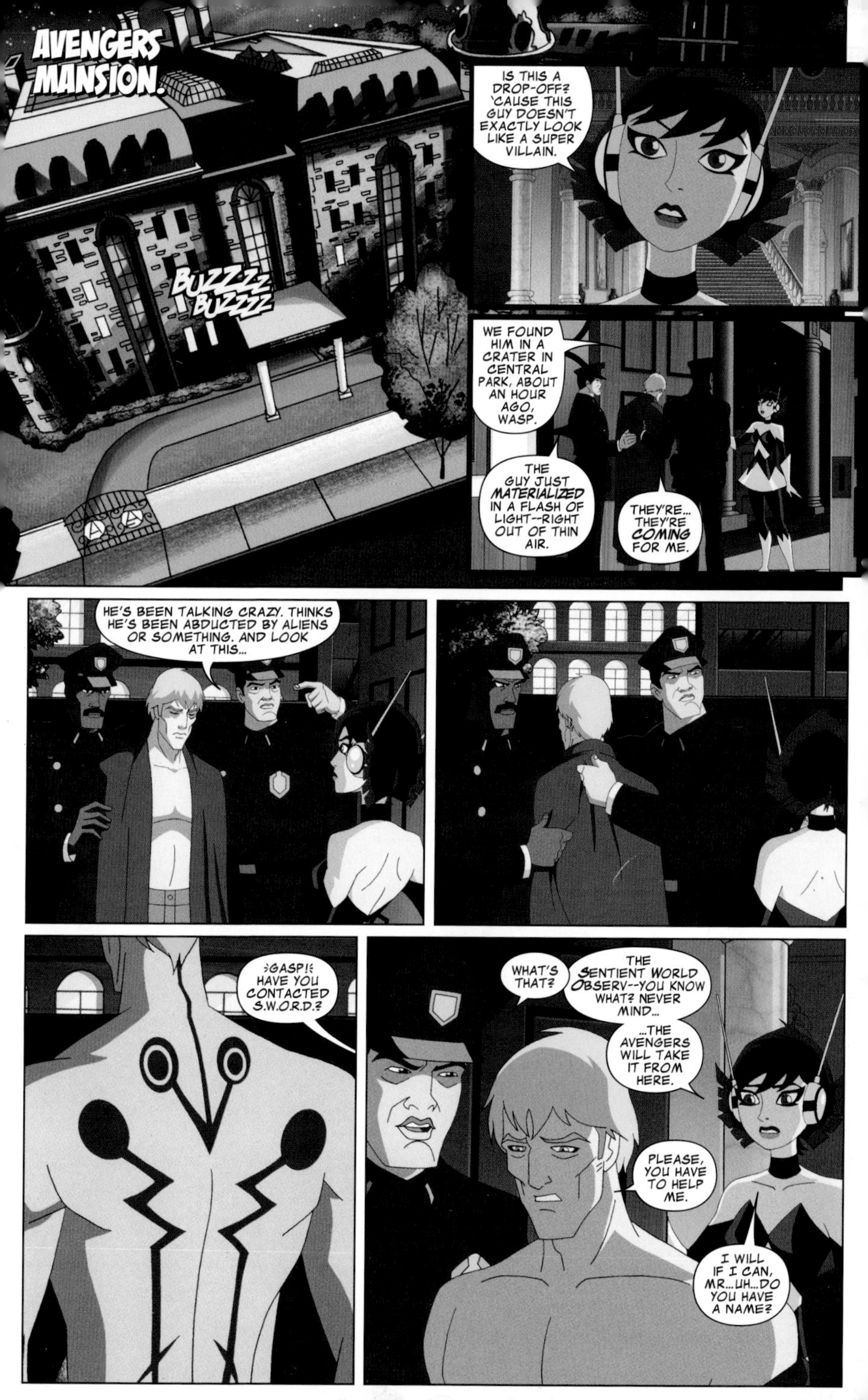
AVENGERS MANSION.
BUZZZZ BUZZZZ
IS THIS A DROP-OFF? 'CAUSE THIS GUY DOESN'T EXACTLY LOOK LIKE A SUPER VILLAIN.
WE FOUND HIM IN A CRATER IN CENTRAL PARK, ABOUT AN HOUR AGO, WASP.
THE GUY JUST MATERIALIZED IN A FLASH OF LIGHT--RIGHT OUT OF THIN AIR.
THEY'RE... THEY'RE COMING FOR ME.
HE'S BEEN TALKING CRAZY. THINKS HE'S BEEN ABDUCTED BY ALIENS OR SOMETHING. AND LOOK AT THIS...
!GASP! HAVE YOU CONTACTED S.W.O.R.D.?
WHAT'S THAT?
THE SENTIENT WORLD OBSERV--YOU KNOW WHAT? NEVER MIND...
...THE AVENGERS WILL TAKE IT FROM HERE.
PLEASE, YOU HAVE TO HELP ME.
I WILL IF I CAN, MR...UH...DO YOU HAVE A NAME?

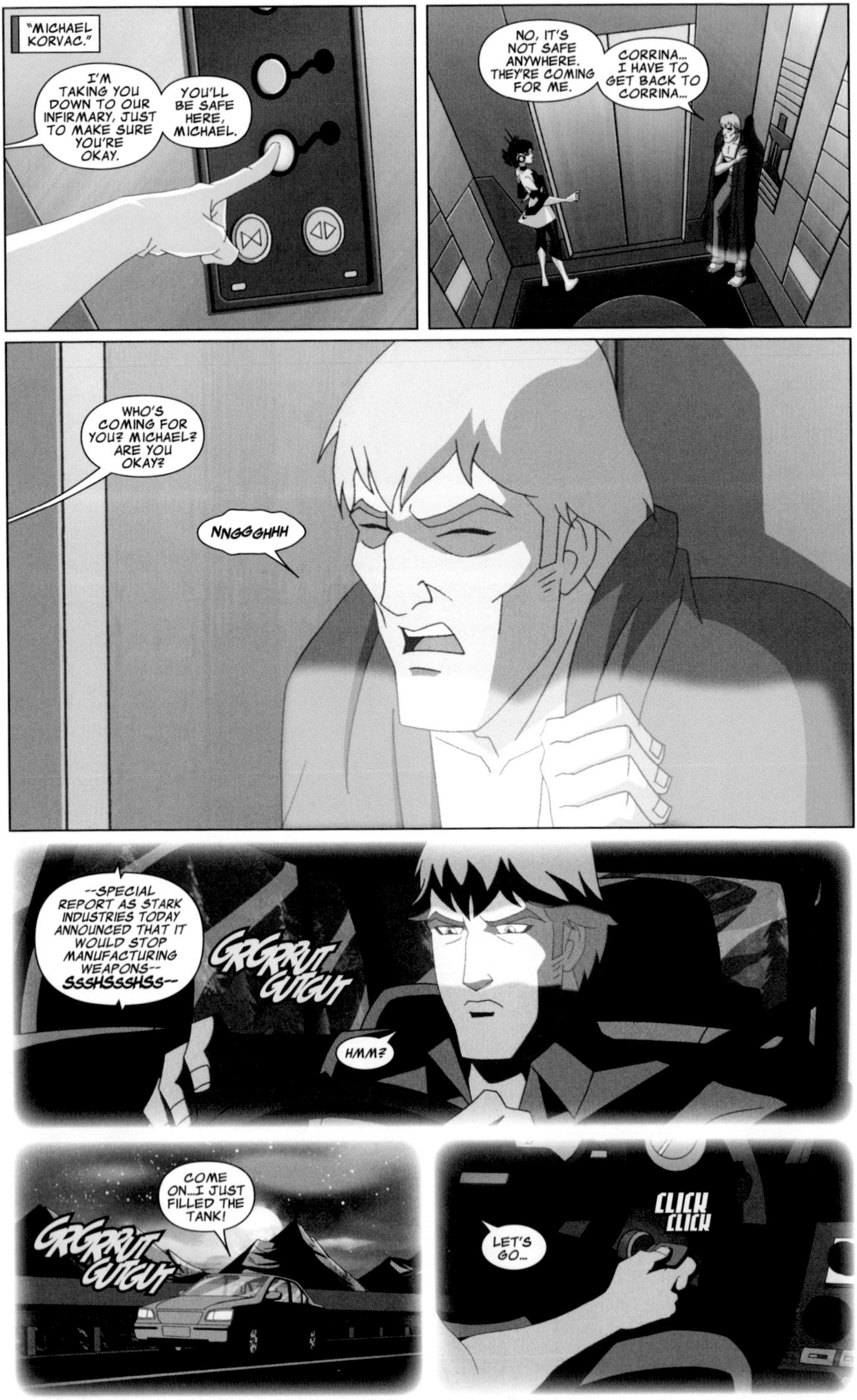
"MICHAEL KORVAC."
I'M TAKING YOU DOWN TO OUR INFIRMARY, JUST TO MAKE SURE YOU'RE OKAY.
YOU'LL BE SAFE HERE, MICHAEL.
NO, IT'S NOT SAFE ANYWHERE. THEY'RE COMING FOR ME.
CORRINA... I HAVE TO GET BACK TO CORRINA...
WHO'S COMING FOR YOU? MICHAEL? ARE YOU OKAY?
NNGGGHHH
--SPECIAL REPORT AS STARK INDUSTRIES TODAY ANNOUNCED THAT IT WOULD STOP MANUFACTURING WEAPONS-- SSSHSSSHSS--
GRGRRUT GUTGUT
HMM?
COME ON...I JUST FILLED THE TANK!
GRGRRUT GUTGUT
CLICK CLICK
LET'S GO...

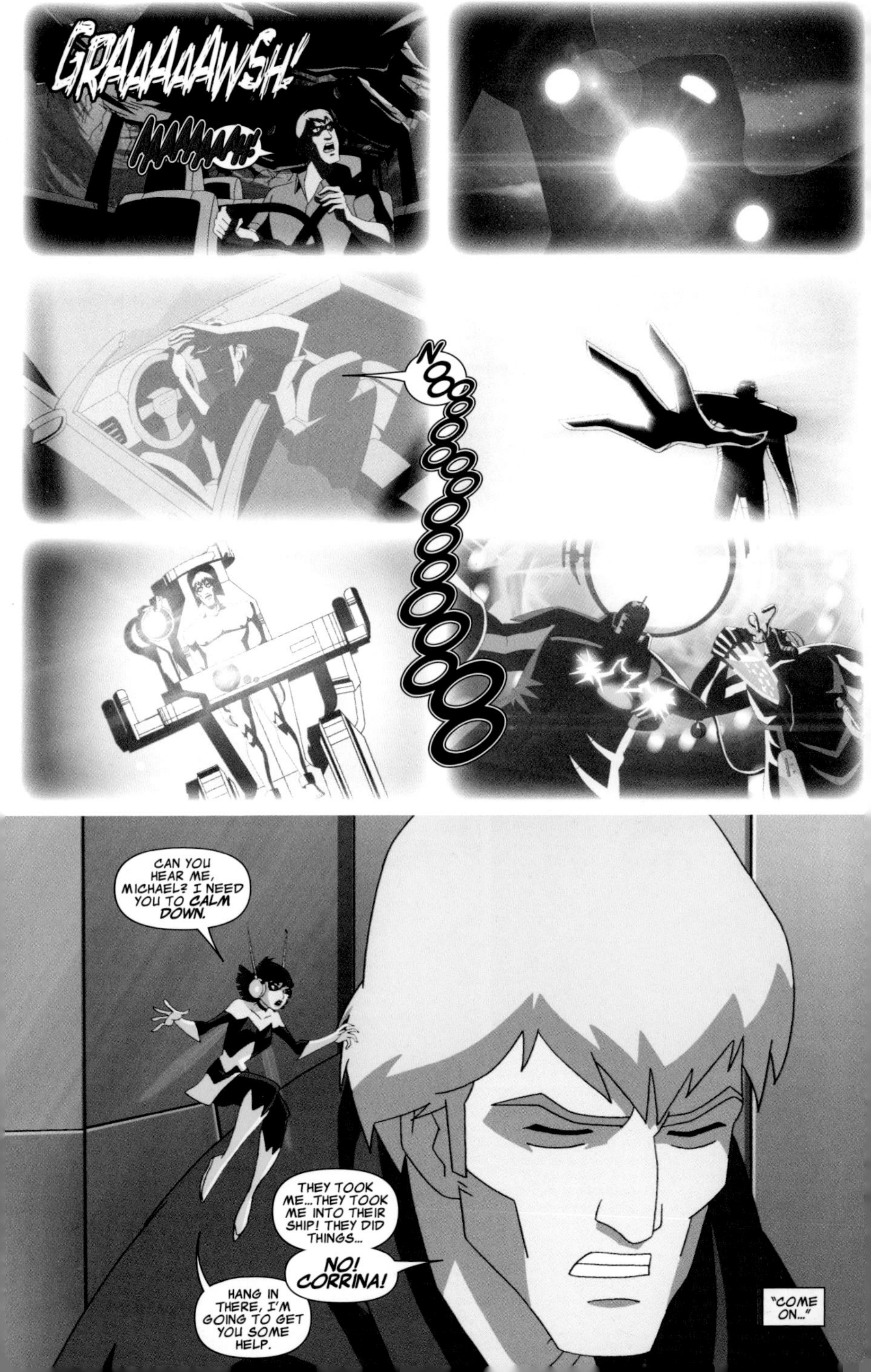
GRAAAAAAWSH!
AAAAAAAH!
NOOOOOOOOOOOOOOOOOO
CAN YOU HEAR ME, MICHAEL? I NEED YOU TO CALM DOWN.
THEY TOOK ME...THEY TOOK ME INTO THEIR SHIP! THEY DID THINGS...
NO! CORRINA!
HANG IN THERE, I'M GOING TO GET YOU SOME HELP.
"COME ON..."

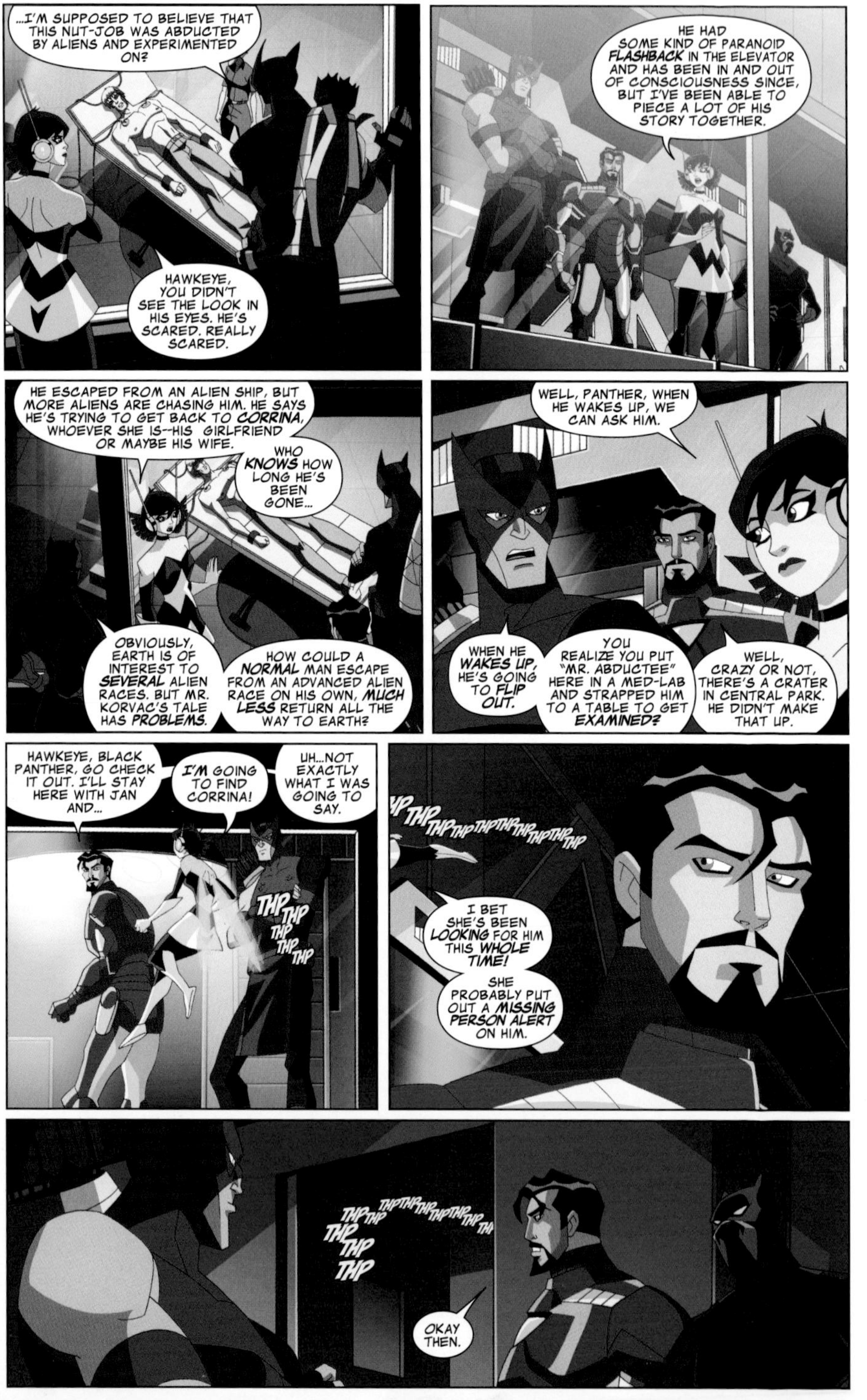
...I'M SUPPOSED TO BELIEVE THAT THIS NUT-JOB WAS ABDUCTED BY ALIENS AND EXPERIMENTED ON?
HAWKEYE, YOU DIDN'T SEE THE LOOK IN HIS EYES. HE'S SCARED. REALLY SCARED.
HE HAD SOME KIND OF PARANOID FLASHBACK IN THE ELEVATOR AND HAS BEEN IN AND OUT OF CONSCIOUSNESS SINCE, BUT I'VE BEEN ABLE TO PIECE A LOT OF HIS STORY TOGETHER.
HE ESCAPED FROM AN ALIEN SHIP, BUT MORE ALIENS ARE CHASING HIM. HE SAYS HE'S TRYING TO GET BACK TO CORRINA, WHOEVER SHE IS--HIS GIRLFRIEND OR MAYBE HIS WIFE.
WHO KNOWS HOW LONG HE'S BEEN GONE...
OBVIOUSLY, EARTH IS OF INTEREST TO SEVERAL ALIEN RACES. BUT MR. KORVAC'S TALE HAS PROBLEMS.
HOW COULD A NORMAL MAN ESCAPE FROM AN ADVANCED ALIEN RACE ON HIS OWN, MUCH LESS RETURN ALL THE WAY TO EARTH?
WELL, PANTHER, WHEN HE WAKES UP, WE CAN ASK HIM.
WHEN HE WAKES UP, HE'S GOING TO FLIP OUT.
YOU REALIZE YOU PUT "MR. ABDUCTEE" HERE IN A MED-LAB AND STRAPPED HIM TO A TABLE TO GET EXAMINED?
WELL, CRAZY OR NOT, THERE'S A CRATER IN CENTRAL PARK. HE DIDN'T MAKE THAT UP.
HAWKEYE, BLACK PANTHER, GO CHECK IT OUT. I'LL STAY HERE WITH JAN AND...
I'M GOING TO FIND CORRINA!
UH...NOT EXACTLY WHAT I WAS GOING TO SAY.
THP THP THP THP THP
THP THP THP THP THP THP THP THP THP THP THP
I BET SHE'S BEEN LOOKING FOR HIM THIS WHOLE TIME!
SHE PROBABLY PUT OUT A MISSING PERSON ALERT ON HIM.
THP THP THP THP THP THP THP THP THP THP
THP THP THP
OKAY THEN.

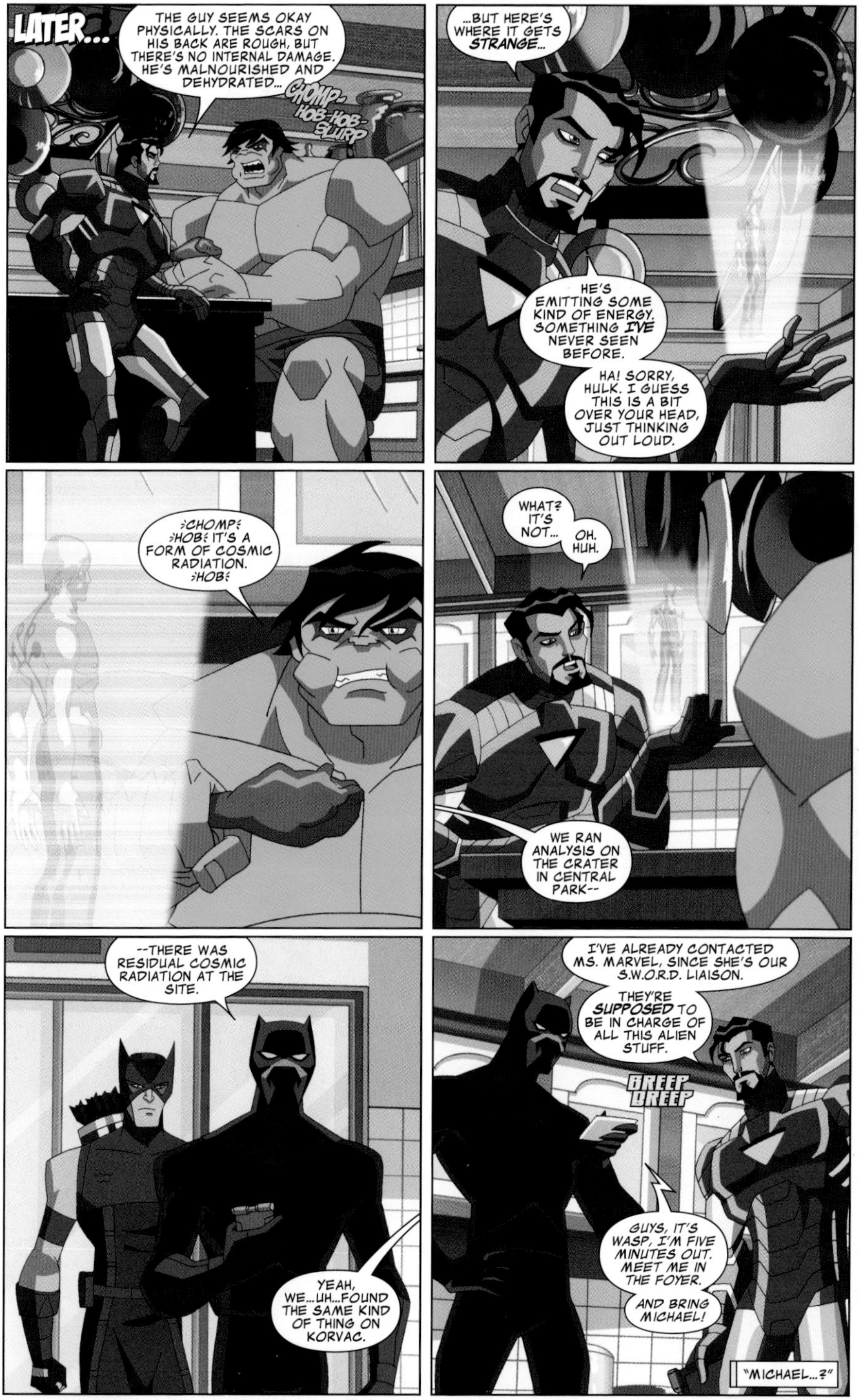

LATER...
THE GUY SEEMS OKAY PHYSICALLY. THE SCARS ON HIS BACK ARE ROUGH, BUT THERE'S NO INTERNAL DAMAGE. HE'S MALNOURISHED AND DEHYDRATED...
CHOMP-HOB-HOB-SLURP
...BUT HERE'S WHERE IT GETS STRANGE...
HE'S EMITTING SOME KIND OF ENERGY. SOMETHING I'VE NEVER SEEN BEFORE.
HA! SORRY, HULK. I GUESS THIS IS A BIT OVER YOUR HEAD. JUST THINKING OUT LOUD.
CHOMP HOB IT'S A FORM OF COSMIC RADIATION. HOB
WHAT? IT'S NOT...
OH. HUH.
WE RAN ANALYSIS ON THE CRATER IN CENTRAL PARK--
--THERE WAS RESIDUAL COSMIC RADIATION AT THE SITE.
YEAH, WE...UH...FOUND THE SAME KIND OF THING ON KORVAC.
I'VE ALREADY CONTACTED MS. MARVEL, SINCE SHE'S OUR S.W.O.R.D. LIAISON.
THEY'RE SUPPOSED TO BE IN CHARGE OF ALL THIS ALIEN STUFF.
BREEP BREEP
GUYS, IT'S WASP, I'M FIVE MINUTES OUT. MEET ME IN THE FOYER.
AND BRING MICHAEL!
"MICHAEL...?"

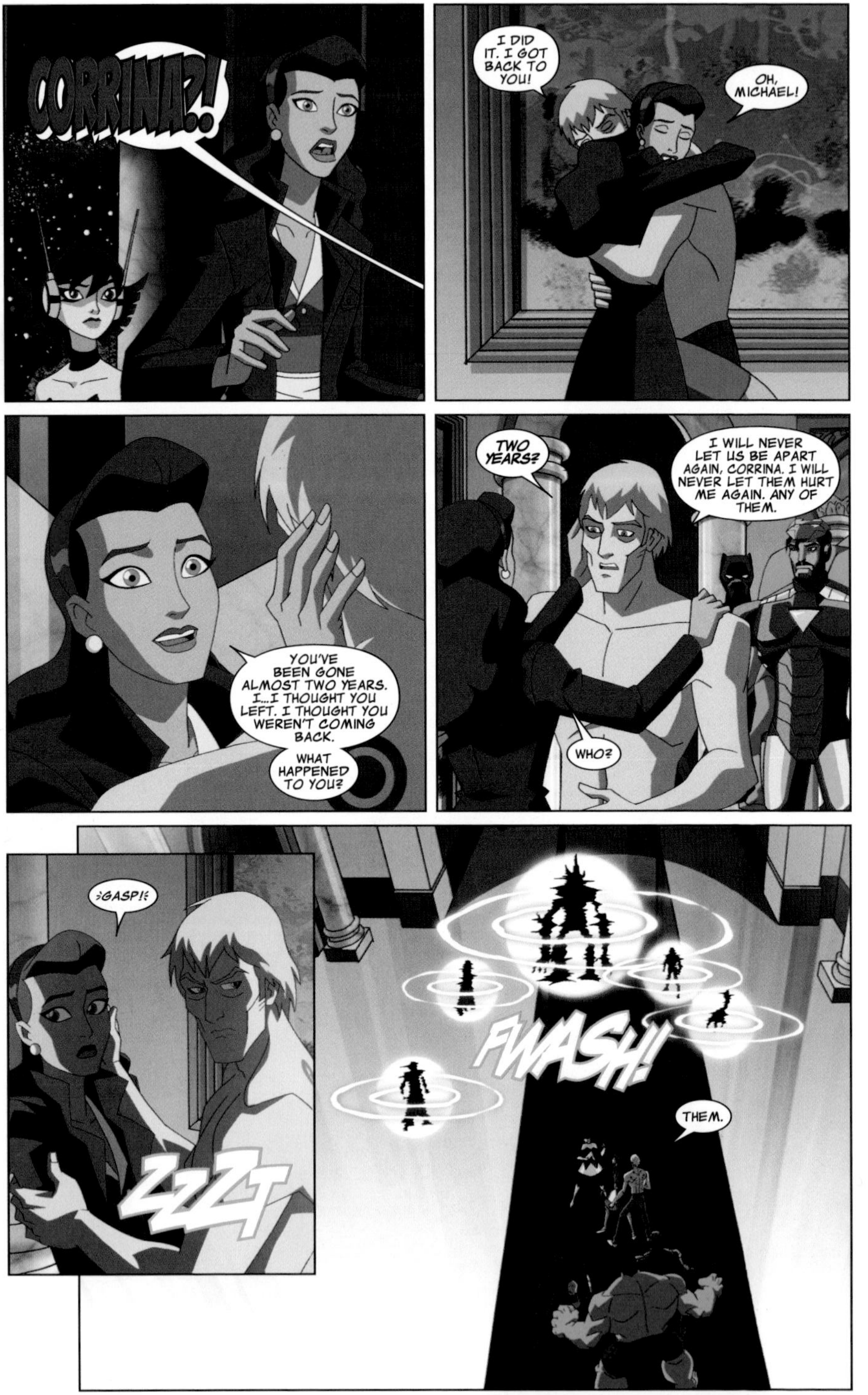
CORRINA?!
I DID IT. I GOT BACK TO YOU!
OH, MICHAEL!
YOU'VE BEEN GONE ALMOST TWO YEARS. I...I THOUGHT YOU LEFT. I THOUGHT YOU WEREN'T COMING BACK.
WHAT HAPPENED TO YOU?
TWO YEARS?
I WILL NEVER LET US BE APART AGAIN, CORRINA. I WILL NEVER LET THEM HURT ME AGAIN. ANY OF THEM.
WHO?
GASP!
ZZZT
FWASH!
THEM.

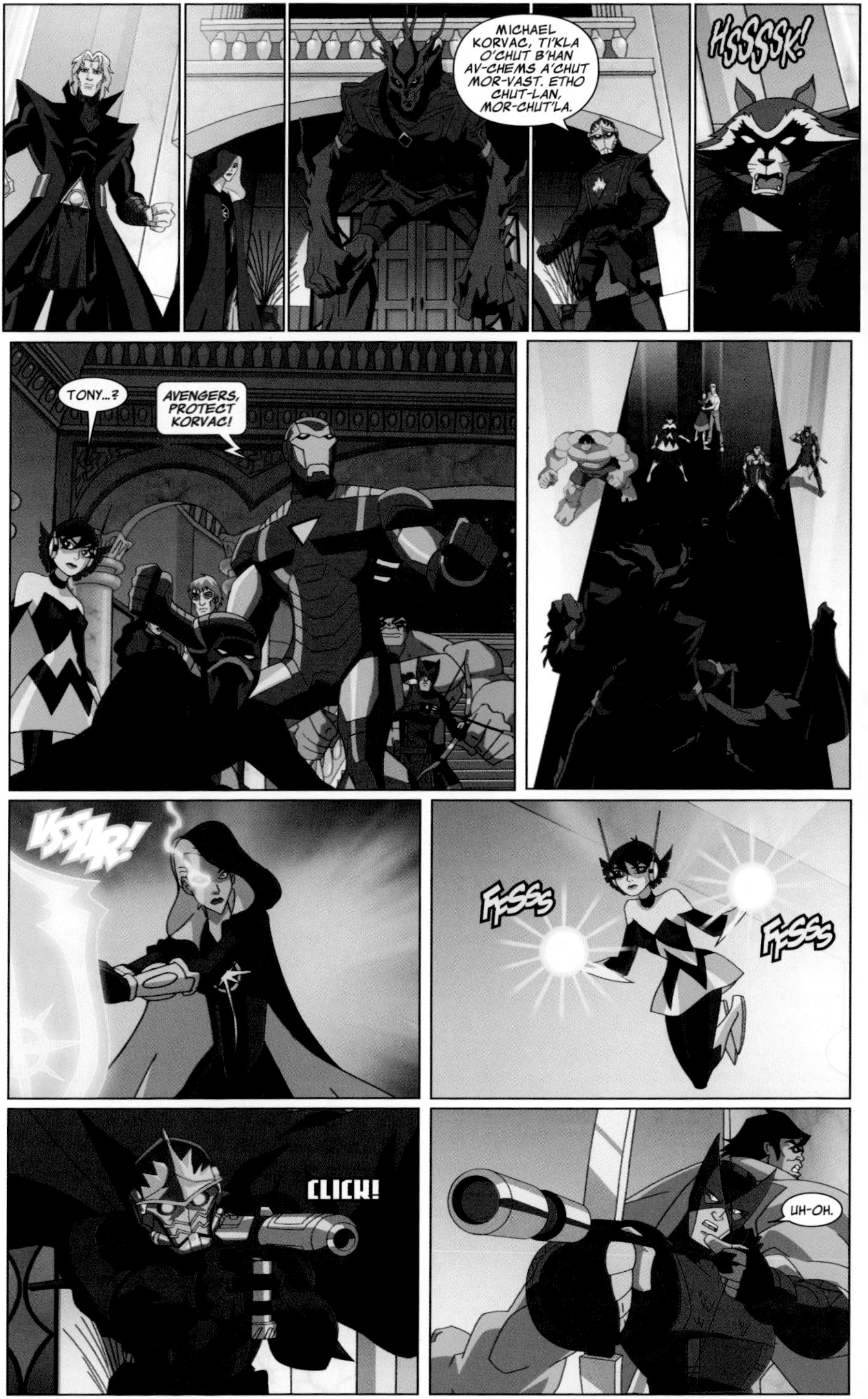
MICHAEL KORVAC, TI'KLA O'CHUT B'HAN AV-CHEMS A'CHUT MOR-VAST. ETHO CHUT-LAN, MOR-CHUT'LA.
HSSSSK!
TONY...?
AVENGERS, PROTECT KORVAC!
VSSAR!
FFSSS
FFSSS
CLICK!
UH-OH.

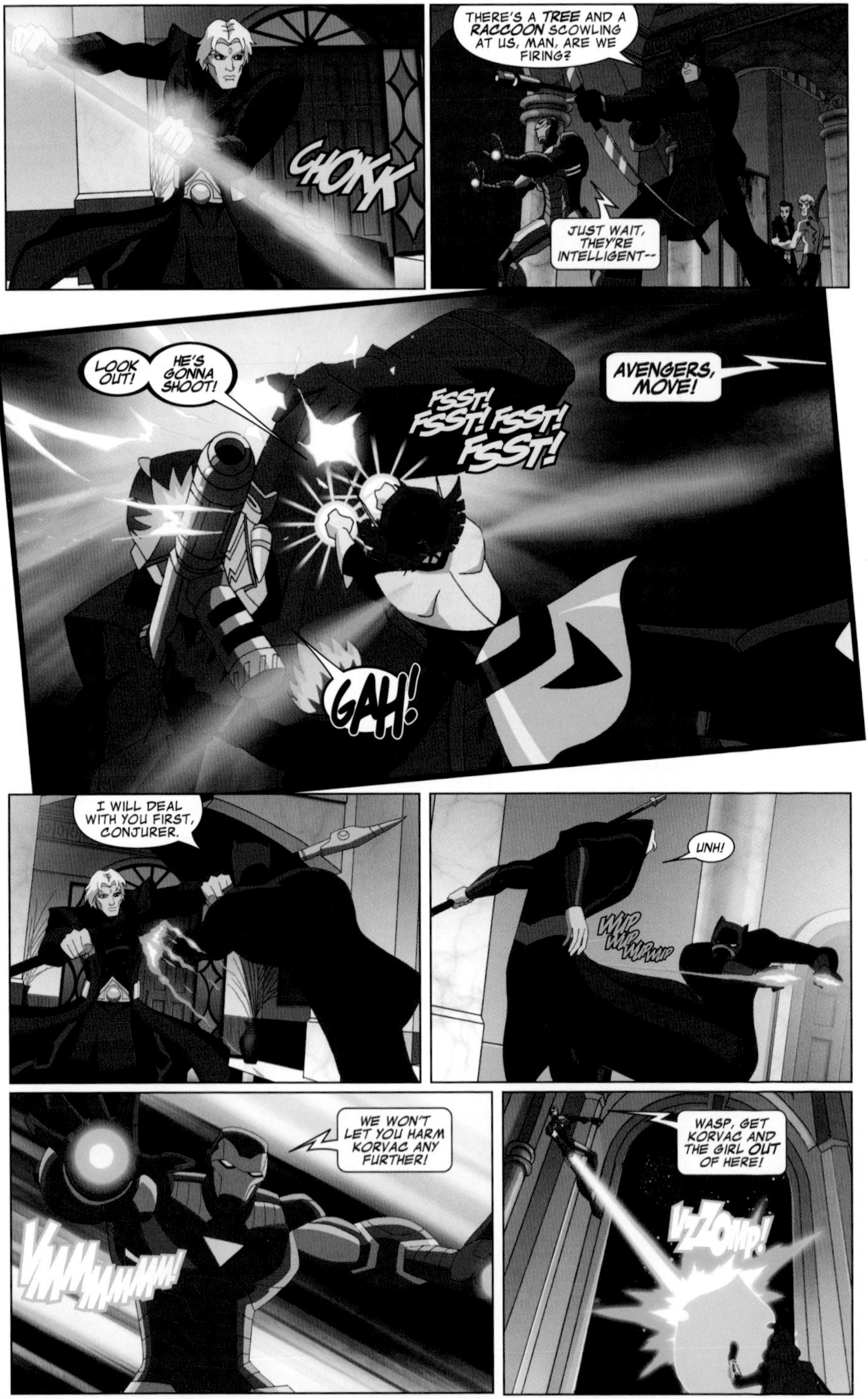
CHOKK
THERE'S A TREE AND A RACCOON SCOWLING AT US, MAN, ARE WE FIRING?
JUST WAIT, THEY'RE INTELLIGENT--
LOOK OUT!
HE'S GONNA SHOOT!
AVENGERS, MOVE!
FSST! FSST! FSST! FSST!
GAH!
I WILL DEAL WITH YOU FIRST, CONJURER.
UNH!
WIP WIP WIPWIP
WE WON'T LET YOU HARM KORVAC ANY FURTHER!
VMMMMMM!
WASP, GET KORVAC AND THE GIRL OUT OF HERE!
VZZOMP!

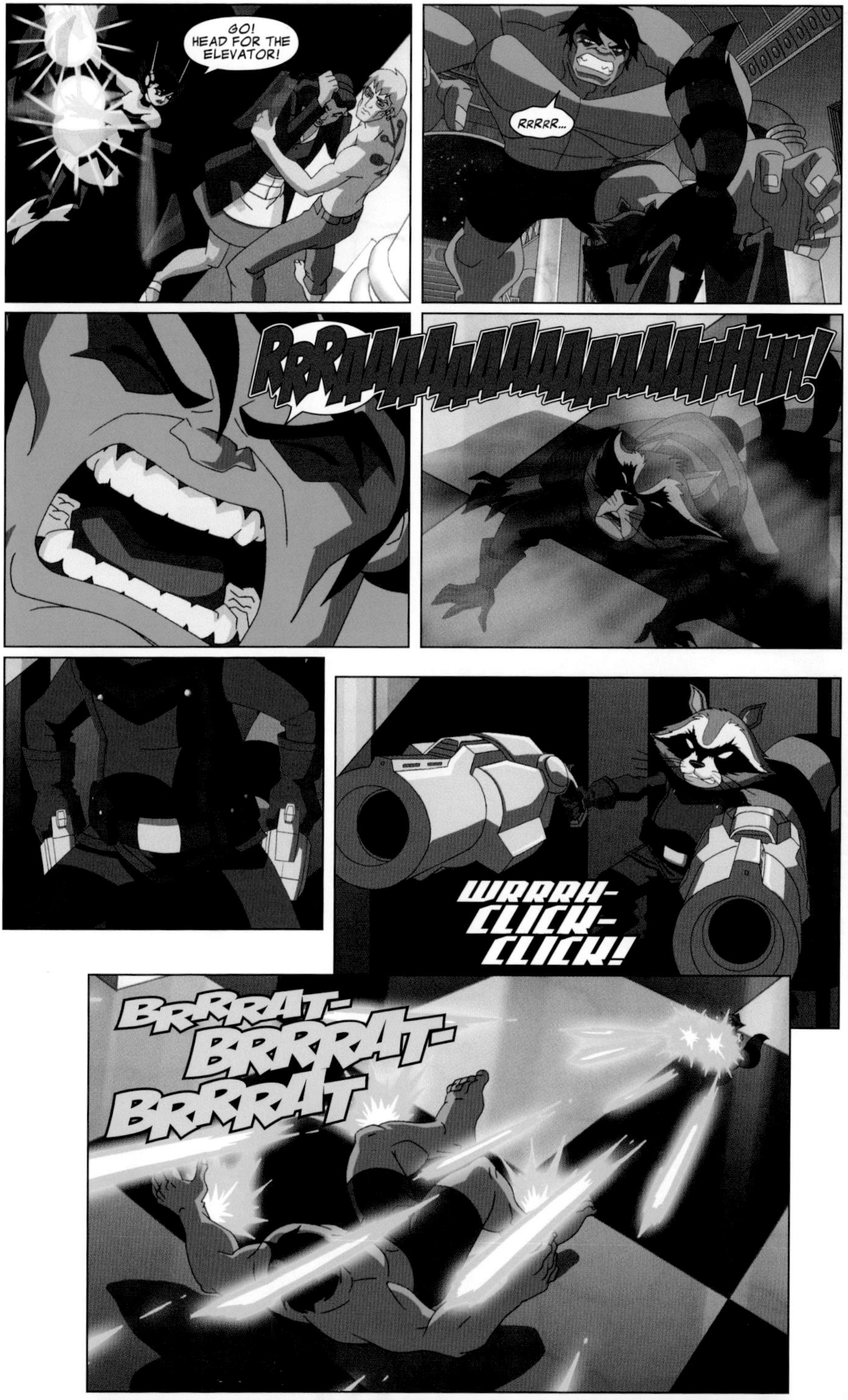
GO! HEAD FOR THE ELEVATOR!
RRRRR...
RRRAAAAAAAAAAAAAAAAHHHH!
WRRRH-CLICK-CLICK!
BRRRAT-BRRRAT-BRRRAT

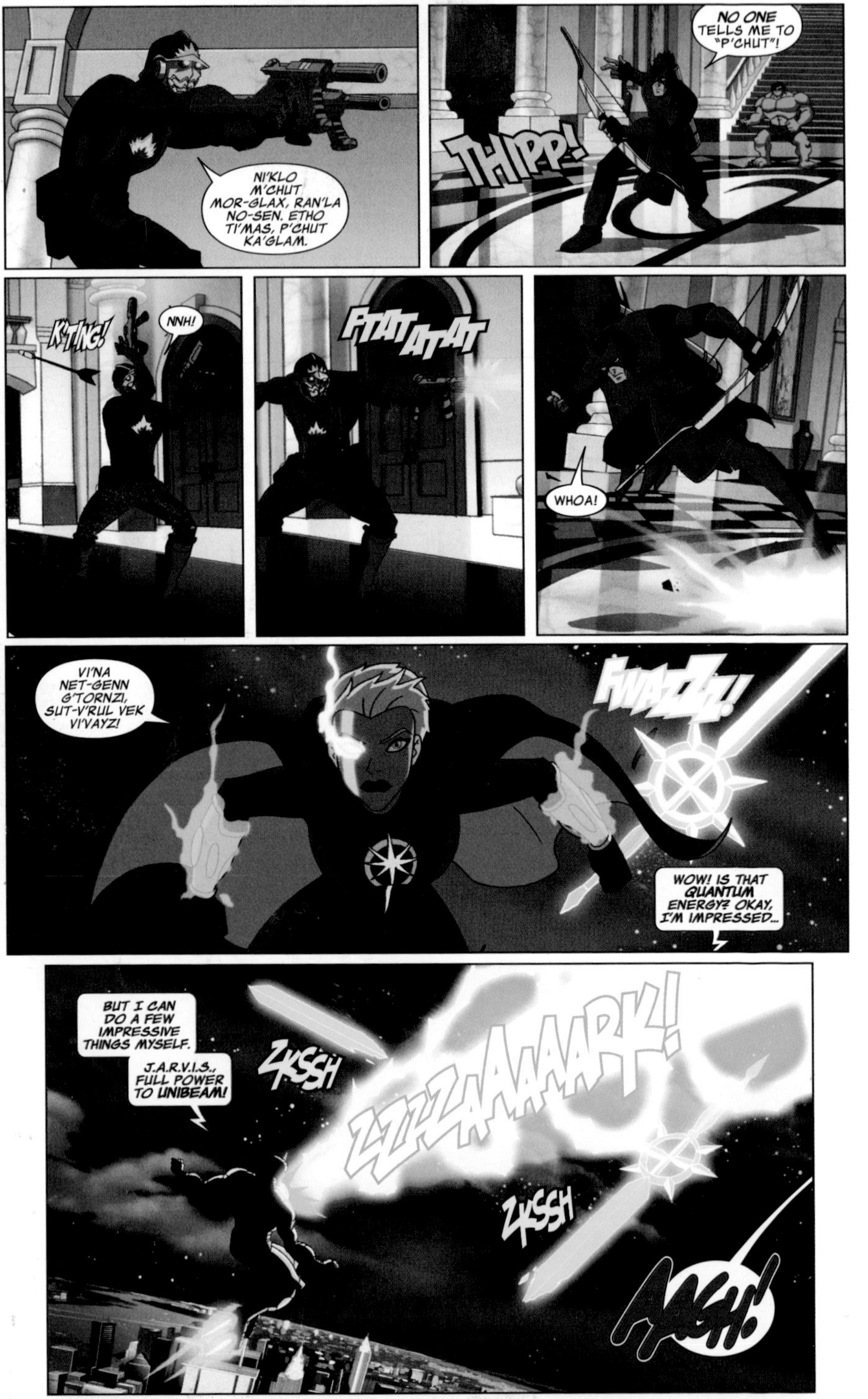
NI'KLO M'CHUT MOR-GLAX, RAN'LA NO-SEN. ETHO TI'MAS, P'CHUT KA'GLAM.
NO ONE TELLS ME TO "P'CHUT"!
THIPP!
K'TING!
NNH!
FTATATAT
WHOA!
VI'NA NET-GENN G'TORNZI, SUT-V'RUL VEK VI'VAYZ!
FWAZZZ!
WOW! IS THAT QUANTUM ENERGY? OKAY, I'M IMPRESSED...
BUT I CAN DO A FEW IMPRESSIVE THINGS MYSELF.
J.A.R.V.I.S., FULL POWER TO UNIBEAM!
ZKSSH
ZZZZAAAAARK!
ZKSSH
AAGH!

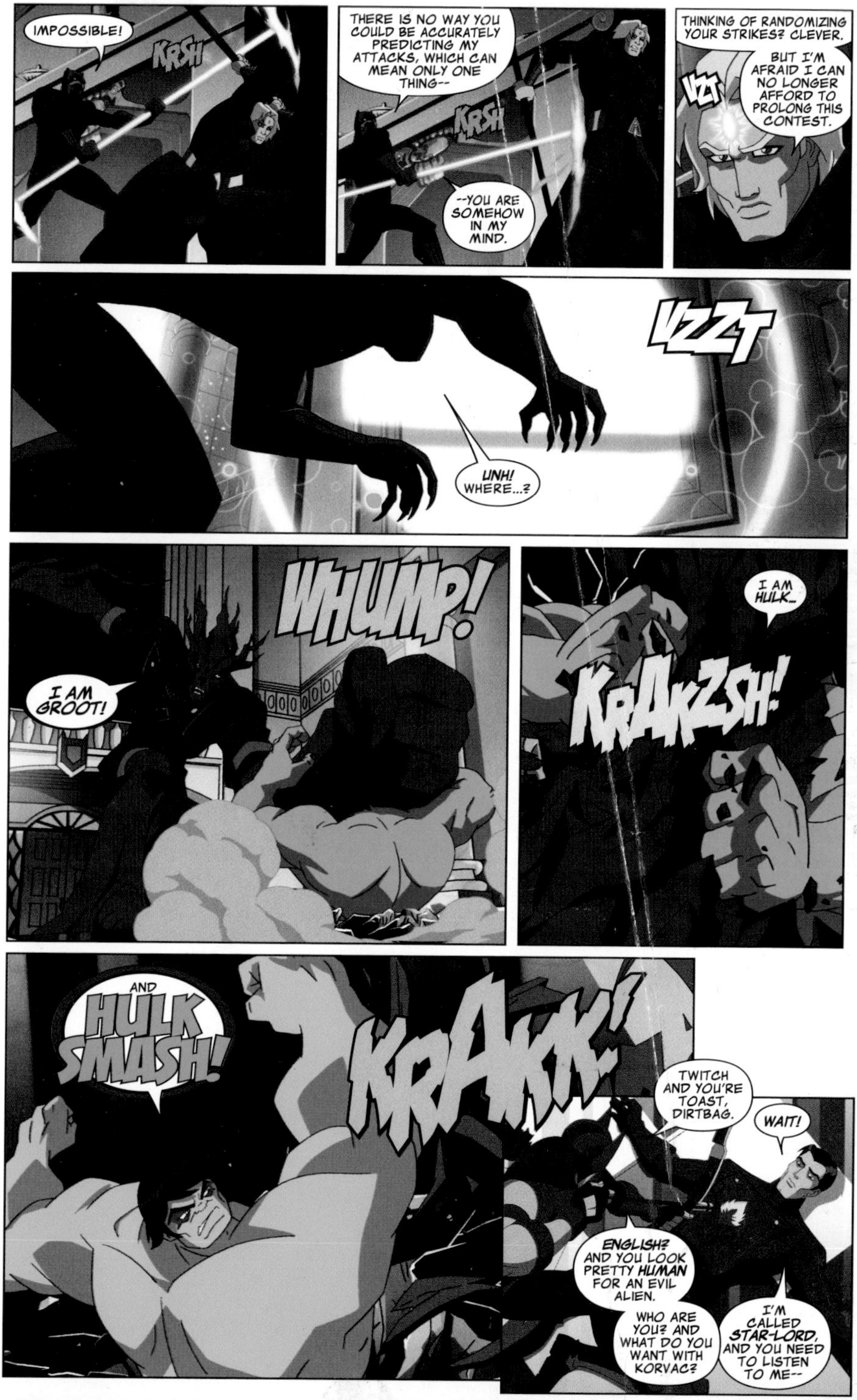
IMPOSSIBLE!
KRSH
THERE IS NO WAY YOU COULD BE ACCURATELY PREDICTING MY ATTACKS, WHICH CAN MEAN ONLY ONE THING--
KRSH
--YOU ARE SOMEHOW IN MY MIND.
THINKING OF RANDOMIZING YOUR STRIKES? CLEVER.
VZT
BUT I'M AFRAID I CAN NO LONGER AFFORD TO PROLONG THIS CONTEST.
VZZT
UNH! WHERE...?
WHUMP!
I AM GROOT!
I AM HULK...
KRAKZSH!
AND HULK SMASH!
KRAKK!
TWITCH AND YOU'RE TOAST, DIRTBAG.
WAIT!
ENGLISH? AND YOU LOOK PRETTY HUMAN FOR AN EVIL ALIEN.
WHO ARE YOU? AND WHAT DO YOU WANT WITH KORVAC?
I'M CALLED STAR-LORD, AND YOU NEED TO LISTEN TO ME--

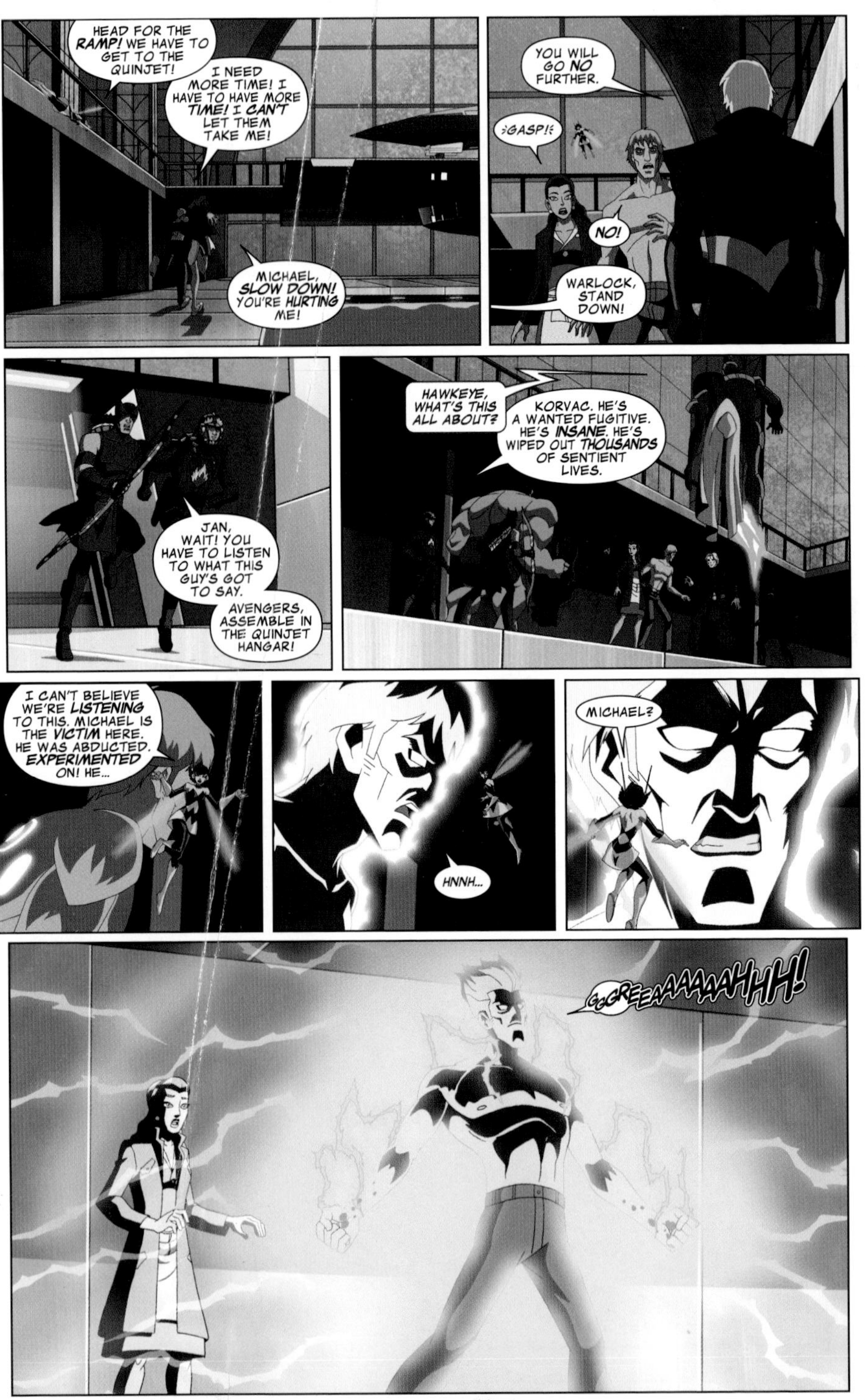
HEAD FOR THE RAMP! WE HAVE TO GET TO THE QUINJET!
I NEED MORE TIME! I HAVE TO HAVE MORE TIME! I CAN'T LET THEM TAKE ME!
MICHAEL, SLOW DOWN! YOU'RE HURTING ME!
YOU WILL GO NO FURTHER.
GASP!
NO!
WARLOCK, STAND DOWN!
JAN, WAIT! YOU HAVE TO LISTEN TO WHAT THIS GUY'S GOT TO SAY.
AVENGERS, ASSEMBLE IN THE QUINJET HANGAR!
HAWKEYE, WHAT'S THIS ALL ABOUT?
KORVAC. HE'S A WANTED FUGITIVE. HE'S INSANE. HE'S WIPED OUT THOUSANDS OF SENTIENT LIVES.
I CAN'T BELIEVE WE'RE LISTENING TO THIS. MICHAEL IS THE VICTIM HERE. HE WAS ABDUCTED. EXPERIMENTED ON! HE...
HNNH...
MICHAEL?
GGGREEAAAAAAHHHH!

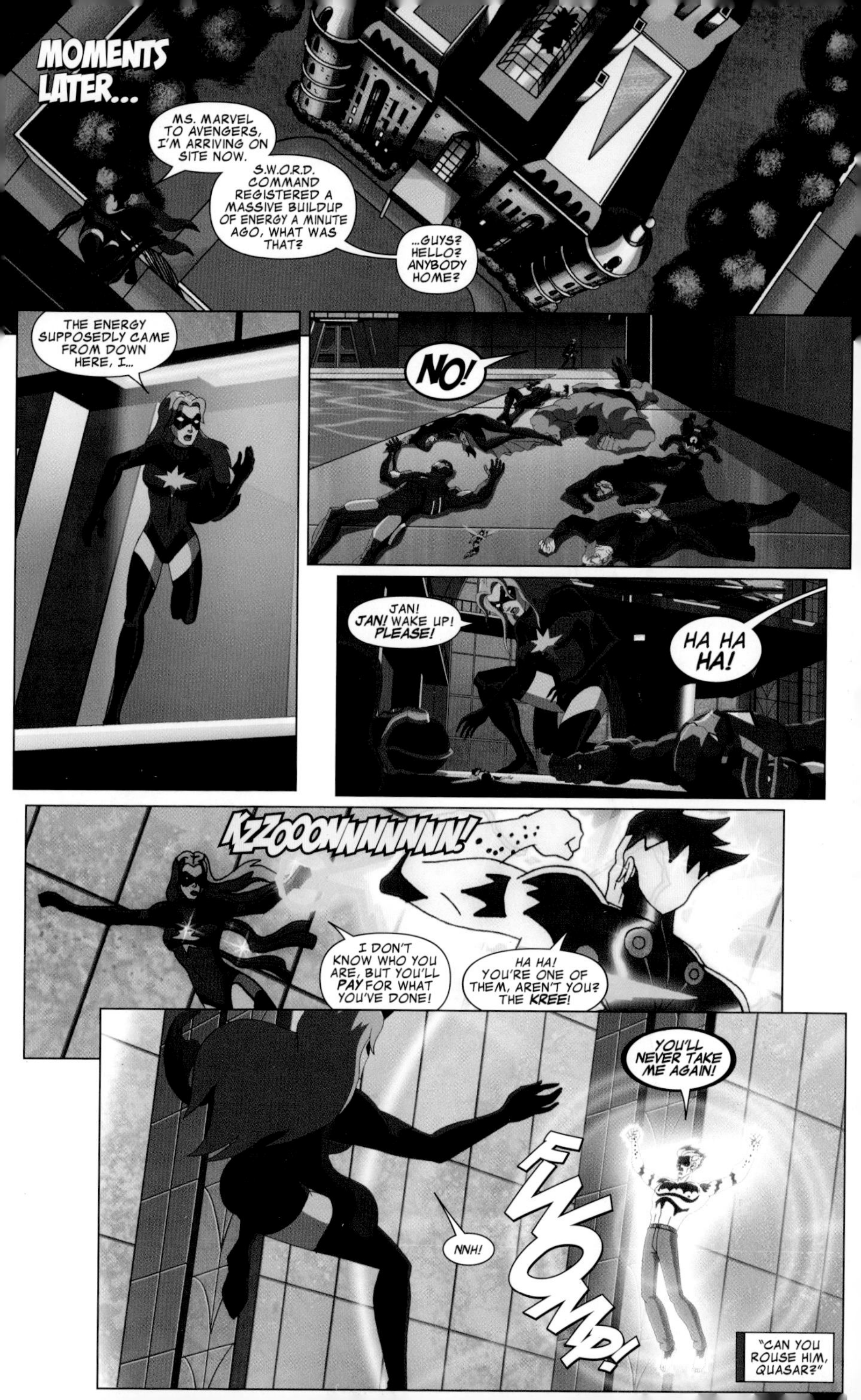
MOMENTS LATER...
MS. MARVEL TO AVENGERS, I'M ARRIVING ON SITE NOW.
S.W.O.R.D. COMMAND REGISTERED A MASSIVE BUILDUP OF ENERGY A MINUTE AGO, WHAT WAS THAT?
...GUYS? HELLO? ANYBODY HOME?
THE ENERGY SUPPOSEDLY CAME FROM DOWN HERE, I...
NO!
JAN! JAN! WAKE UP! PLEASE!
HA HA HA!
KZZOOONNNNNNN!
I DON'T KNOW WHO YOU ARE, BUT YOU'LL PAY FOR WHAT YOU'VE DONE!
HA HA! YOU'RE ONE OF THEM, AREN'T YOU? THE KREE!
YOU'LL NEVER TAKE ME AGAIN!
FWOMP!
NNH!
"CAN YOU ROUSE HIM, QUASAR?"

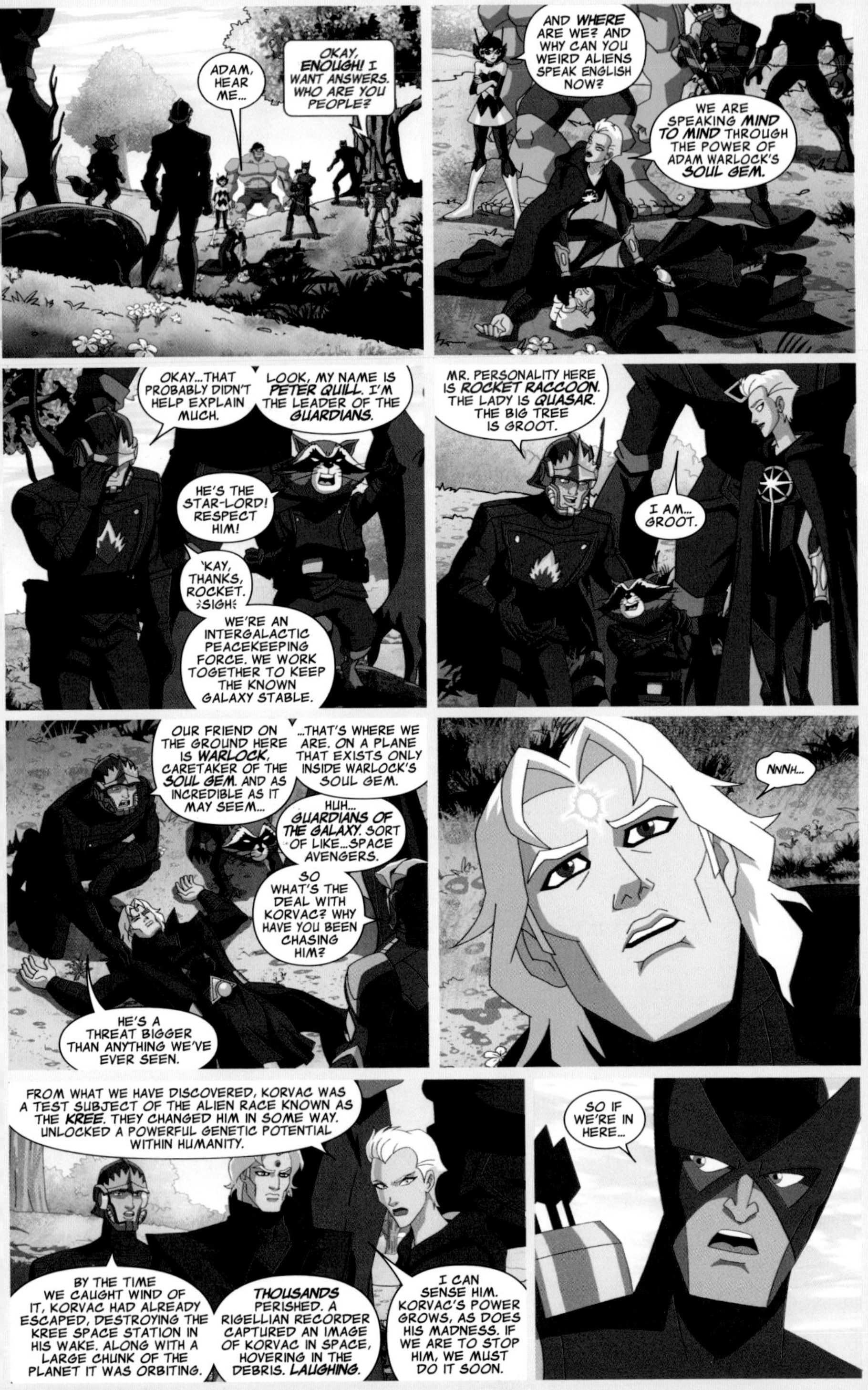

ADAM, HEAR ME...
OKAY, ENOUGH! I WANT ANSWERS. WHO ARE YOU PEOPLE?
AND WHERE ARE WE? AND WHY CAN YOU WEIRD ALIENS SPEAK ENGLISH NOW?
WE ARE SPEAKING MIND TO MIND THROUGH THE POWER OF ADAM WARLOCK'S SOUL GEM.
OKAY...THAT PROBABLY DIDN'T HELP EXPLAIN MUCH.
LOOK, MY NAME IS PETER QUILL. I'M THE LEADER OF THE GUARDIANS.
HE'S THE STAR-LORD! RESPECT HIM!
'KAY, THANKS, ROCKET. *SIGH*
WE'RE AN INTERGALACTIC PEACEKEEPING FORCE. WE WORK TOGETHER TO KEEP THE KNOWN GALAXY STABLE.
MR. PERSONALITY HERE IS ROCKET RACCOON. THE LADY IS QUASAR. THE BIG TREE IS GROOT.
I AM... GROOT.
OUR FRIEND ON THE GROUND HERE IS WARLOCK, CARETAKER OF THE SOUL GEM. AND AS INCREDIBLE AS IT MAY SEEM...
...THAT'S WHERE WE ARE. ON A PLANE THAT EXISTS ONLY INSIDE WARLOCK'S SOUL GEM.
HUH... GUARDIANS OF THE GALAXY. SORT OF LIKE...SPACE AVENGERS.
SO WHAT'S THE DEAL WITH KORVAC? WHY HAVE YOU BEEN CHASING HIM?
HE'S A THREAT BIGGER THAN ANYTHING WE'VE EVER SEEN.
NNNH...
FROM WHAT WE HAVE DISCOVERED, KORVAC WAS A TEST SUBJECT OF THE ALIEN RACE KNOWN AS THE KREE. THEY CHANGED HIM IN SOME WAY. UNLOCKED A POWERFUL GENETIC POTENTIAL WITHIN HUMANITY.
BY THE TIME WE CAUGHT WIND OF IT, KORVAC HAD ALREADY ESCAPED, DESTROYING THE KREE SPACE STATION IN HIS WAKE. ALONG WITH A LARGE CHUNK OF THE PLANET IT WAS ORBITING.
THOUSANDS PERISHED. A RIGELLIAN RECORDER CAPTURED AN IMAGE OF KORVAC IN SPACE, HOVERING IN THE DEBRIS. LAUGHING.
I CAN SENSE HIM. KORVAC'S POWER GROWS, AS DOES HIS MADNESS. IF WE ARE TO STOP HIM, WE MUST DO IT SOON.
SO IF WE'RE IN HERE...

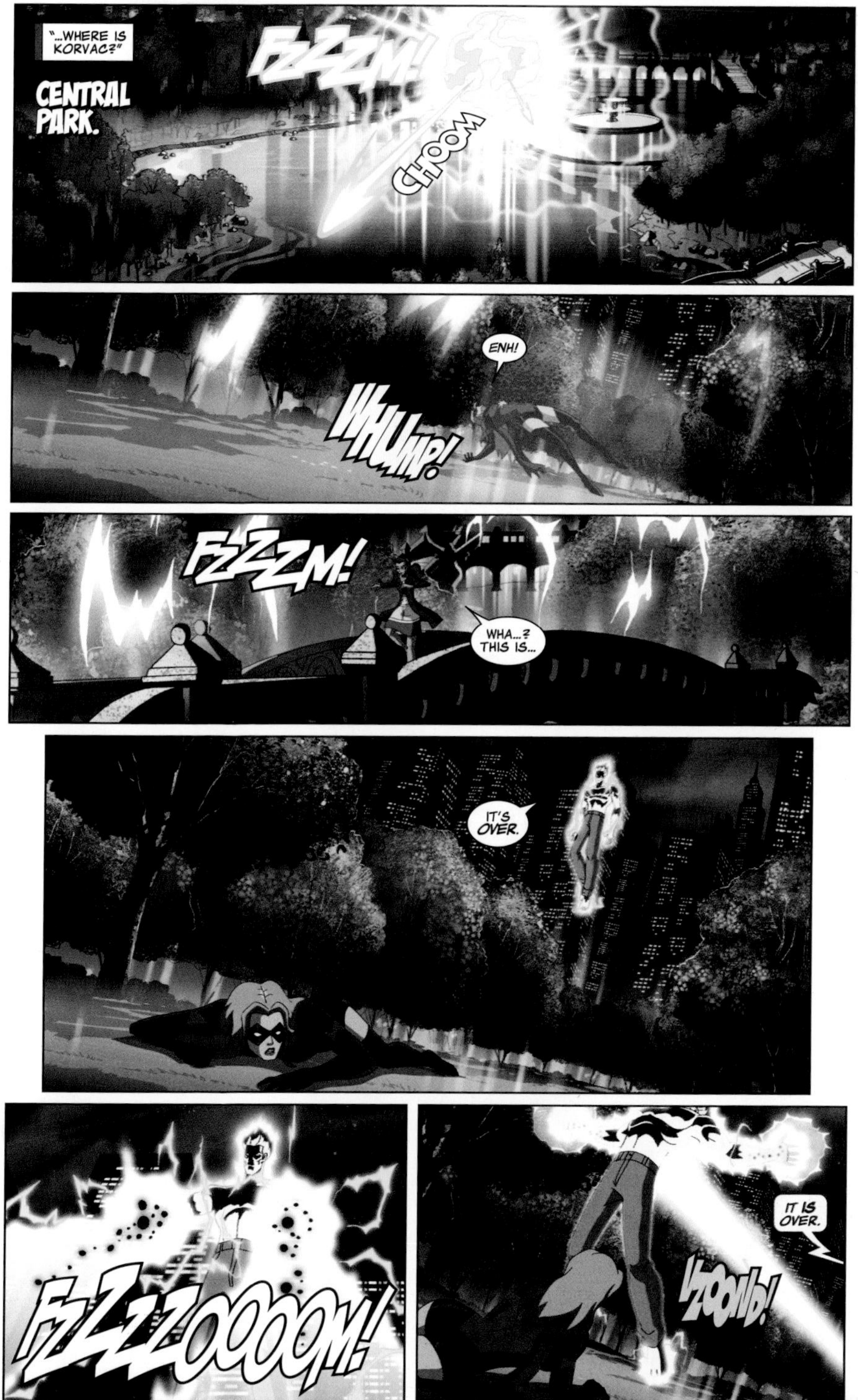
"...WHERE IS KORVAC?"
CENTRAL PARK.
FZZZM!
CHOOM
ENH!
WHUMP!
FZZZM!
WHA...? THIS IS...
IT'S OVER.
FZZZOOOOM!
IT IS OVER.
VZOOMB!

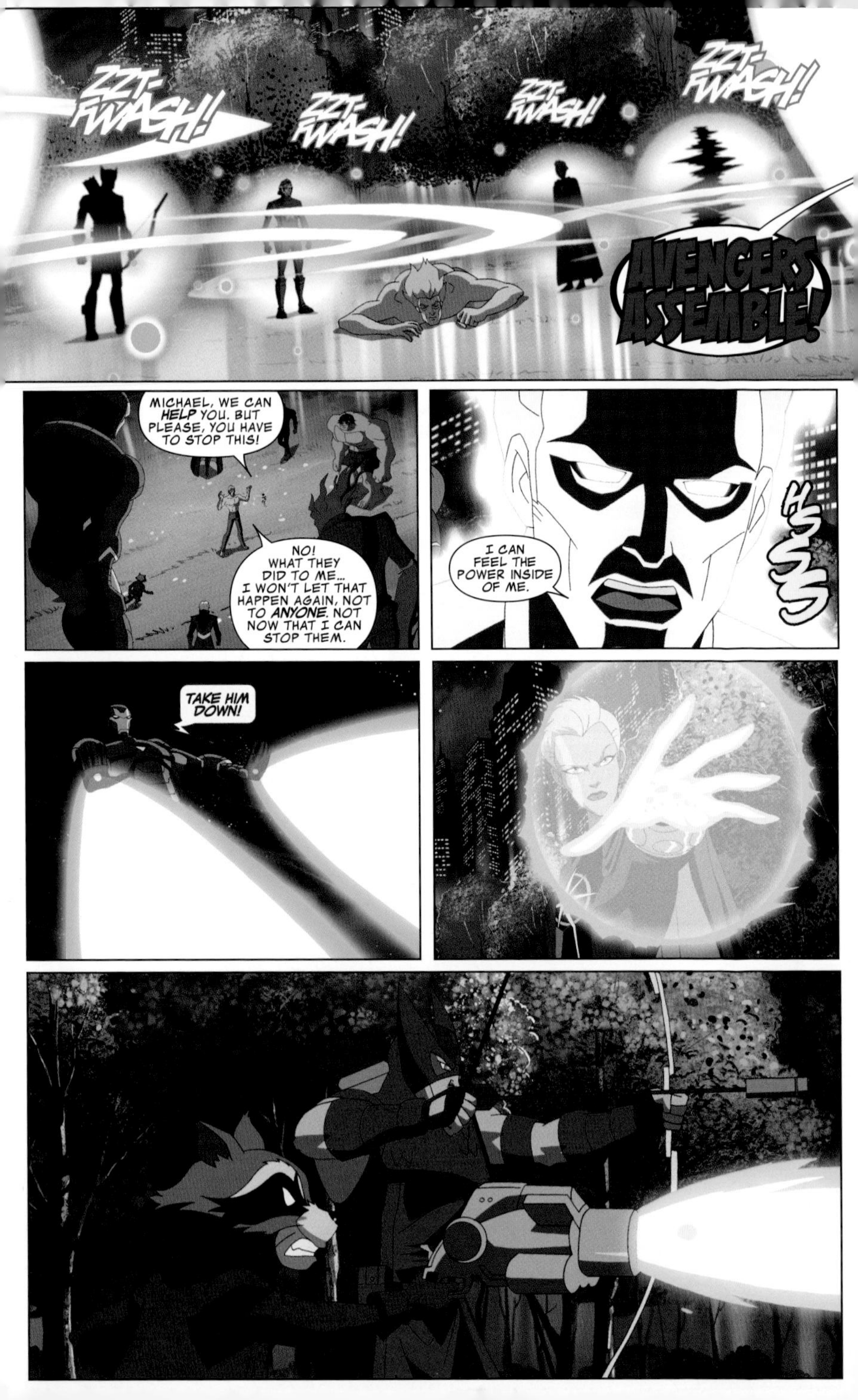
ZZT-FWASH!
ZZT-FWASH!
ZZT-FWASH!
ZZT-FWASH!
AVENGERS ASSEMBLE!
MICHAEL, WE CAN HELP YOU. BUT PLEASE, YOU HAVE TO STOP THIS!
NO! WHAT THEY DID TO ME... I WON'T LET THAT HAPPEN AGAIN, NOT TO ANYONE. NOT NOW THAT I CAN STOP THEM.
I CAN FEEL THE POWER INSIDE OF ME.
HSSS
TAKE HIM DOWN!

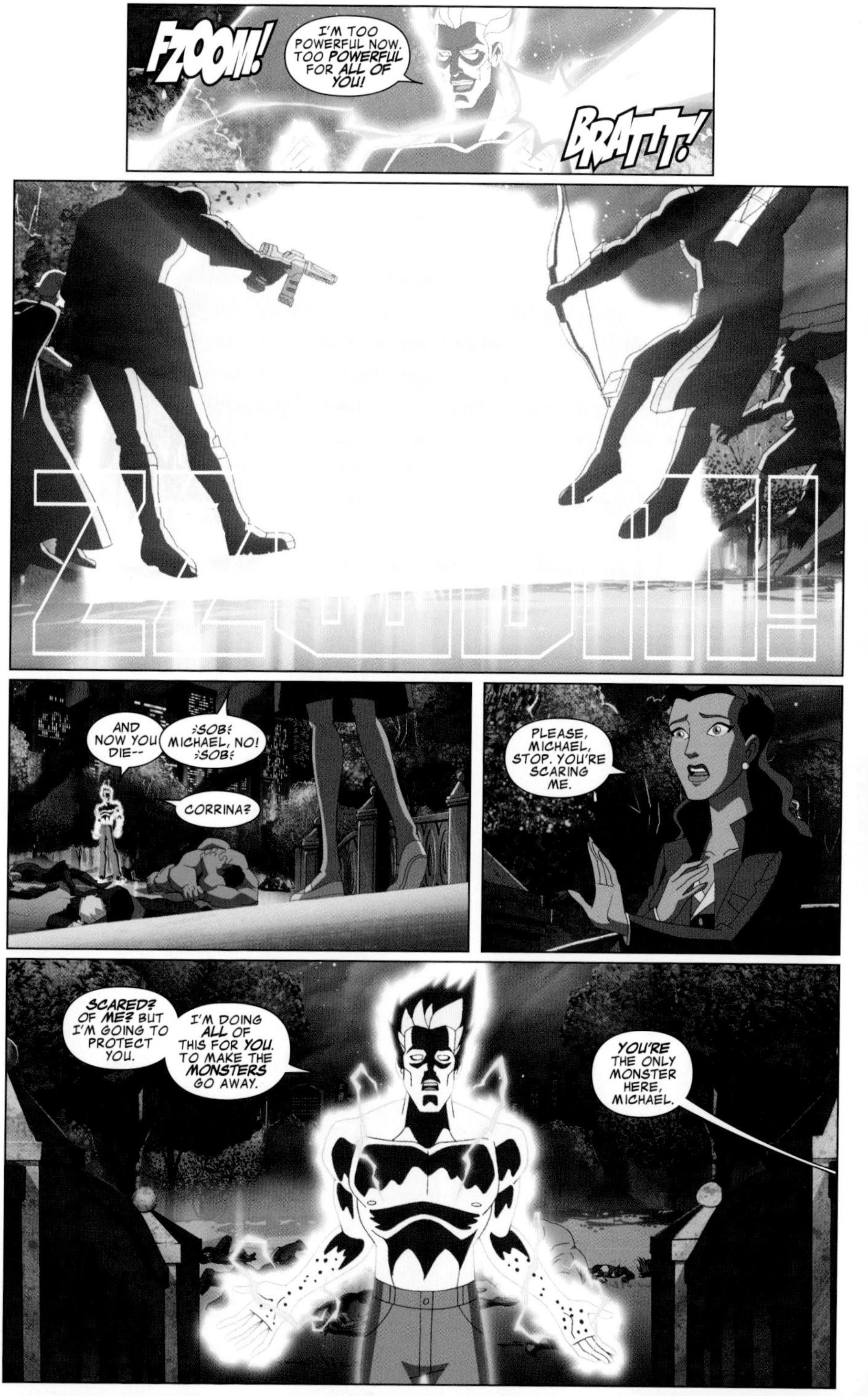
FZOOM!
I'M TOO POWERFUL NOW. TOO POWERFUL FOR ALL OF YOU!
BRATTT!
AND NOW YOU DIE--
>SOB< MICHAEL, NO! >SOB<
CORRINA?
PLEASE, MICHAEL, STOP. YOU'RE SCARING ME.
SCARED? OF ME? BUT I'M GOING TO PROTECT YOU.
I'M DOING ALL OF THIS FOR YOU. TO MAKE THE MONSTERS GO AWAY.
YOU'RE THE ONLY MONSTER HERE, MICHAEL.

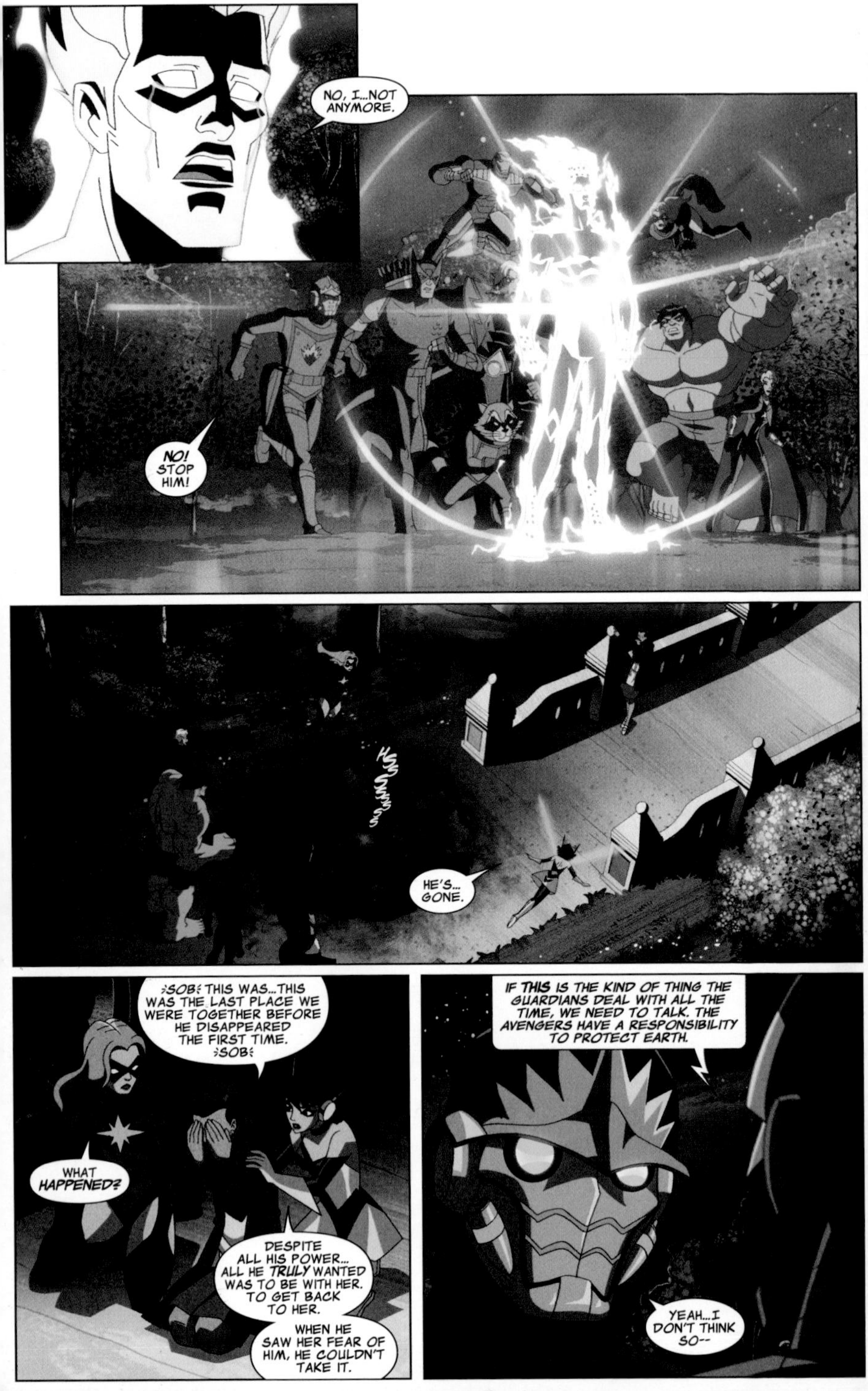
NO, I...NOT ANYMORE.
NO! STOP HIM!
HSSSSSSSSS
HE'S... GONE.
SOB THIS WAS...THIS WAS THE LAST PLACE WE WERE TOGETHER BEFORE HE DISAPPEARED THE FIRST TIME. SOB
WHAT HAPPENED?
DESPITE ALL HIS POWER... ALL HE TRULY WANTED WAS TO BE WITH HER. TO GET BACK TO HER.
WHEN HE SAW HER FEAR OF HIM, HE COULDN'T TAKE IT.
IF THIS IS THE KIND OF THING THE GUARDIANS DEAL WITH ALL THE TIME, WE NEED TO TALK. THE AVENGERS HAVE A RESPONSIBILITY TO PROTECT EARTH.
YEAH...I DON'T THINK SO--

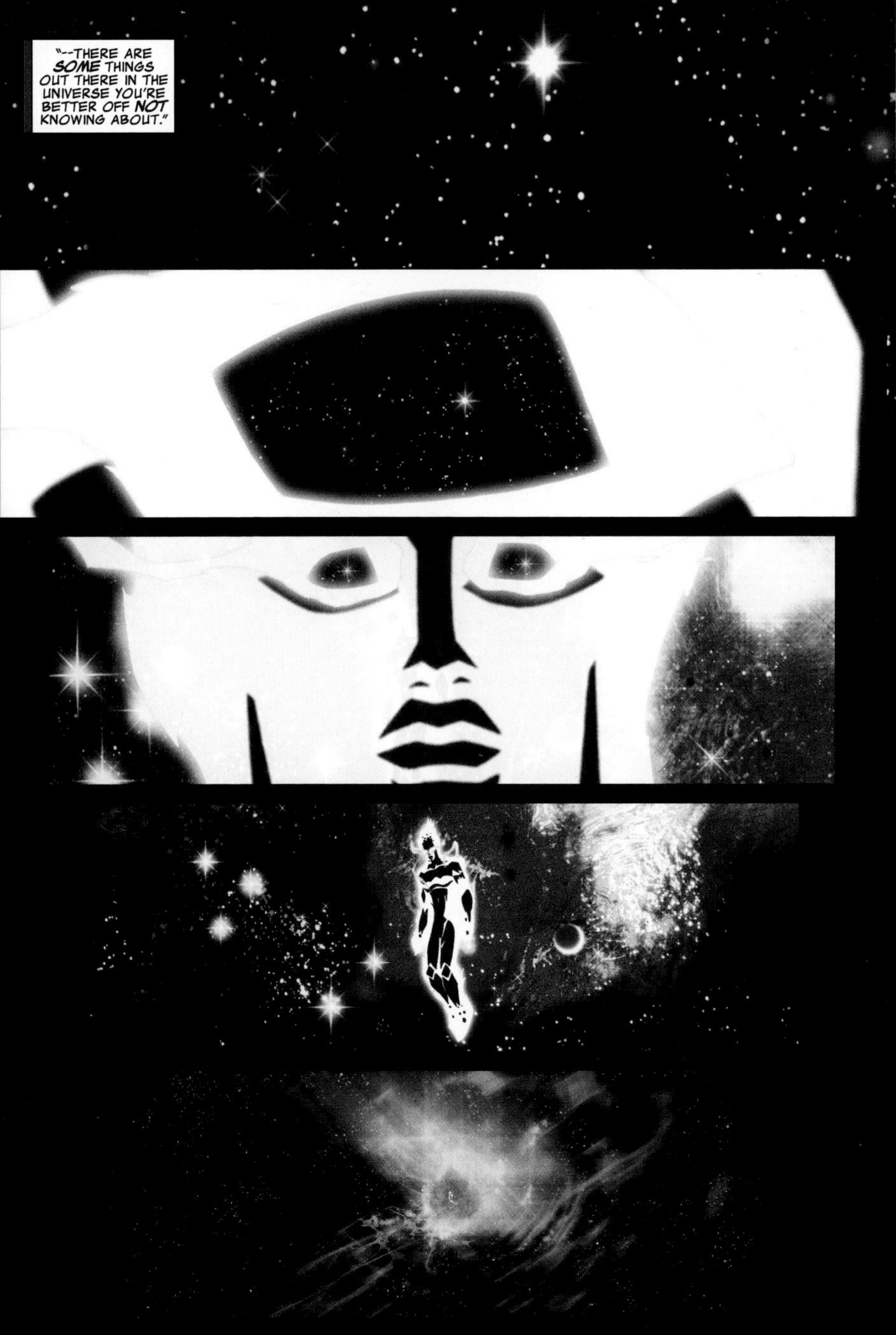
"--THERE ARE SOME THINGS OUT THERE IN THE UNIVERSE YOU'RE BETTER OFF NOT KNOWING ABOUT."

IN LOVING MEMORY OF

BOYD KIRKLAND

FRIEND, FATHER, DIRECTOR, AVENGER

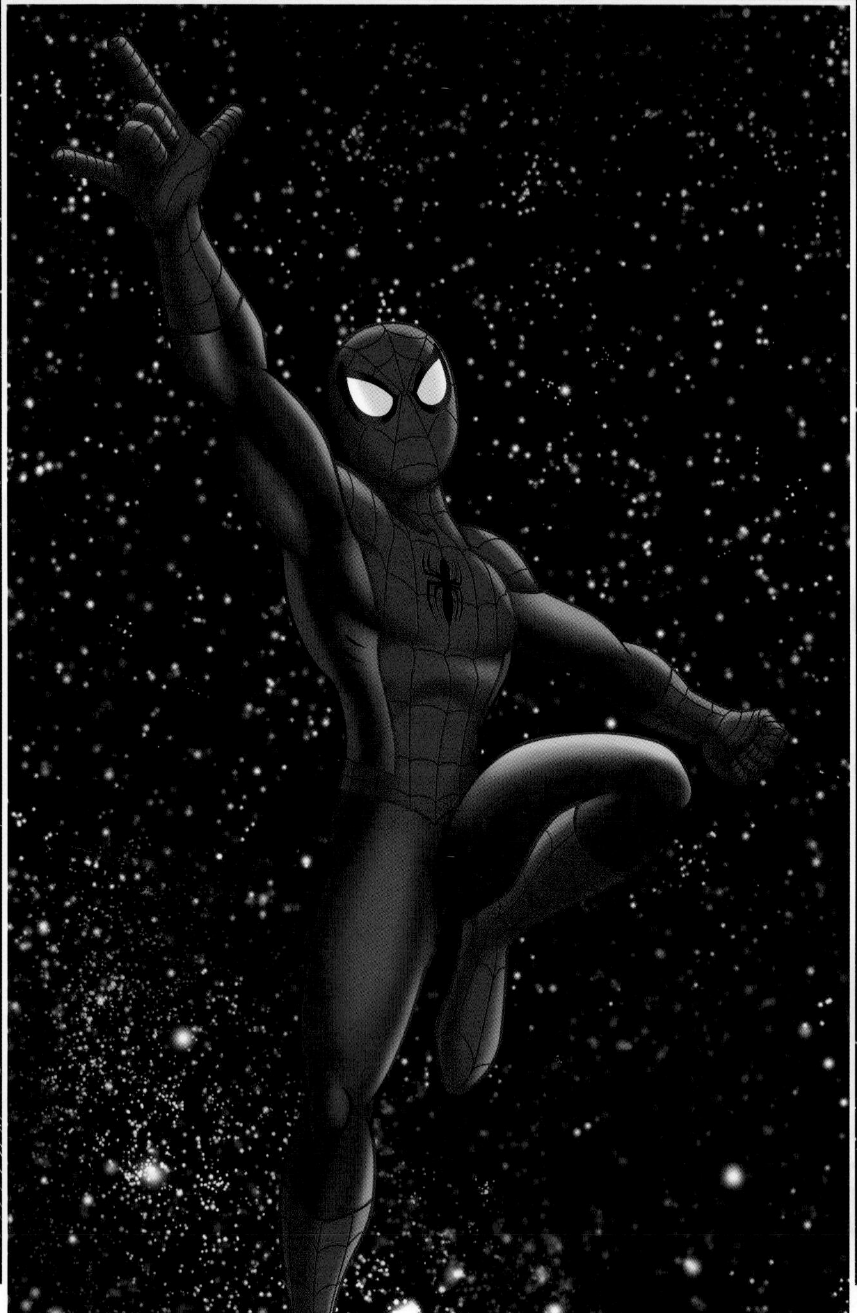

While attending a radiology demonstration, high school student Peter Parker was bitten by a radioactive spider and gained the spider's powers! Now he is training with a superspy organization called S.H.I.E.L.D. to become the...

Marvel Ultimate Spider-Man™

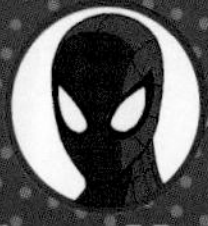

Spider-Man

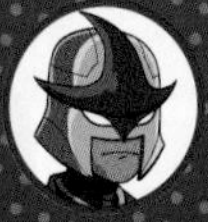

Nova

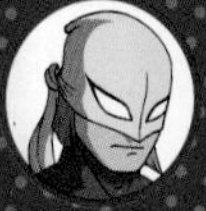

Iron Fist

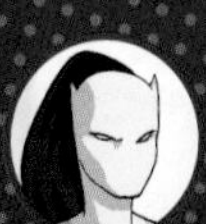

White Tiger

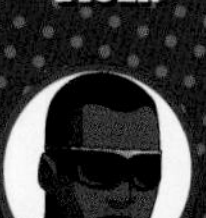

Luke Cage

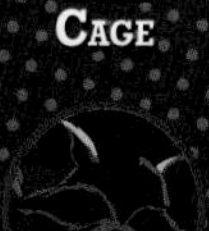

Rocket Raccoon

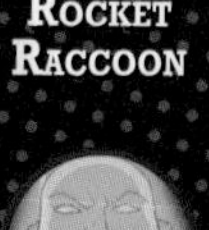

Korvac

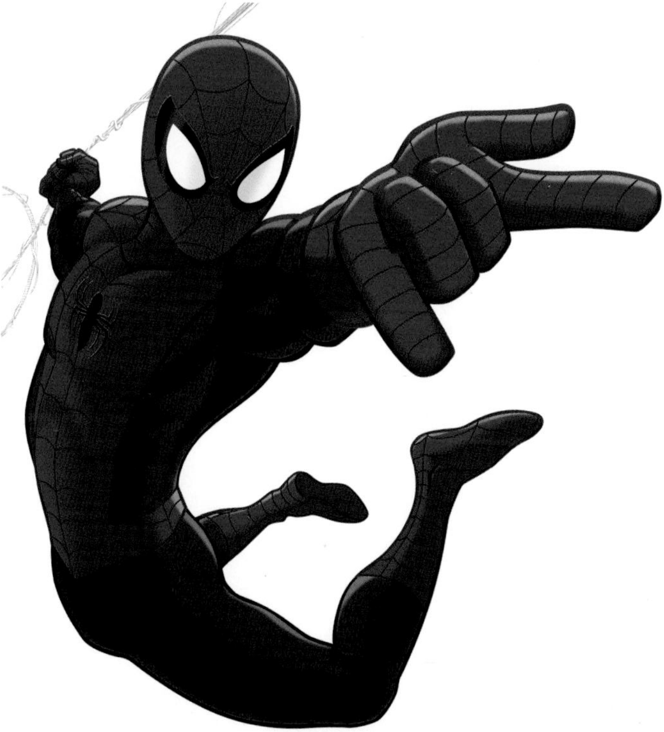

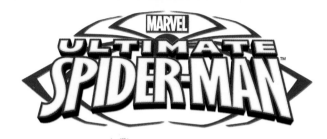

BASED ON

"GUARDIANS OF THE GALAXY"

BY BRIAN MICHAEL BENDIS

ADAPTED BY JOE CARAMAGNA

SEBASTIAN GIRNER editor **JON MOISAN** consulting editor
MARK PANICCIA senior editor
AXEL ALONSO editor in chief **JOE QUESADA** chief creative officer
DAN BUCKLEY publisher **ALAN FINE** executive producer

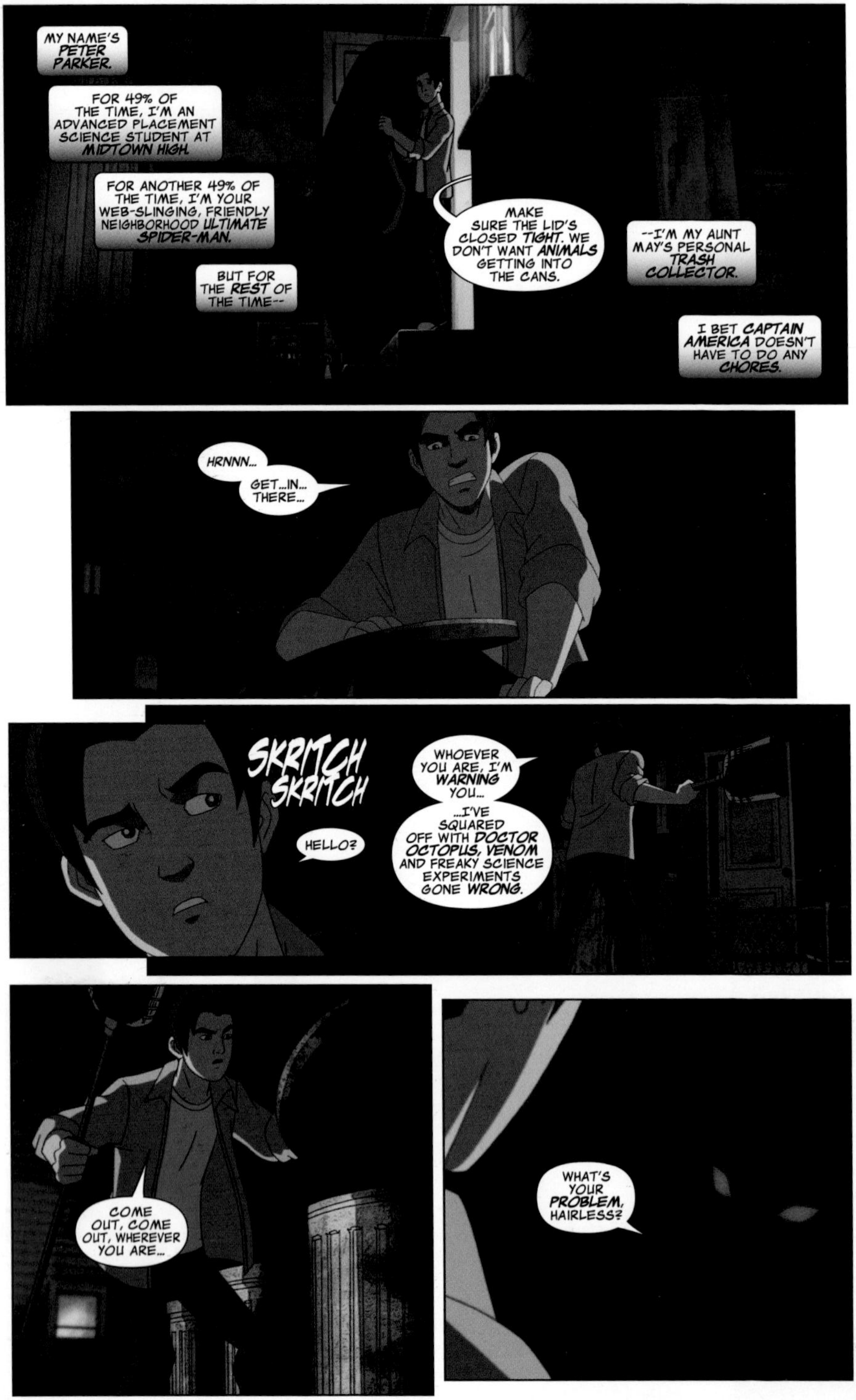
MY NAME'S PETER PARKER.
FOR 49% OF THE TIME, I'M AN ADVANCED PLACEMENT SCIENCE STUDENT AT MIDTOWN HIGH.
FOR ANOTHER 49% OF THE TIME, I'M YOUR WEB-SLINGING, FRIENDLY NEIGHBORHOOD ULTIMATE SPIDER-MAN.
BUT FOR THE REST OF THE TIME--
MAKE SURE THE LID'S CLOSED TIGHT. WE DON'T WANT ANIMALS GETTING INTO THE CANS.
--I'M MY AUNT MAY'S PERSONAL TRASH COLLECTOR.
I BET CAPTAIN AMERICA DOESN'T HAVE TO DO ANY CHORES.
HRNNN... GET...IN... THERE...
SKRITCH SKRITCH
HELLO?
WHOEVER YOU ARE, I'M WARNING YOU...
...I'VE SQUARED OFF WITH DOCTOR OCTOPUS, VENOM AND FREAKY SCIENCE EXPERIMENTS GONE WRONG.
COME OUT, COME OUT, WHEREVER YOU ARE...
WHAT'S YOUR PROBLEM, HAIRLESS?

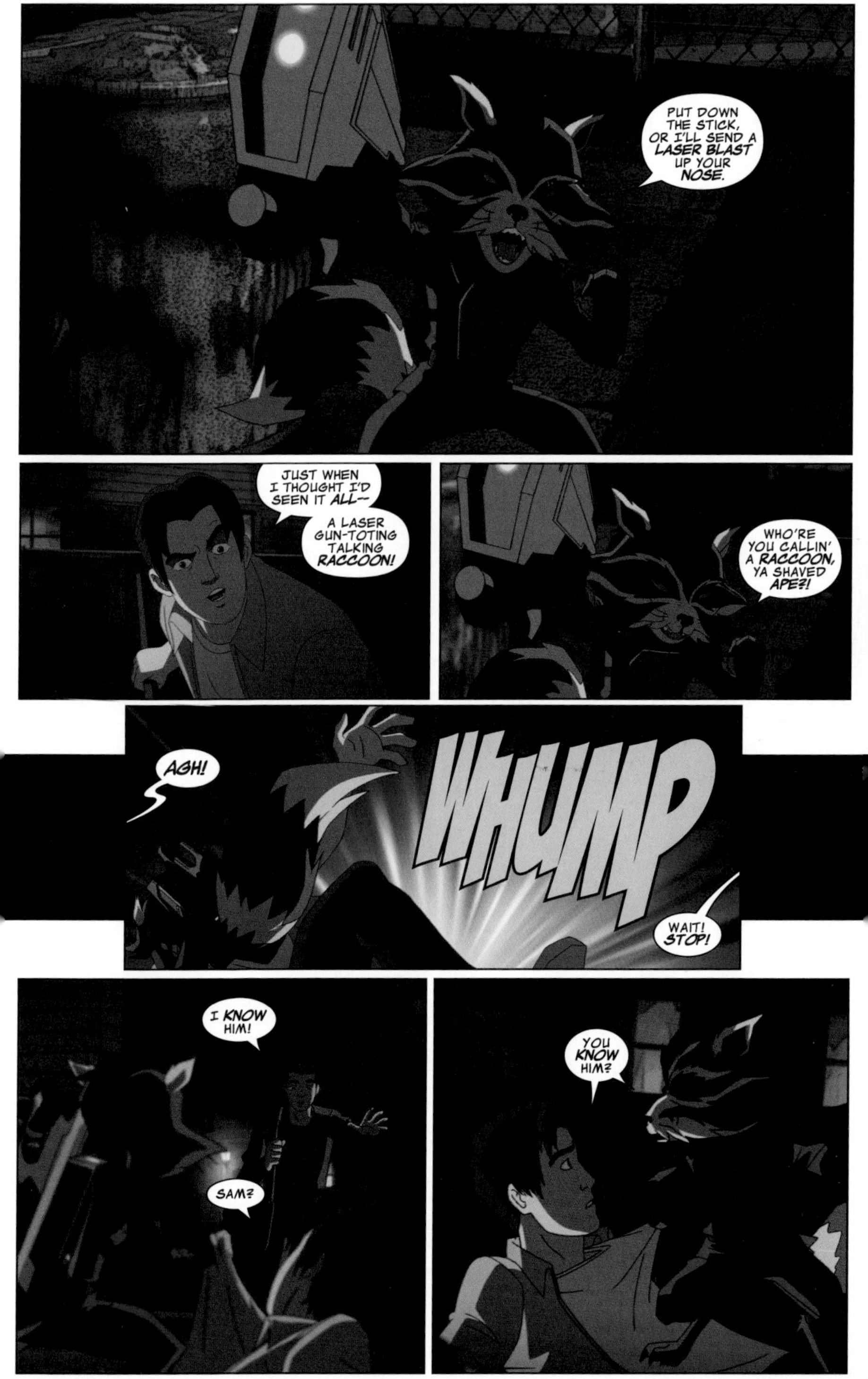
PUT DOWN THE STICK, OR I'LL SEND A LASER BLAST UP YOUR NOSE.
JUST WHEN I THOUGHT I'D SEEN IT ALL--
A LASER GUN-TOTING TALKING RACCOON!
WHO'RE YOU CALLIN' A RACCOON, YA SHAVED APE?!
AGH!
WHUMP
WAIT! STOP!
I KNOW HIM!
SAM?
YOU KNOW HIM?

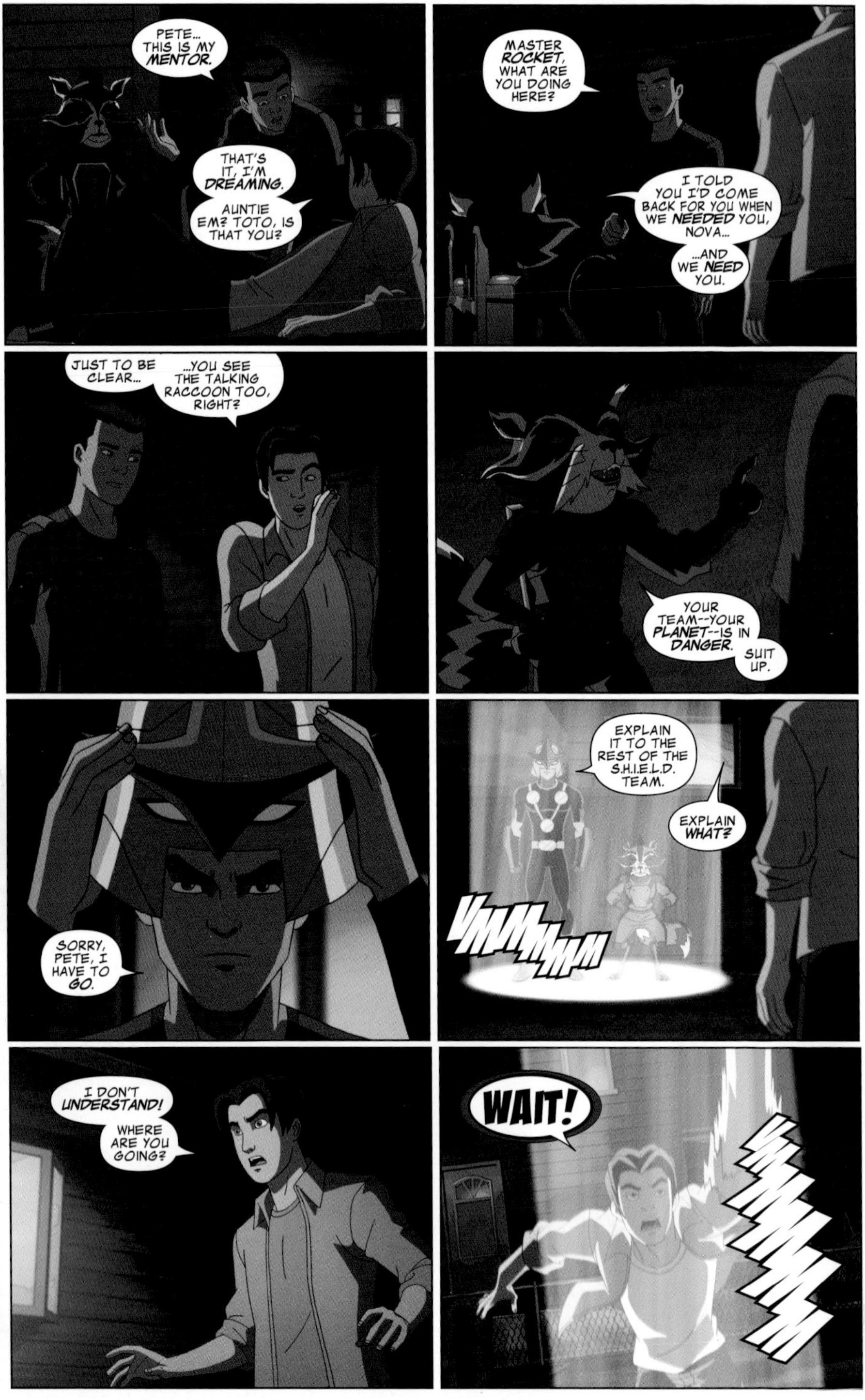
PETE... THIS IS MY MENTOR.
THAT'S IT, I'M DREAMING.
AUNTIE EM? TOTO, IS THAT YOU?
MASTER ROCKET, WHAT ARE YOU DOING HERE?
I TOLD YOU I'D COME BACK FOR YOU WHEN WE NEEDED YOU, NOVA...
...AND WE NEED YOU.
JUST TO BE CLEAR...
...YOU SEE THE TALKING RACCOON TOO, RIGHT?
YOUR TEAM--YOUR PLANET--IS IN DANGER.
SUIT UP.
SORRY, PETE, I HAVE TO GO.
EXPLAIN IT TO THE REST OF THE S.H.I.E.L.D. TEAM.
EXPLAIN WHAT?
VMMMMMM
I DON'T UNDERSTAND!
WHERE ARE YOU GOING?
WAIT!

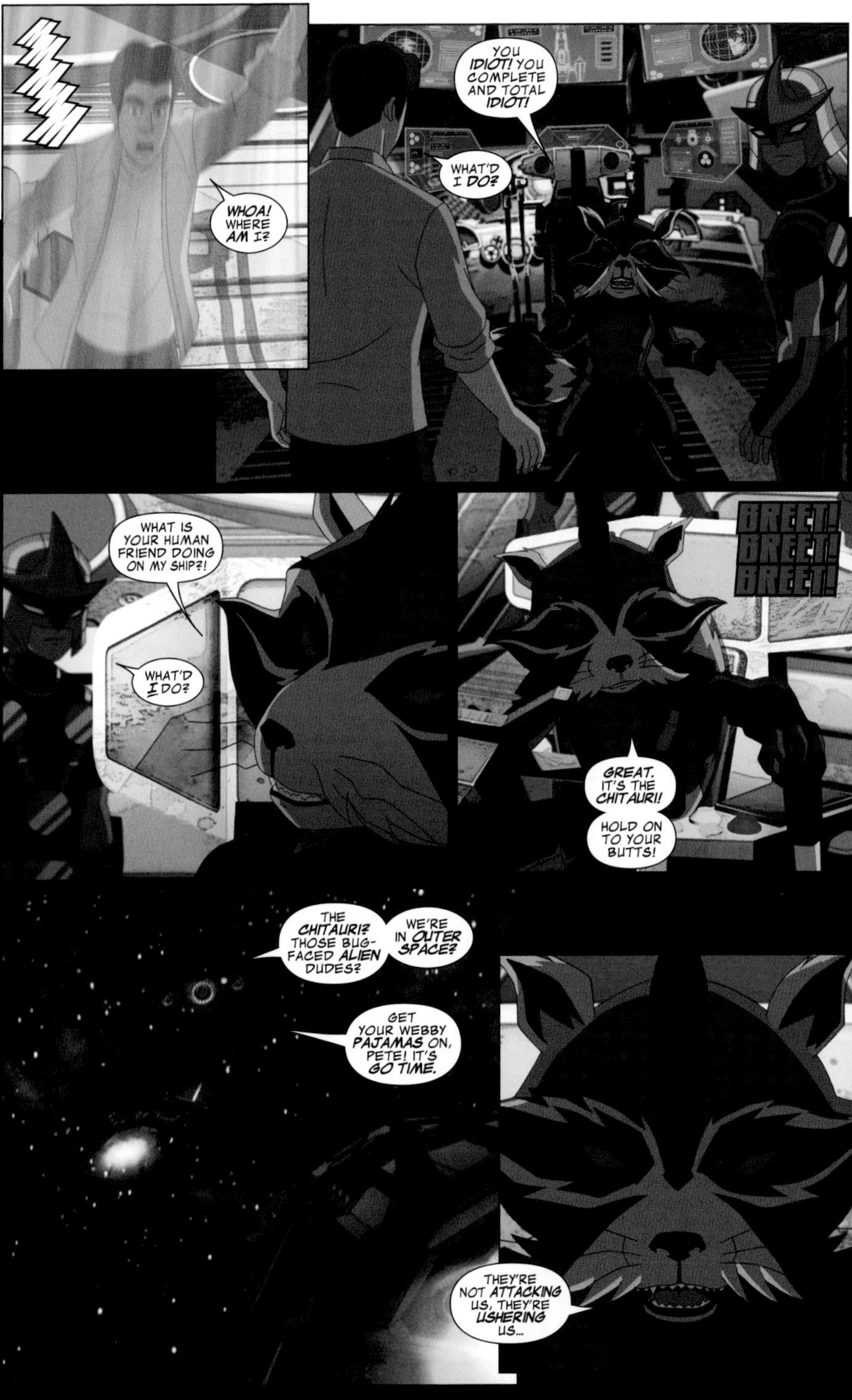
WHOA! WHERE AM I?
YOU IDIOT! YOU COMPLETE AND TOTAL IDIOT!
WHAT'D I DO?
WHAT IS YOUR HUMAN FRIEND DOING ON MY SHIP?!
WHAT'D I DO?
BREET! BREET! BREET!
GREAT. IT'S THE CHITAURI!
HOLD ON TO YOUR BUTTS!
THE CHITAURI? THOSE BUG-FACED ALIEN DUDES?
WE'RE IN OUTER SPACE?
GET YOUR WEBBY PAJAMAS ON, PETE! IT'S GO TIME.
THEY'RE NOT ATTACKING US, THEY'RE USHERING US...

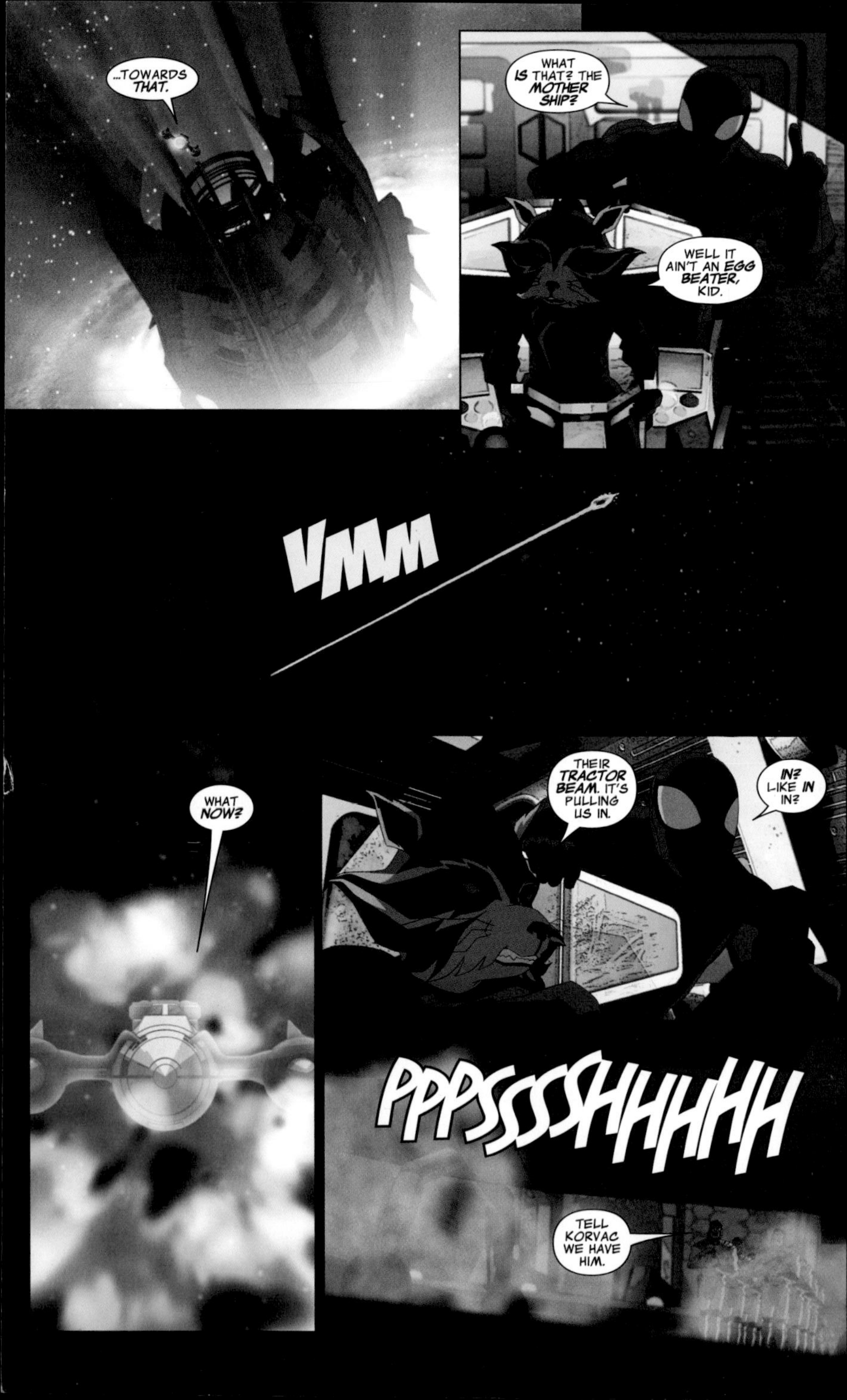
...TOWARDS THAT.
WHAT IS THAT? THE MOTHER SHIP?
WELL IT AIN'T AN EGG BEATER, KID.
VMM
WHAT NOW?
THEIR TRACTOR BEAM. IT'S PULLING US IN.
IN? LIKE IN IN?
PPPSSSSHHHHHH
TELL KORVAC WE HAVE HIM.

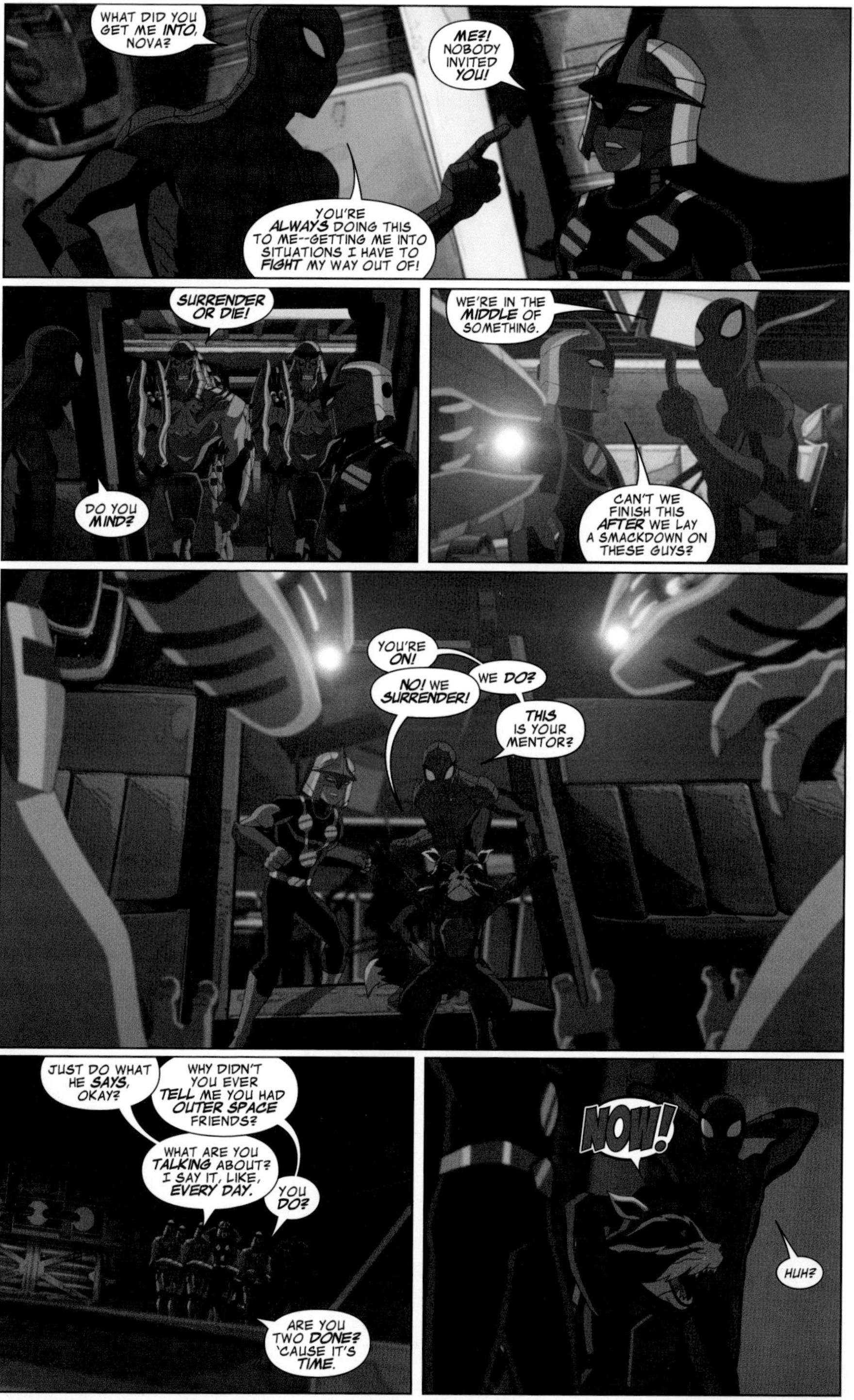
WHAT DID YOU GET ME INTO, NOVA?
ME?! NOBODY INVITED YOU!
YOU'RE ALWAYS DOING THIS TO ME--GETTING ME INTO SITUATIONS I HAVE TO FIGHT MY WAY OUT OF!
SURRENDER OR DIE!
DO YOU MIND?
WE'RE IN THE MIDDLE OF SOMETHING.
CAN'T WE FINISH THIS AFTER WE LAY A SMACKDOWN ON THESE GUYS?
YOU'RE ON!
NO! WE SURRENDER!
WE DO?
THIS IS YOUR MENTOR?
JUST DO WHAT HE SAYS, OKAY?
WHY DIDN'T YOU EVER TELL ME YOU HAD OUTER SPACE FRIENDS?
WHAT ARE YOU TALKING ABOUT? I SAY IT, LIKE, EVERY DAY.
YOU DO?
ARE YOU TWO DONE? 'CAUSE IT'S TIME.
NOW!
HUH?

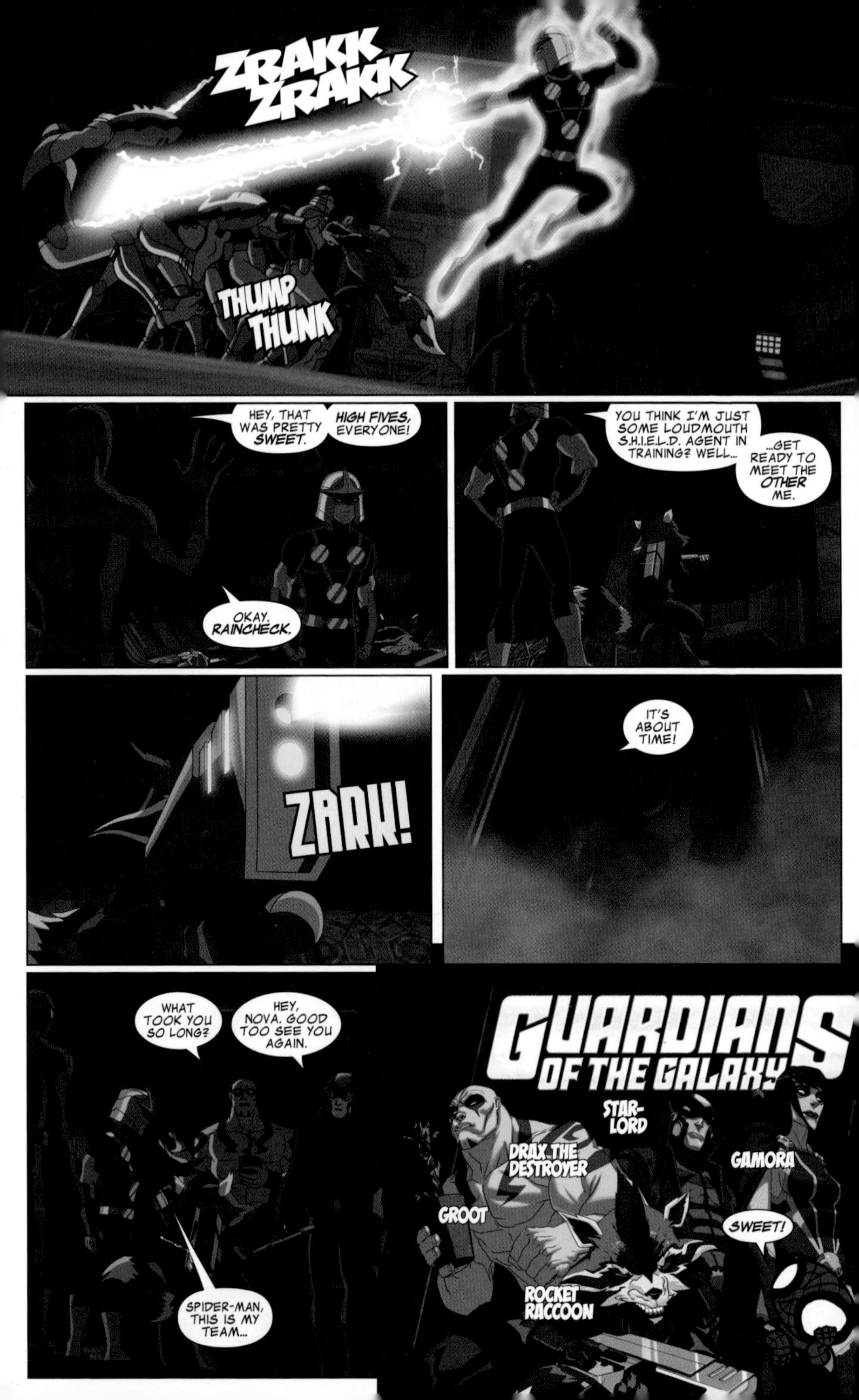
ZRAKK ZRAKK
THUMP THUNK
HEY, THAT WAS PRETTY SWEET.
HIGH FIVES, EVERYONE!
OKAY. RAINCHECK.
YOU THINK I'M JUST SOME LOUDMOUTH S.H.I.E.L.D. AGENT IN TRAINING? WELL...
...GET READY TO MEET THE OTHER ME.
ZARK!
IT'S ABOUT TIME!
WHAT TOOK YOU SO LONG?
HEY, NOVA. GOOD TOO SEE YOU AGAIN.
GUARDIANS OF THE GALAXY
STAR-LORD
DRAX THE DESTROYER
GAMORA
GROOT
SWEET!
SPIDER-MAN, THIS IS MY TEAM...
ROCKET RACCOON

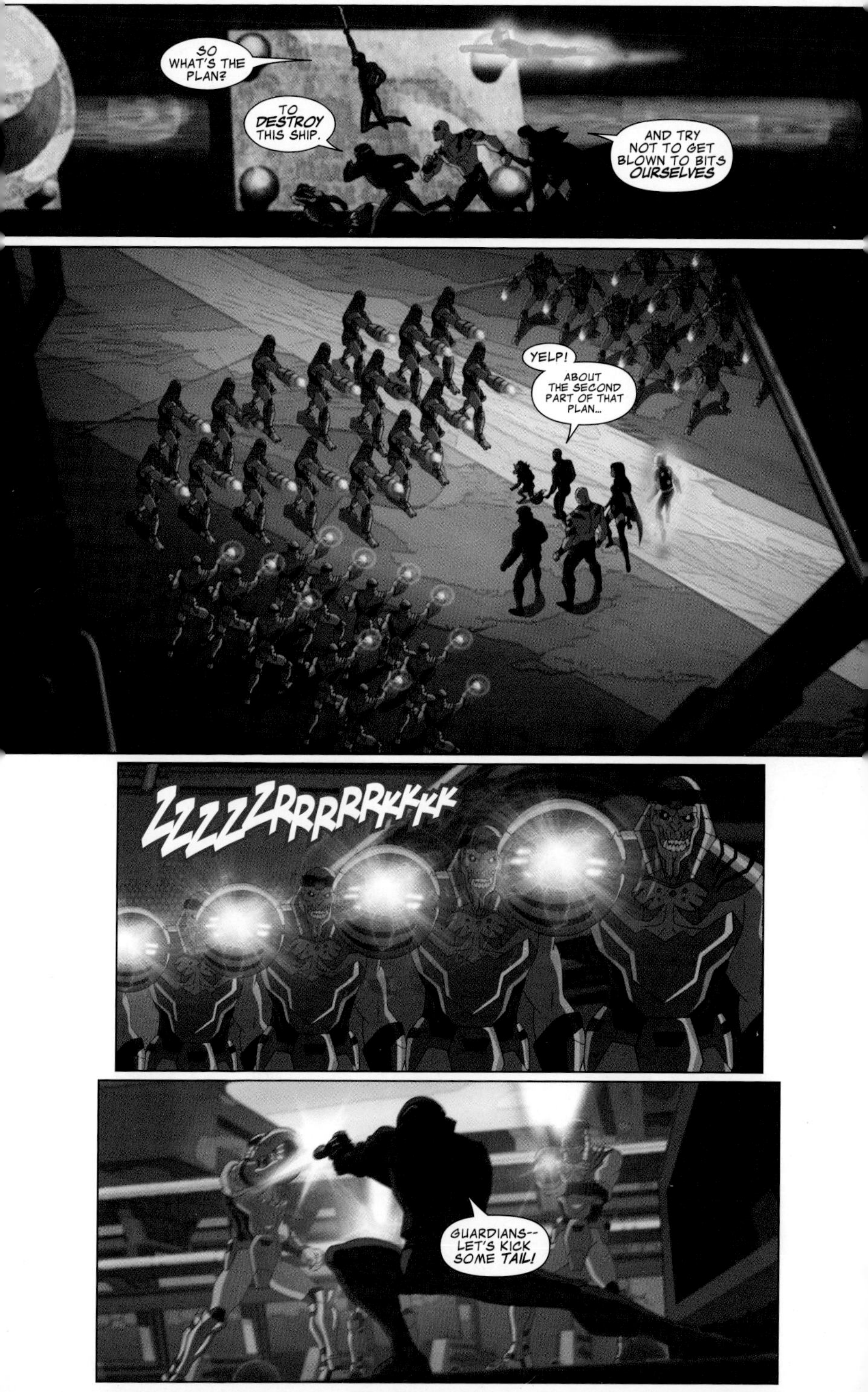
SO WHAT'S THE PLAN?
TO DESTROY THIS SHIP.
AND TRY NOT TO GET BLOWN TO BITS OURSELVES
YELP!
ABOUT THE SECOND PART OF THAT PLAN...
ZZZZZRRRRRKKKK
GUARDIANS-- LET'S KICK SOME TAIL!

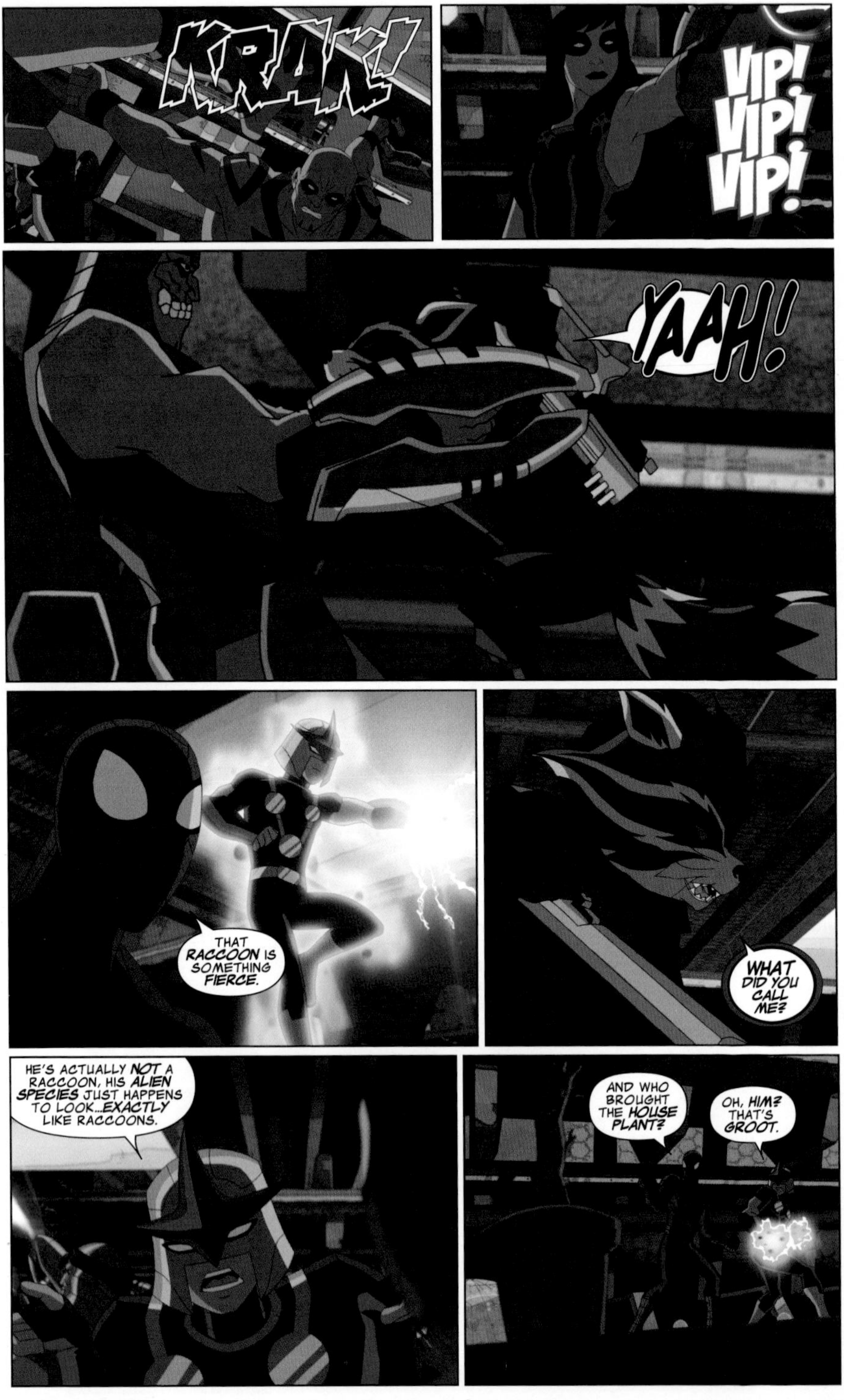
KRAK!
VIP! VIP! VIP!
YAAH!
THAT RACCOON IS SOMETHING FIERCE.
WHAT DID YOU CALL ME?
HE'S ACTUALLY NOT A RACCOON, HIS ALIEN SPECIES JUST HAPPENS TO LOOK...EXACTLY LIKE RACCOONS.
AND WHO BROUGHT THE HOUSE PLANT?
OH, HIM? THAT'S GROOT.

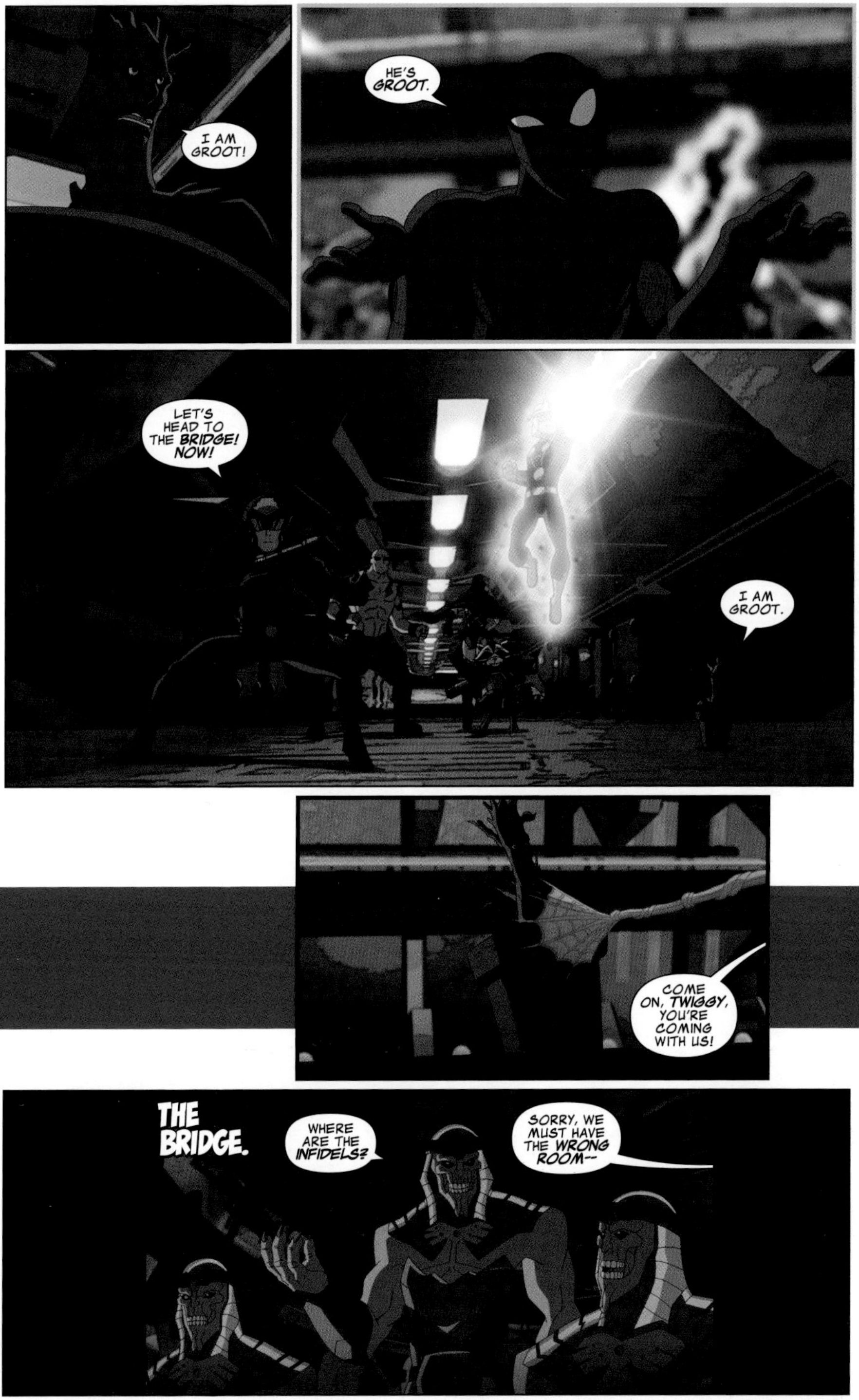
I AM GROOT!
HE'S GROOT.
LET'S HEAD TO THE BRIDGE! NOW!
I AM GROOT.
COME ON, TWIGGY, YOU'RE COMING WITH US!
THE BRIDGE.
WHERE ARE THE INFIDELS?
SORRY, WE MUST HAVE THE WRONG ROOM--

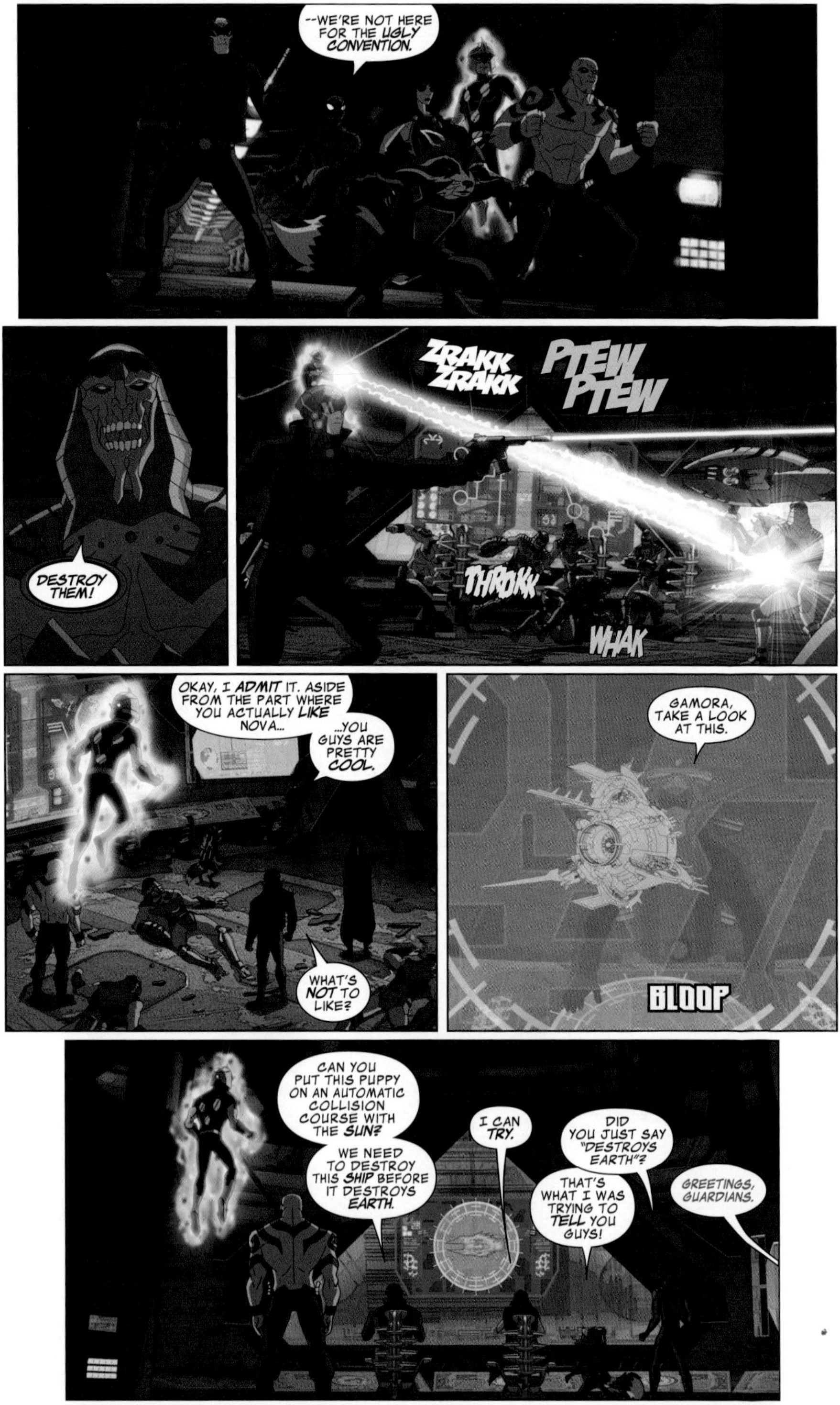
--WE'RE NOT HERE FOR THE UGLY CONVENTION.
DESTROY THEM!
ZRAKK ZRAKK
PTEW PTEW
THROKK
WHAK
OKAY, I ADMIT IT. ASIDE FROM THE PART WHERE YOU ACTUALLY LIKE NOVA...
...YOU GUYS ARE PRETTY COOL.
WHAT'S NOT TO LIKE?
GAMORA, TAKE A LOOK AT THIS.
BLOOP
CAN YOU PUT THIS PUPPY ON AN AUTOMATIC COLLISION COURSE WITH THE SUN?
WE NEED TO DESTROY THIS SHIP BEFORE IT DESTROYS EARTH.
I CAN TRY.
DID YOU JUST SAY "DESTROYS EARTH"?
THAT'S WHAT I WAS TRYING TO TELL YOU GUYS!
GREETINGS, GUARDIANS.

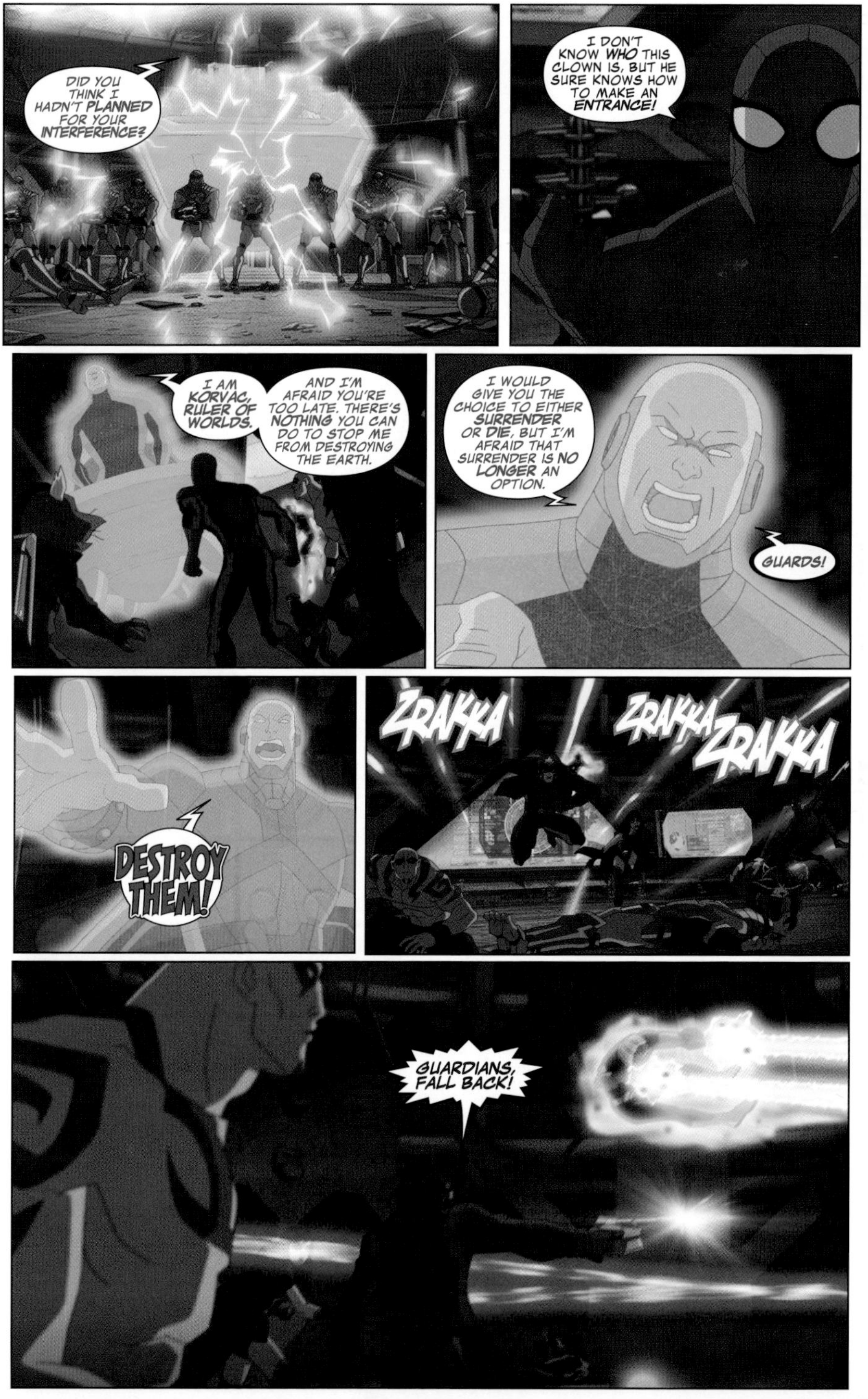
DID YOU THINK I HADN'T PLANNED FOR YOUR INTERFERENCE?
I DON'T KNOW WHO THIS CLOWN IS, BUT HE SURE KNOWS HOW TO MAKE AN ENTRANCE!
I AM KORVAC, RULER OF WORLDS.
AND I'M AFRAID YOU'RE TOO LATE. THERE'S NOTHING YOU CAN DO TO STOP ME FROM DESTROYING THE EARTH.
I WOULD GIVE YOU THE CHOICE TO EITHER SURRENDER OR DIE, BUT I'M AFRAID THAT SURRENDER IS NO LONGER AN OPTION.
GUARDS!
DESTROY THEM!
ZRAKKA
ZRAKKA
ZRAKKA
GUARDIANS, FALL BACK!

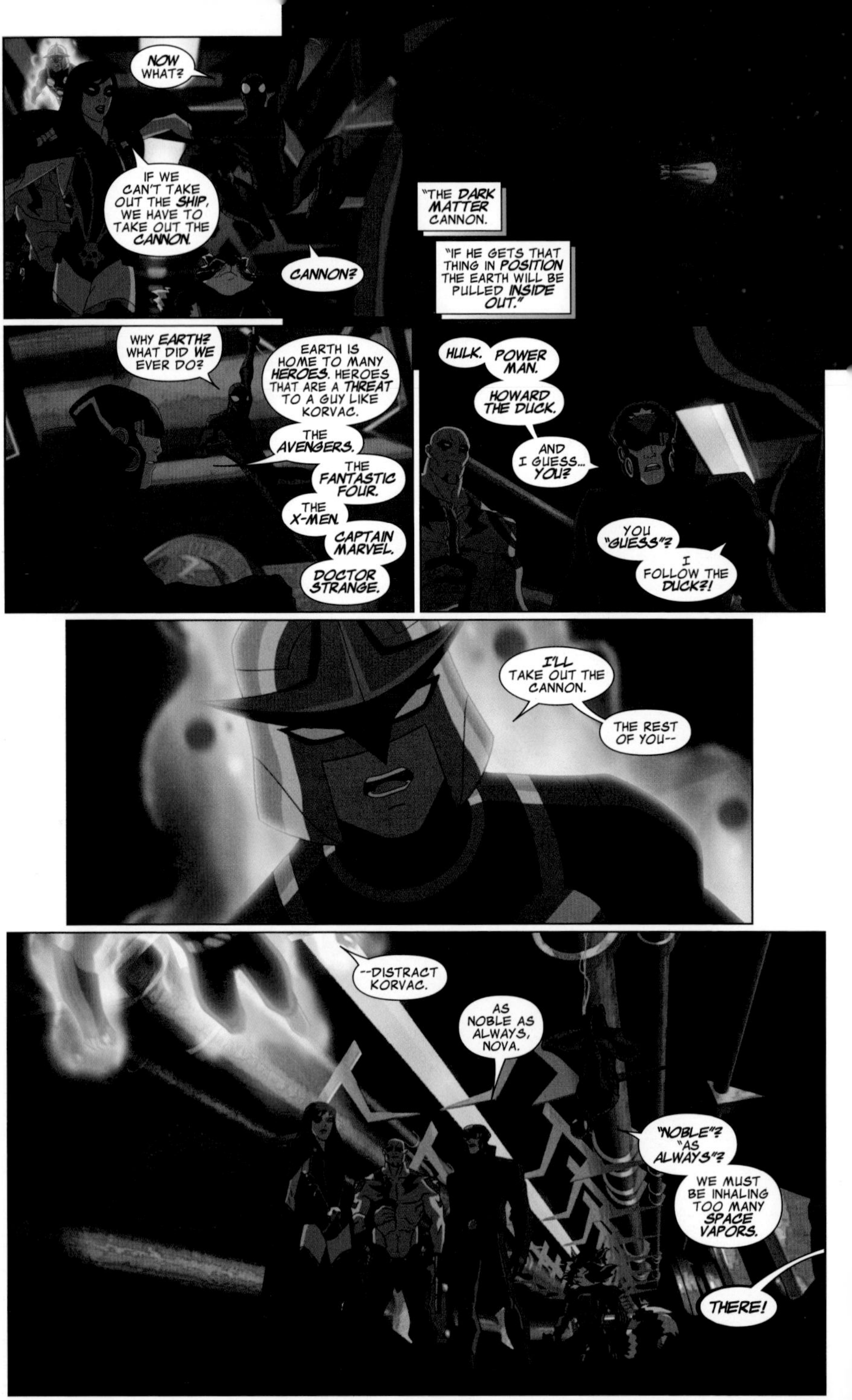
NOW WHAT?
IF WE CAN'T TAKE OUT THE SHIP, WE HAVE TO TAKE OUT THE CANNON.
CANNON?
"THE DARK MATTER CANNON.
"IF HE GETS THAT THING IN POSITION THE EARTH WILL BE PULLED INSIDE OUT."
WHY EARTH? WHAT DID WE EVER DO?
EARTH IS HOME TO MANY HEROES. HEROES THAT ARE A THREAT TO A GUY LIKE KORVAC.
THE AVENGERS.
THE FANTASTIC FOUR.
THE X-MEN.
CAPTAIN MARVEL.
DOCTOR STRANGE.
HULK.
POWER MAN.
HOWARD THE DUCK.
AND I GUESS... YOU?
YOU "GUESS"?
I FOLLOW THE DUCK?!
I'LL TAKE OUT THE CANNON.
THE REST OF YOU--
--DISTRACT KORVAC.
AS NOBLE AS ALWAYS, NOVA.
"NOBLE"? "AS ALWAYS"?
WE MUST BE INHALING TOO MANY SPACE VAPORS.
THERE!

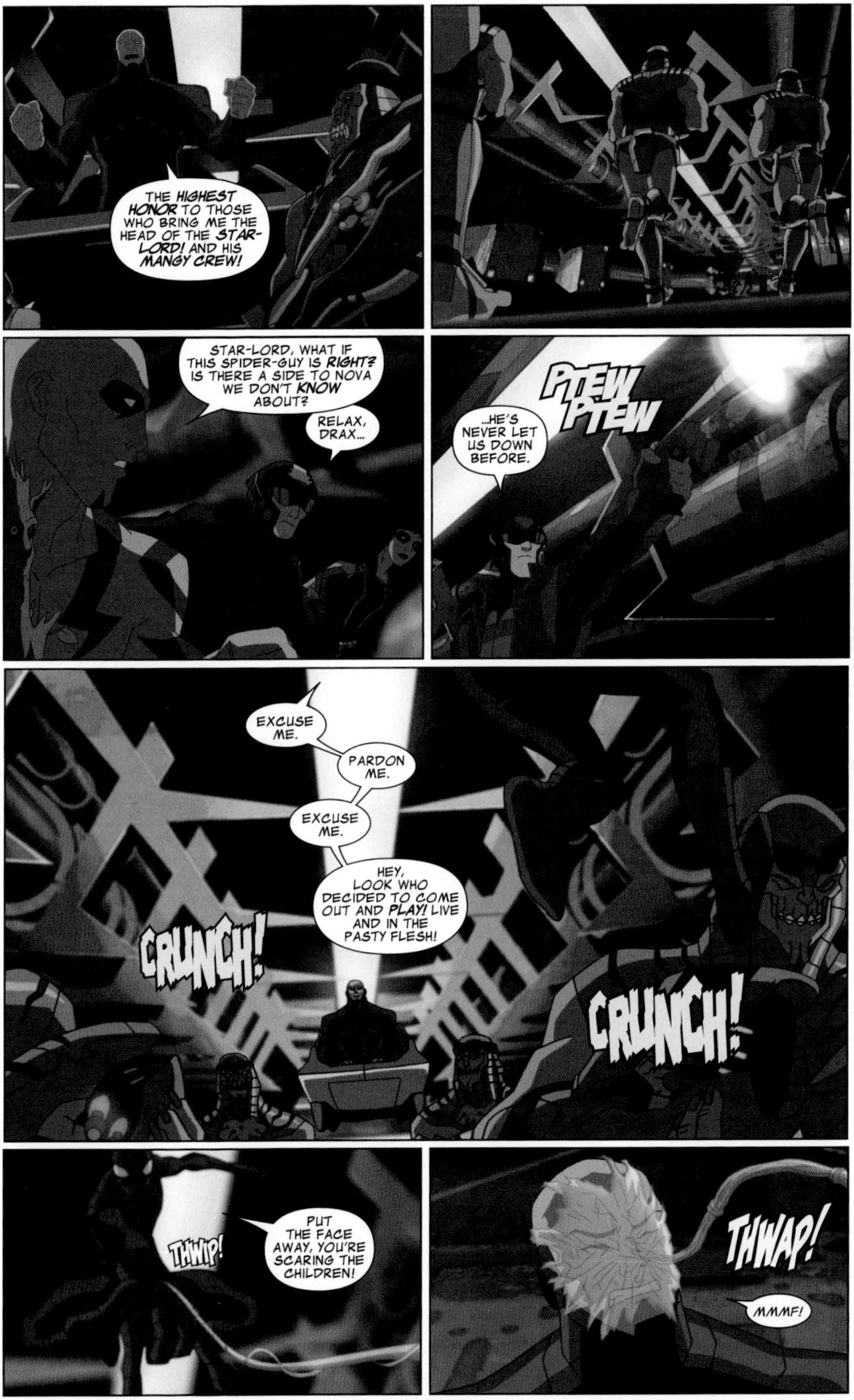
THE HIGHEST HONOR TO THOSE WHO BRING ME THE HEAD OF THE STAR-LORD! AND HIS MANGY CREW!
STAR-LORD, WHAT IF THIS SPIDER-GUY IS RIGHT? IS THERE A SIDE TO NOVA WE DON'T KNOW ABOUT?
RELAX, DRAX...
PTEW PTEW
...HE'S NEVER LET US DOWN BEFORE.
EXCUSE ME.
PARDON ME.
EXCUSE ME.
HEY, LOOK WHO DECIDED TO COME OUT AND PLAY! LIVE AND IN THE PASTY FLESH!
CRUNCH!
CRUNCH!
THWIP!
PUT THE FACE AWAY, YOU'RE SCARING THE CHILDREN!
THWAP!
MMMF!

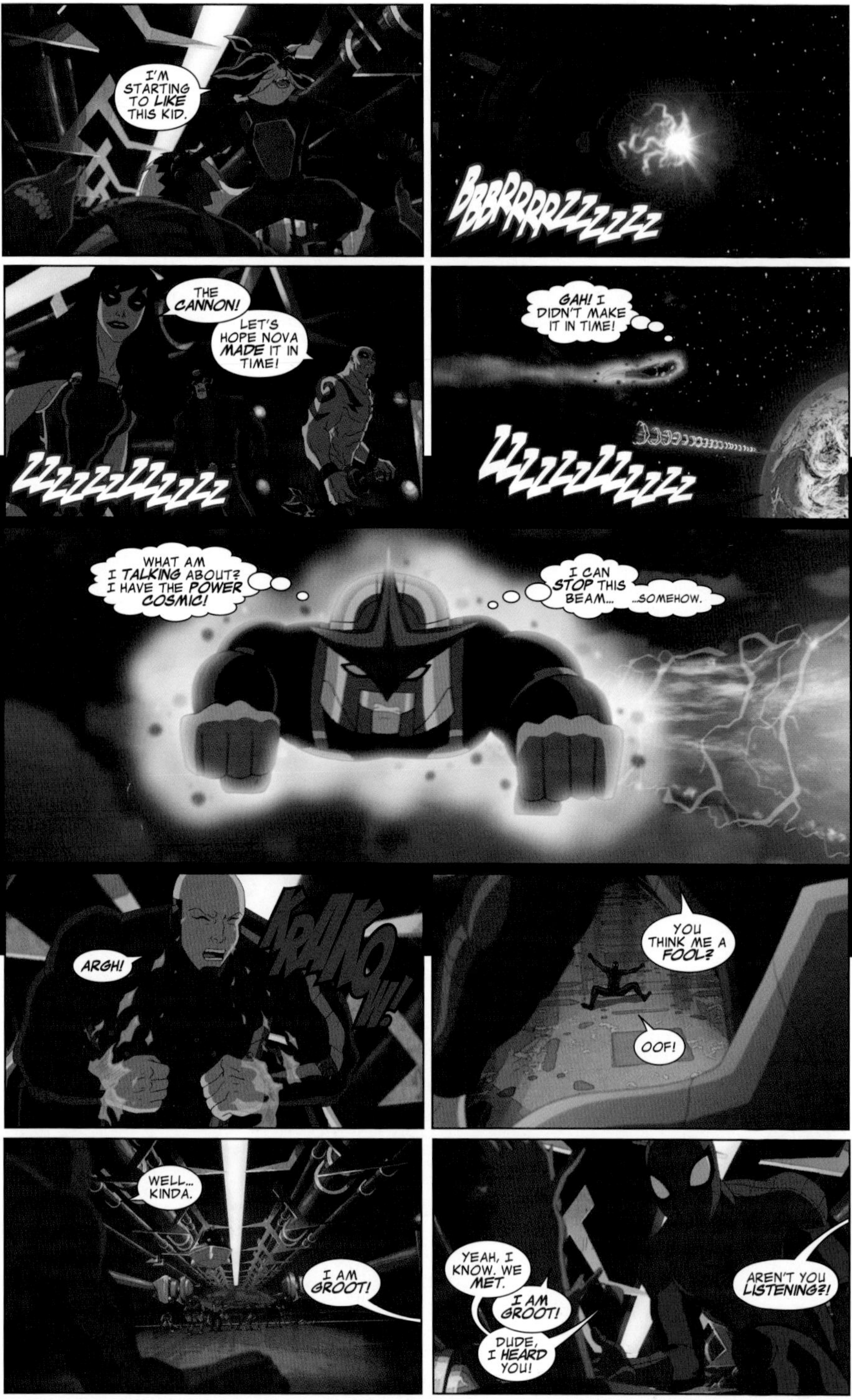
I'M STARTING TO LIKE THIS KID.
BBBRRRRZZZZZZ
THE CANNON!
LET'S HOPE NOVA MADE IT IN TIME!
ZZZZZZZZZZZZZ
GAH! I DIDN'T MAKE IT IN TIME!
ZZZZZZZZZZZZZ
WHAT AM I TALKING ABOUT? I HAVE THE POWER COSMIC!
I CAN STOP THIS BEAM...
...SOMEHOW.
ARGH!
YOU THINK ME A FOOL?
OOF!
WELL... KINDA.
I AM GROOT!
YEAH, I KNOW. WE MET.
I AM GROOT!
DUDE, I HEARD YOU!
AREN'T YOU LISTENING?!

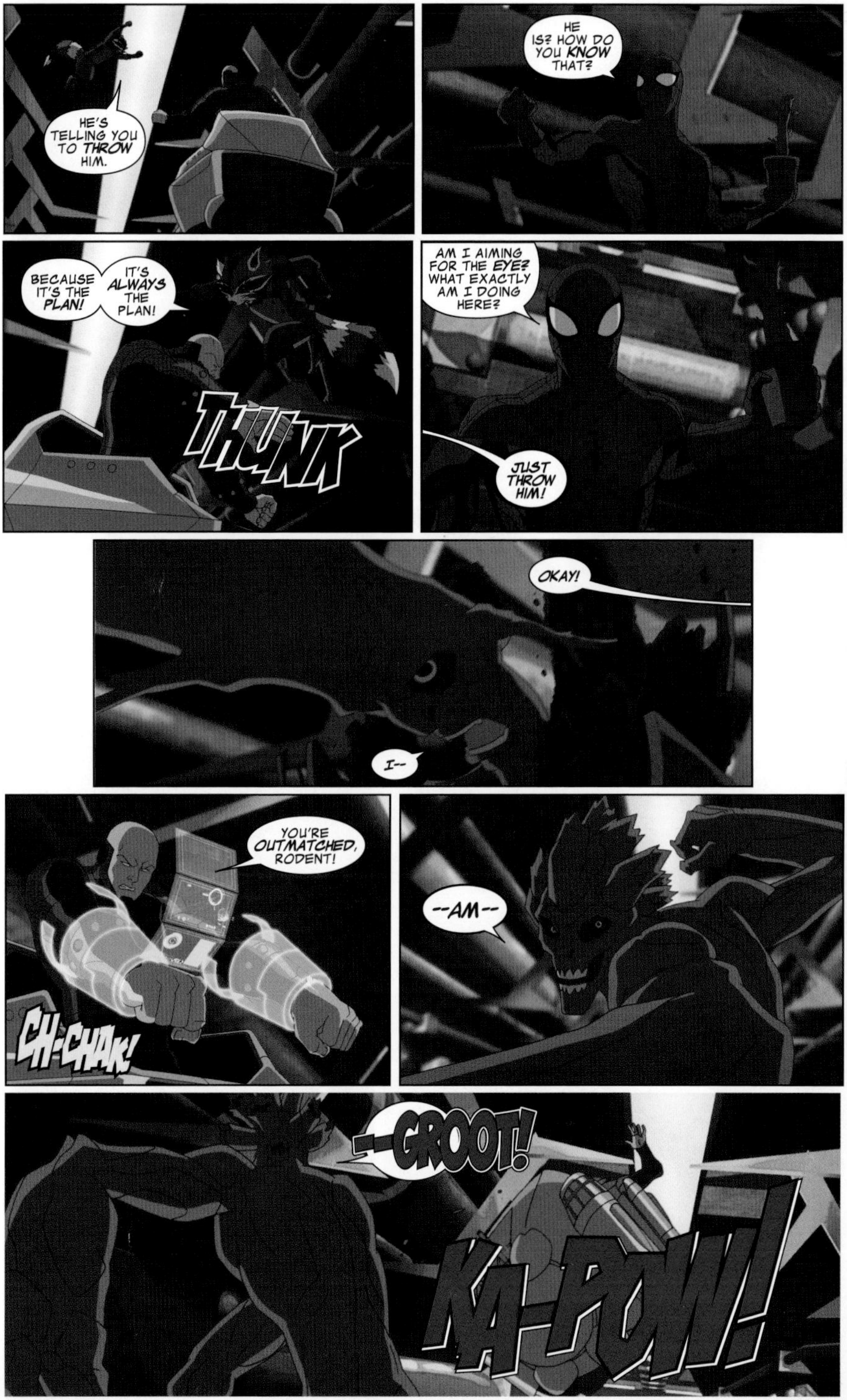
HE'S TELLING YOU TO THROW HIM.
HE IS? HOW DO YOU KNOW THAT?
BECAUSE IT'S THE PLAN!
IT'S ALWAYS THE PLAN!
THUNK
AM I AIMING FOR THE EYE? WHAT EXACTLY AM I DOING HERE?
JUST THROW HIM!
OKAY!
I--
YOU'RE OUTMATCHED, RODENT!
CH-CHAK!
--AM--
--GROOT!
KA-POW!

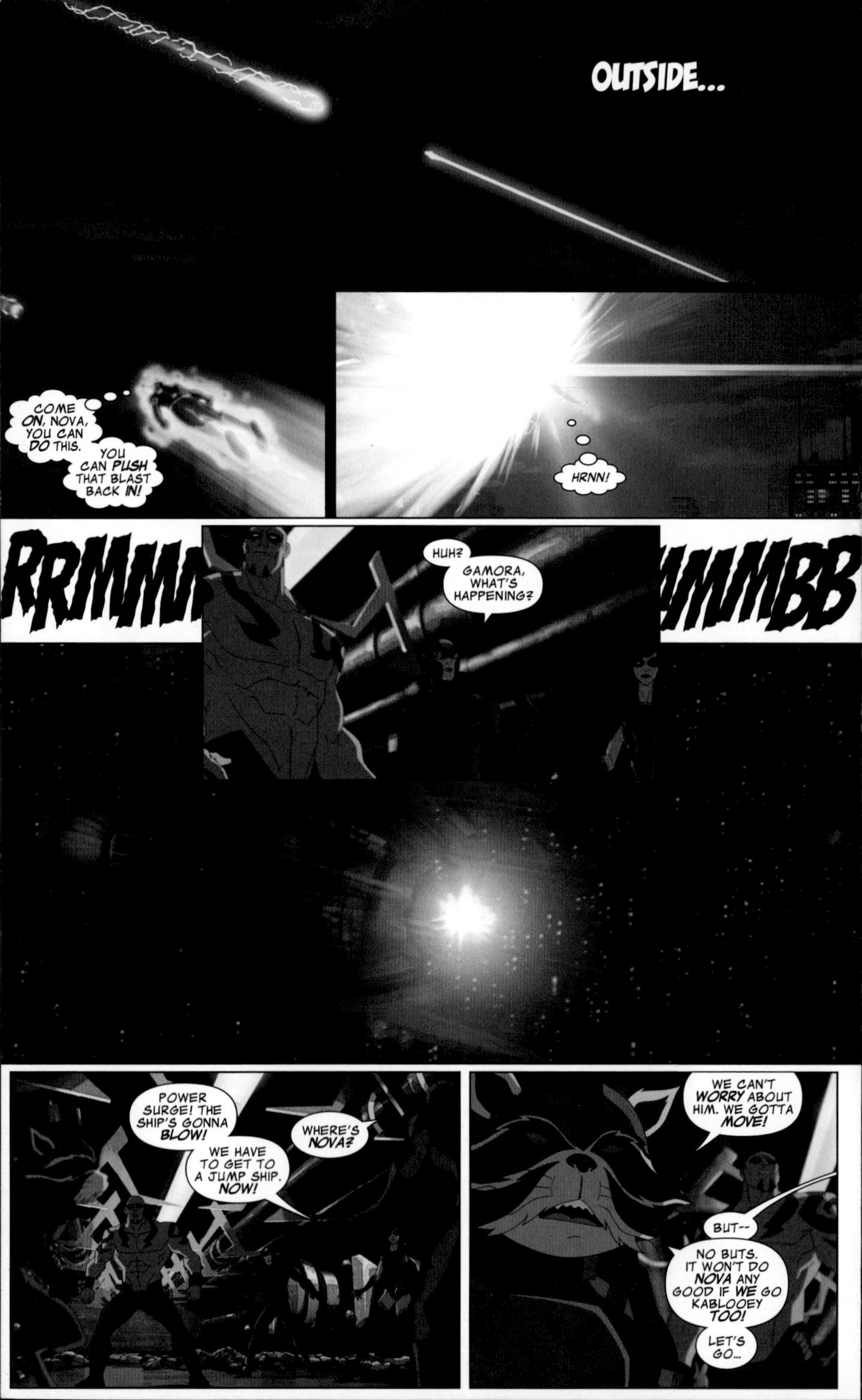
OUTSIDE...
COME ON, NOVA, YOU CAN DO THIS.
YOU CAN PUSH THAT BLAST BACK IN!
HRNN!
HUH? GAMORA, WHAT'S HAPPENING?
POWER SURGE! THE SHIP'S GONNA BLOW!
WHERE'S NOVA?
WE HAVE TO GET TO A JUMP SHIP. NOW!
WE CAN'T WORRY ABOUT HIM. WE GOTTA MOVE!
BUT--
NO BUTS. IT WON'T DO NOVA ANY GOOD IF WE GO KABLOOEY TOO!
LET'S GO...

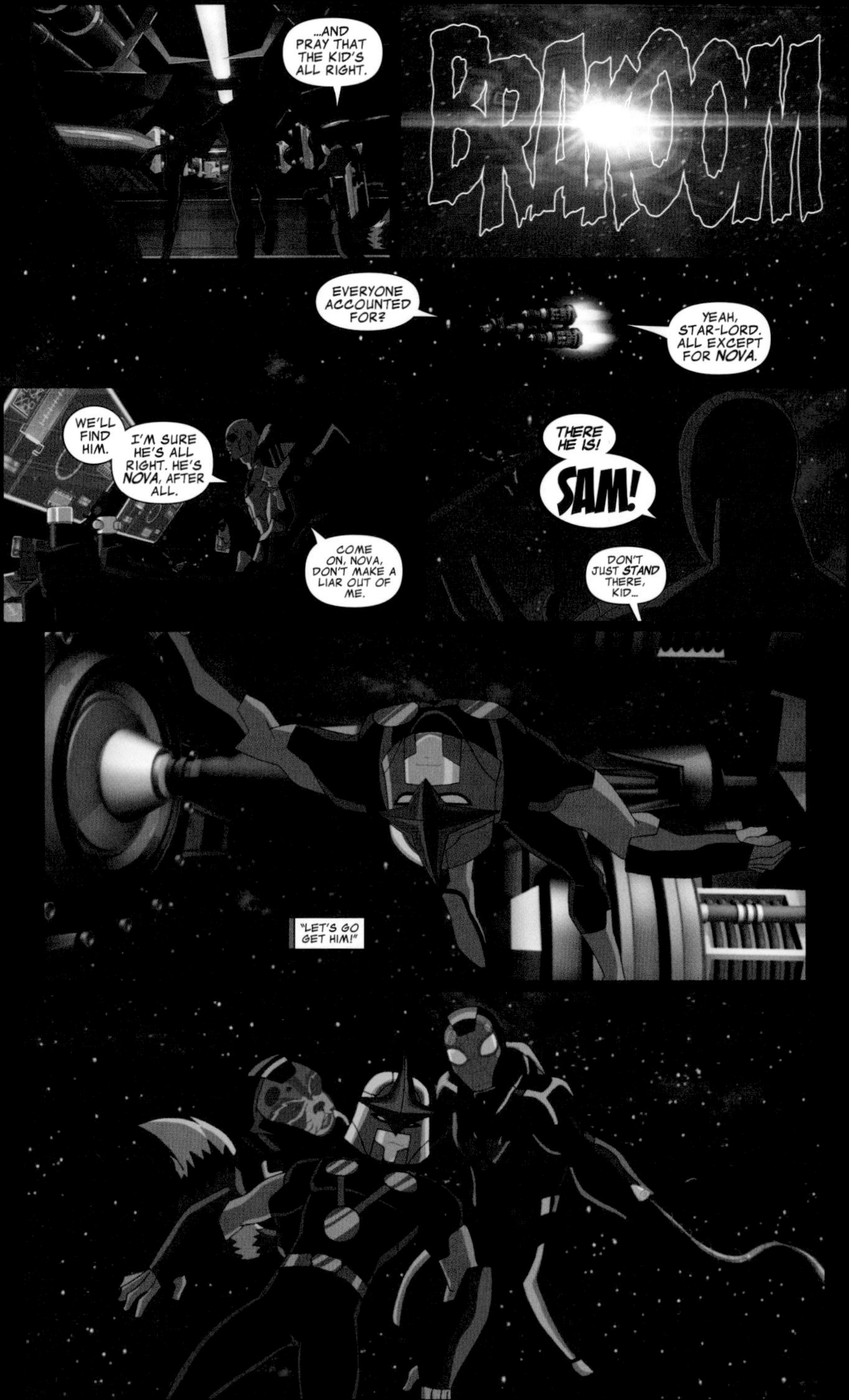
...AND PRAY THAT THE KID'S ALL RIGHT.
BRAKOOM
EVERYONE ACCOUNTED FOR?
YEAH, STAR-LORD. ALL EXCEPT FOR NOVA.
WE'LL FIND HIM.
I'M SURE HE'S ALL RIGHT. HE'S NOVA, AFTER ALL.
COME ON, NOVA, DON'T MAKE A LIAR OUT OF ME.
THERE HE IS!
SAM!
DON'T JUST STAND THERE, KID...
"LET'S GO GET HIM!"

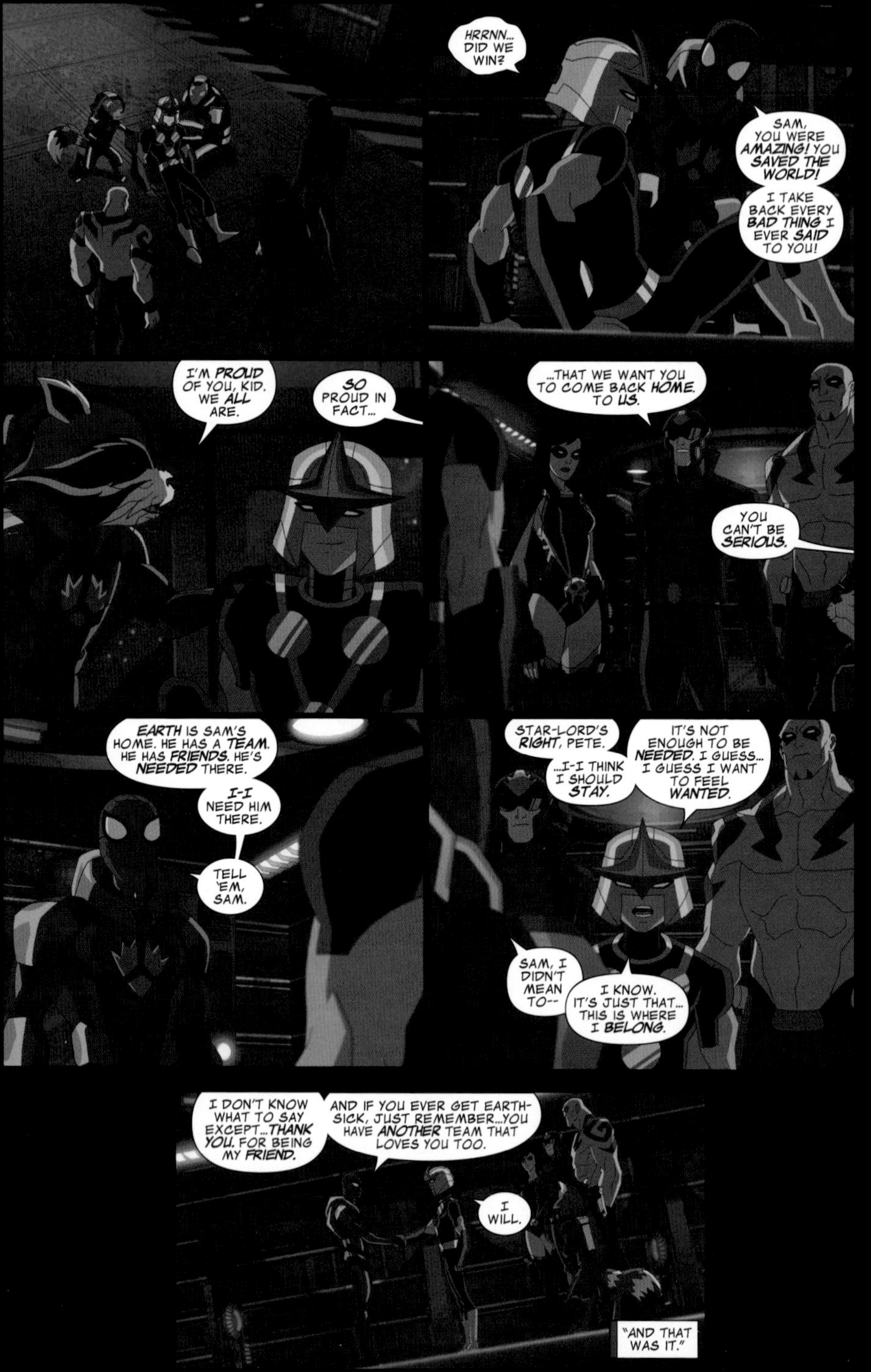
HRRNN... DID WE WIN?
SAM, YOU WERE AMAZING! YOU SAVED THE WORLD!
I TAKE BACK EVERY BAD THING I EVER SAID TO YOU!
I'M PROUD OF YOU, KID. WE ALL ARE.
SO PROUD IN FACT...
...THAT WE WANT YOU TO COME BACK HOME. TO US.
YOU CAN'T BE SERIOUS.
EARTH IS SAM'S HOME. HE HAS A TEAM. HE HAS FRIENDS. HE'S NEEDED THERE.
I-I NEED HIM THERE.
TELL 'EM, SAM.
STAR-LORD'S RIGHT, PETE.
...I-I THINK I SHOULD STAY.
IT'S NOT ENOUGH TO BE NEEDED. I GUESS... I GUESS I WANT TO FEEL WANTED.
SAM, I DIDN'T MEAN TO--
I KNOW. IT'S JUST THAT... THIS IS WHERE I BELONG.
I DON'T KNOW WHAT TO SAY EXCEPT... THANK YOU. FOR BEING MY FRIEND.
AND IF YOU EVER GET EARTH-SICK, JUST REMEMBER... YOU HAVE ANOTHER TEAM THAT LOVES YOU TOO.
I WILL.
"AND THAT WAS IT."

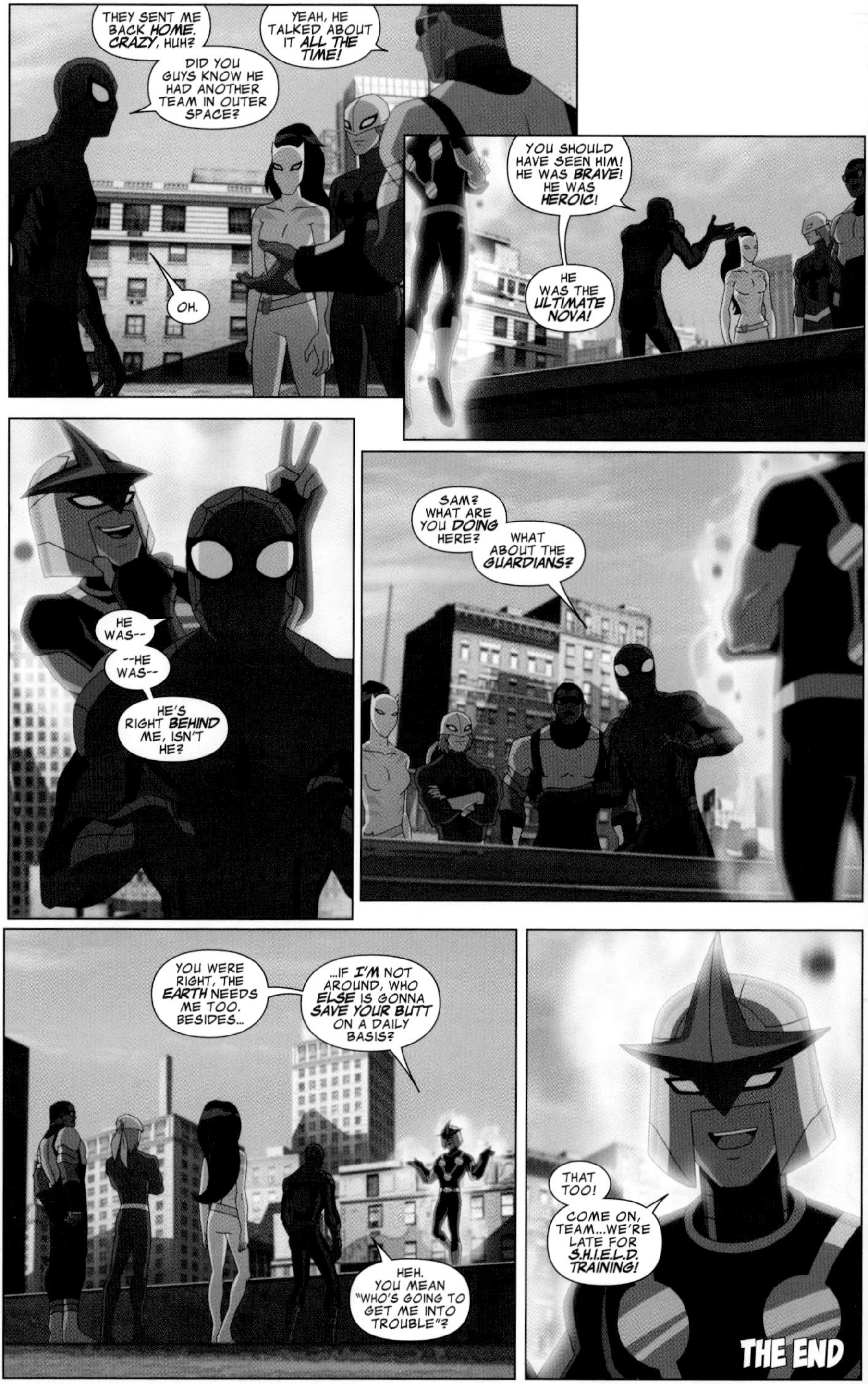
THEY SENT ME BACK HOME. CRAZY, HUH?
DID YOU GUYS KNOW HE HAD ANOTHER TEAM IN OUTER SPACE?
YEAH, HE TALKED ABOUT IT ALL THE TIME!
OH.
YOU SHOULD HAVE SEEN HIM! HE WAS BRAVE! HE WAS HEROIC!
HE WAS THE ULTIMATE NOVA!
HE WAS--
--HE WAS--
HE'S RIGHT BEHIND ME, ISN'T HE?
SAM? WHAT ARE YOU DOING HERE?
WHAT ABOUT THE GUARDIANS?
YOU WERE RIGHT, THE EARTH NEEDS ME TOO. BESIDES...
...IF I'M NOT AROUND, WHO ELSE IS GONNA SAVE YOUR BUTT ON A DAILY BASIS?
HEH. YOU MEAN "WHO'S GOING TO GET ME INTO TROUBLE"?
THAT TOO!
COME ON, TEAM...WE'RE LATE FOR S.H.I.E.L.D. TRAINING!
THE END

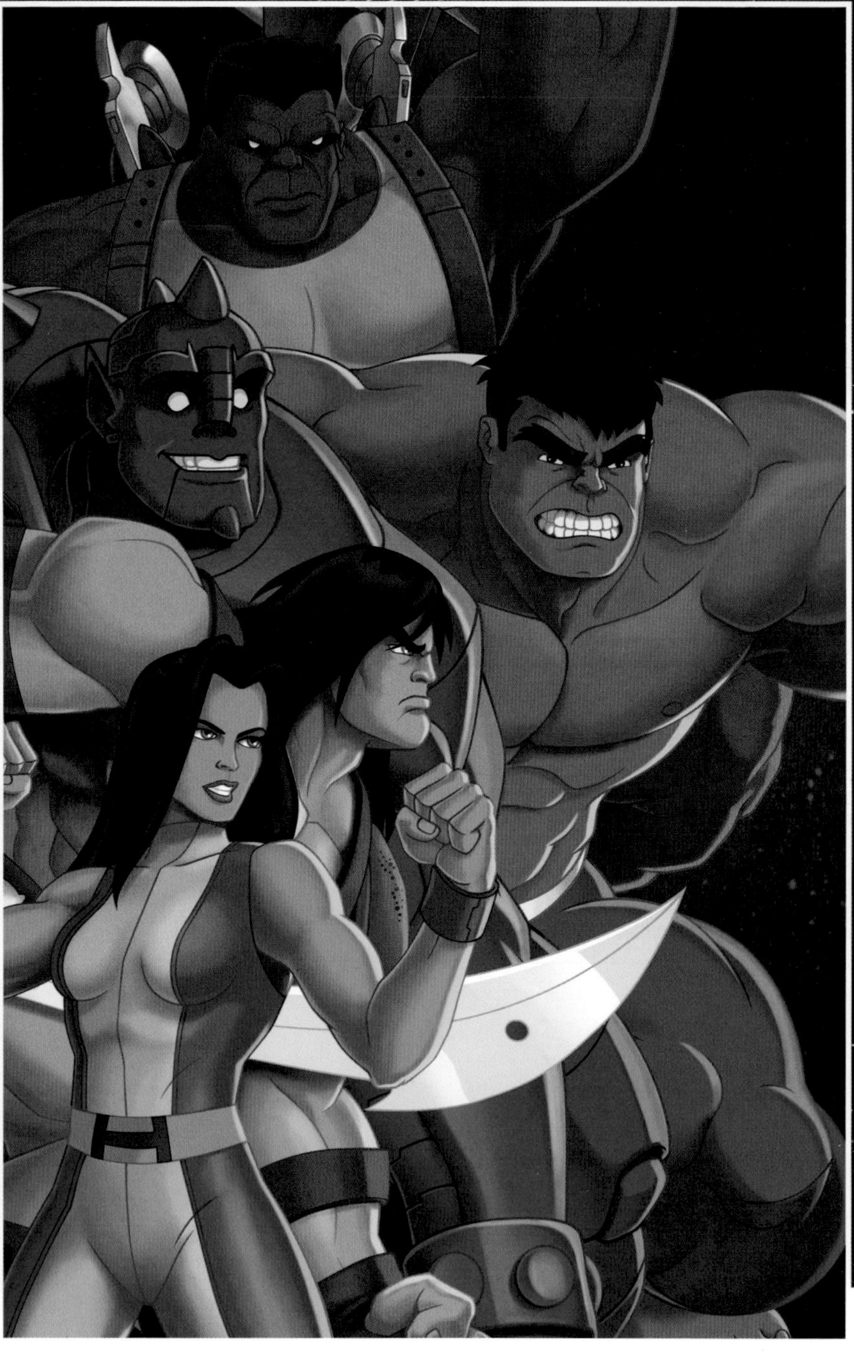

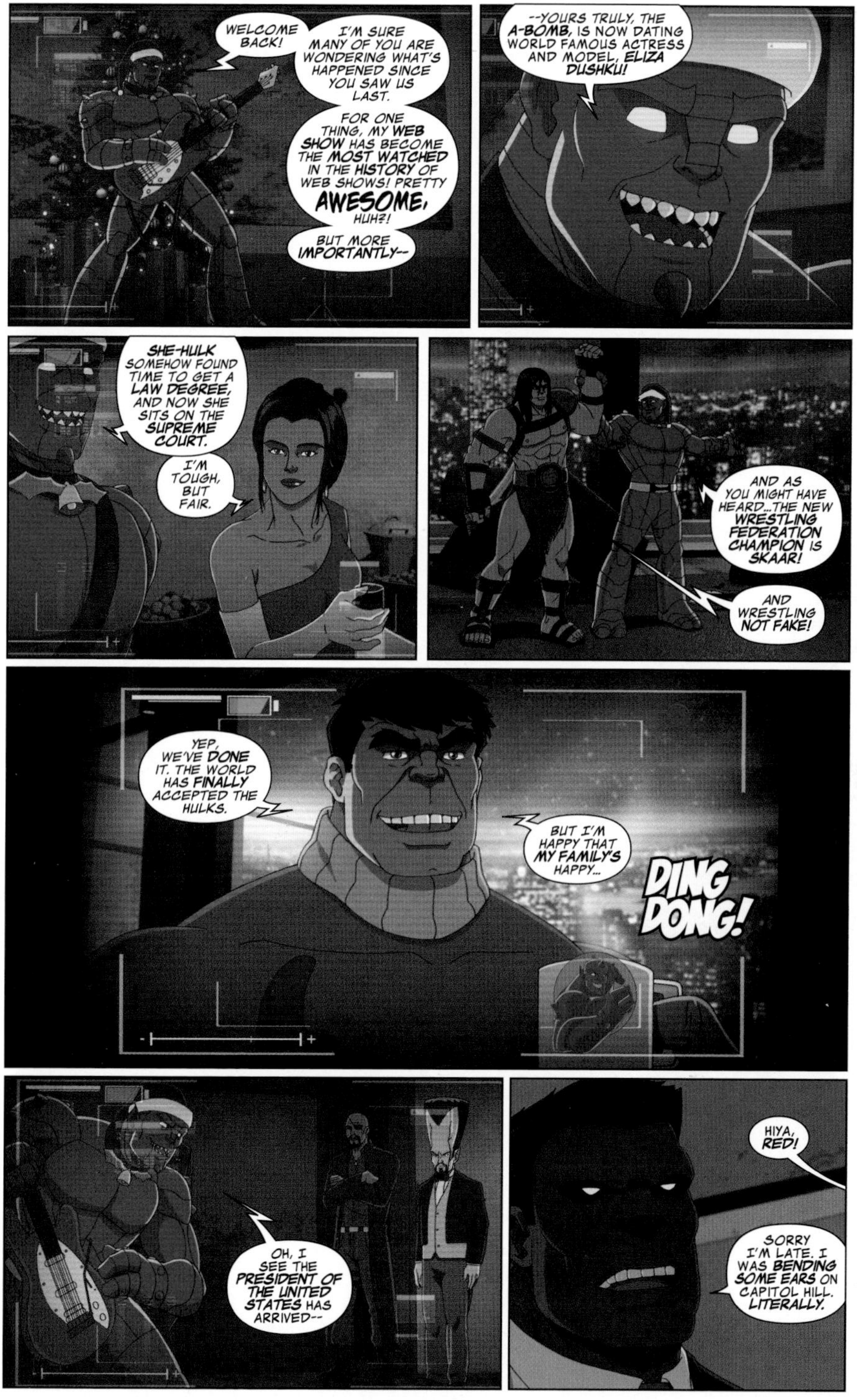
WELCOME BACK!
I'M SURE MANY OF YOU ARE WONDERING WHAT'S HAPPENED SINCE YOU SAW US LAST.
FOR ONE THING, MY WEB SHOW HAS BECOME THE MOST WATCHED IN THE HISTORY OF WEB SHOWS! PRETTY AWESOME, HUH?!
BUT MORE IMPORTANTLY--
--YOURS TRULY, THE A-BOMB, IS NOW DATING WORLD FAMOUS ACTRESS AND MODEL, ELIZA DUSHKU!
SHE-HULK SOMEHOW FOUND TIME TO GET A LAW DEGREE, AND NOW SHE SITS ON THE SUPREME COURT.
I'M TOUGH, BUT FAIR.
AND AS YOU MIGHT HAVE HEARD...THE NEW WRESTLING FEDERATION CHAMPION IS SKAAR!
AND WRESTLING NOT FAKE!
YEP, WE'VE DONE IT. THE WORLD HAS FINALLY ACCEPTED THE HULKS.
BUT I'M HAPPY THAT MY FAMILY'S HAPPY...
DING DONG!
OH, I SEE THE PRESIDENT OF THE UNITED STATES HAS ARRIVED--
HIYA, RED!
SORRY I'M LATE. I WAS BENDING SOME EARS ON CAPITOL HILL. LITERALLY.

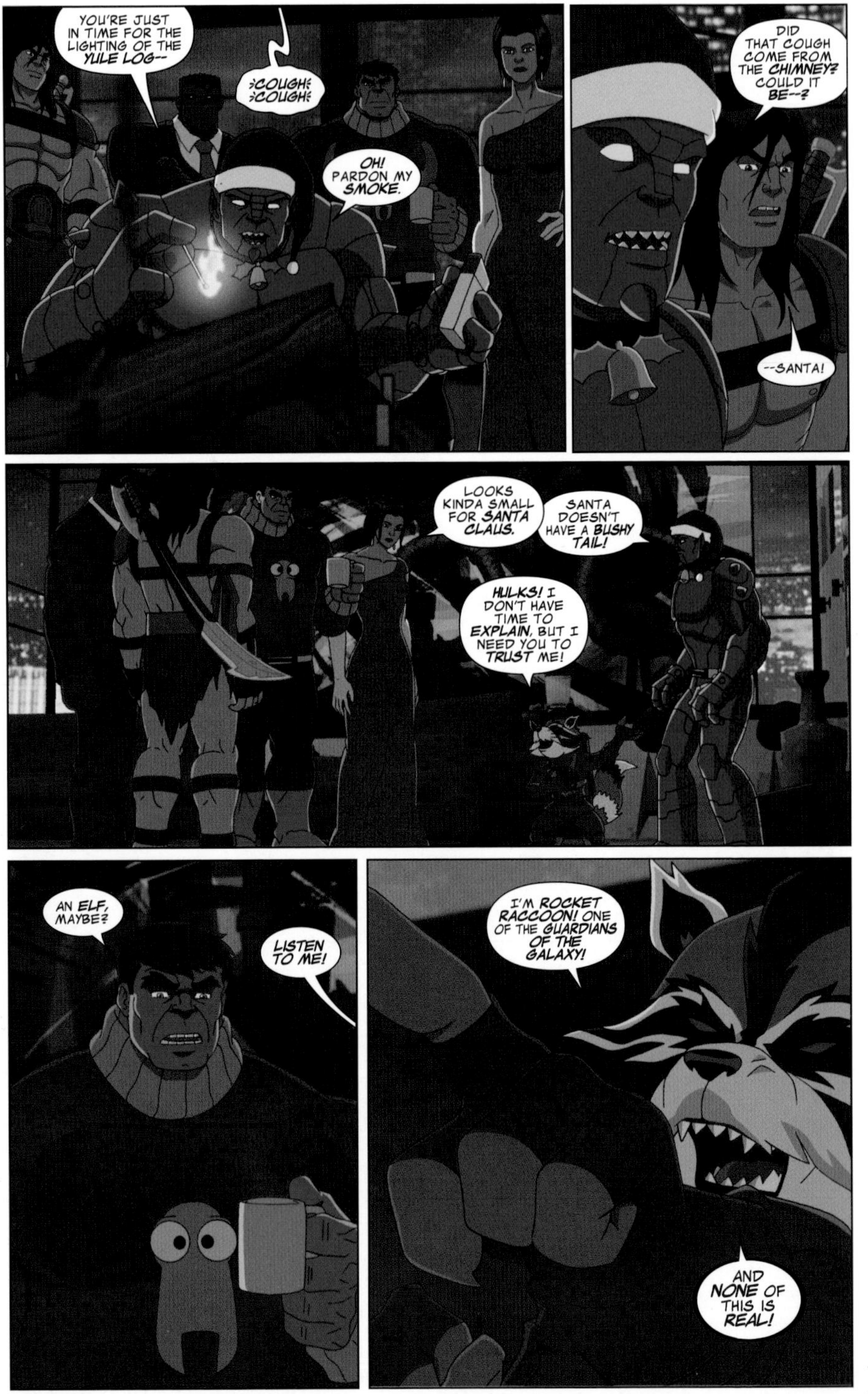
YOU'RE JUST IN TIME FOR THE LIGHTING OF THE YULE LOG--
COUGH COUGH
OH! PARDON MY SMOKE.
DID THAT COUGH COME FROM THE CHIMNEY? COULD IT BE--?
--SANTA!
LOOKS KINDA SMALL FOR SANTA CLAUS.
SANTA DOESN'T HAVE A BUSHY TAIL!
HULKS! I DON'T HAVE TIME TO EXPLAIN, BUT I NEED YOU TO TRUST ME!
AN ELF, MAYBE?
LISTEN TO ME!
I'M ROCKET RACCOON! ONE OF THE GUARDIANS OF THE GALAXY!
AND NONE OF THIS IS REAL!

MARVEL
HULK
AND THE AGENTS OF
S.M.A.S.H.

HULK   **A-BOMB**   **SHE-HULK**   **RED HULK**   **SKAAR**

BASED ON
"IT'S A WONDERFUL SMASH"
WRITTEN BY Steven Melching

ADAPTED BY
Joe Caramagna

Sebastian Girner
EDITOR

Jon Moisan
CONSULTING EDITOR

Mark Paniccia
SENIOR EDITOR

Axel Alonso
EDITOR IN CHIEF

Joe Quesada
CHIEF CREATIVE OFFICER

Dan Buckley
PUBLISHER

Alan Fine
EXECUTIVE PRODUCER

MARVEL
ON XD

DISNEY

MARVEL
UNIVERSE

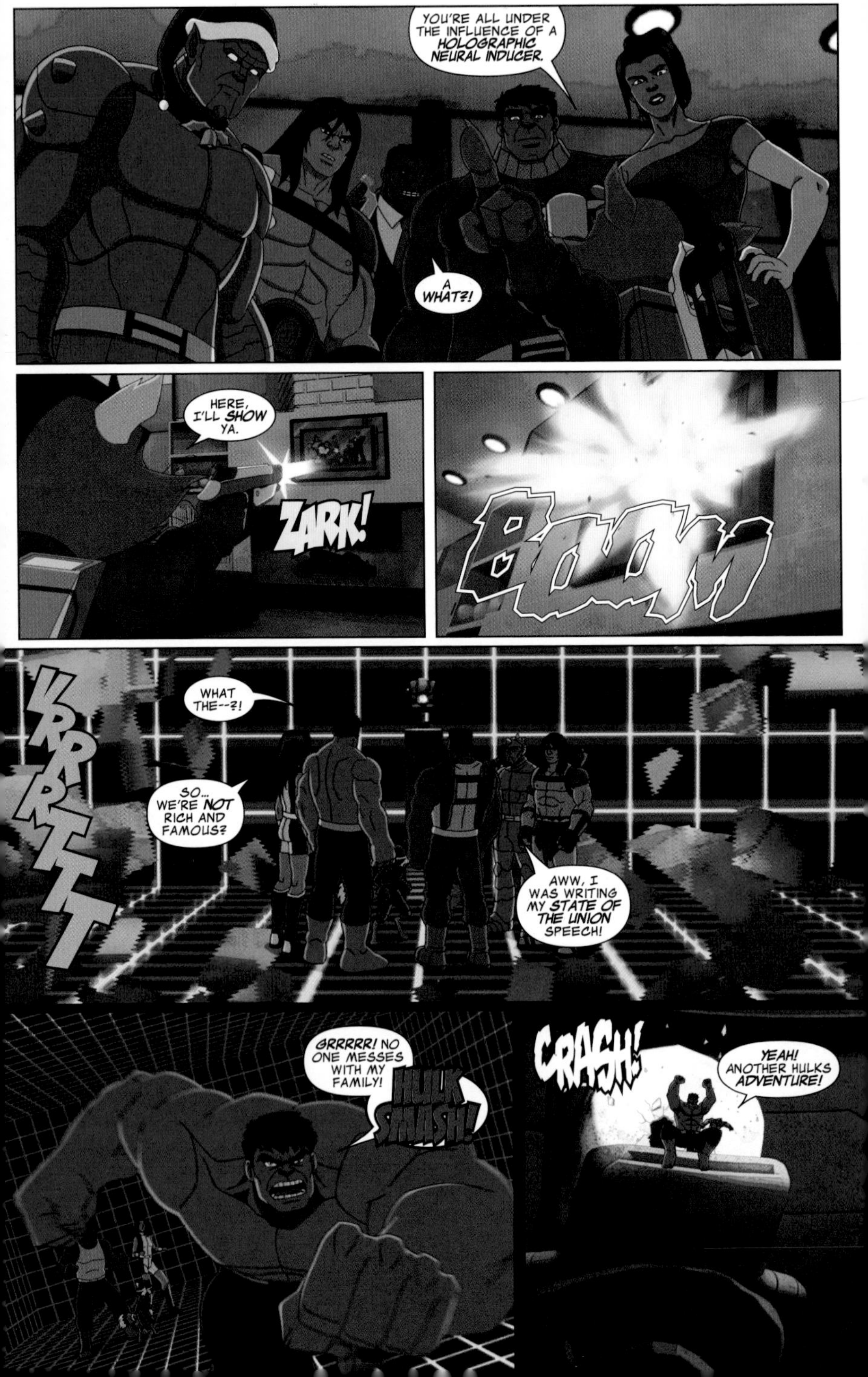
YOU'RE ALL UNDER THE INFLUENCE OF A HOLOGRAPHIC NEURAL INDUCER.
A WHAT?!
HERE, I'LL SHOW YA.
ZARK!
BOOM
KRRRTTT
WHAT THE--?!
SO... WE'RE NOT RICH AND FAMOUS?
AWW, I WAS WRITING MY STATE OF THE UNION SPEECH!
GRRRRR! NO ONE MESSES WITH MY FAMILY!
HULK SMASH!
CRASH!
YEAH! ANOTHER HULKS ADVENTURE!

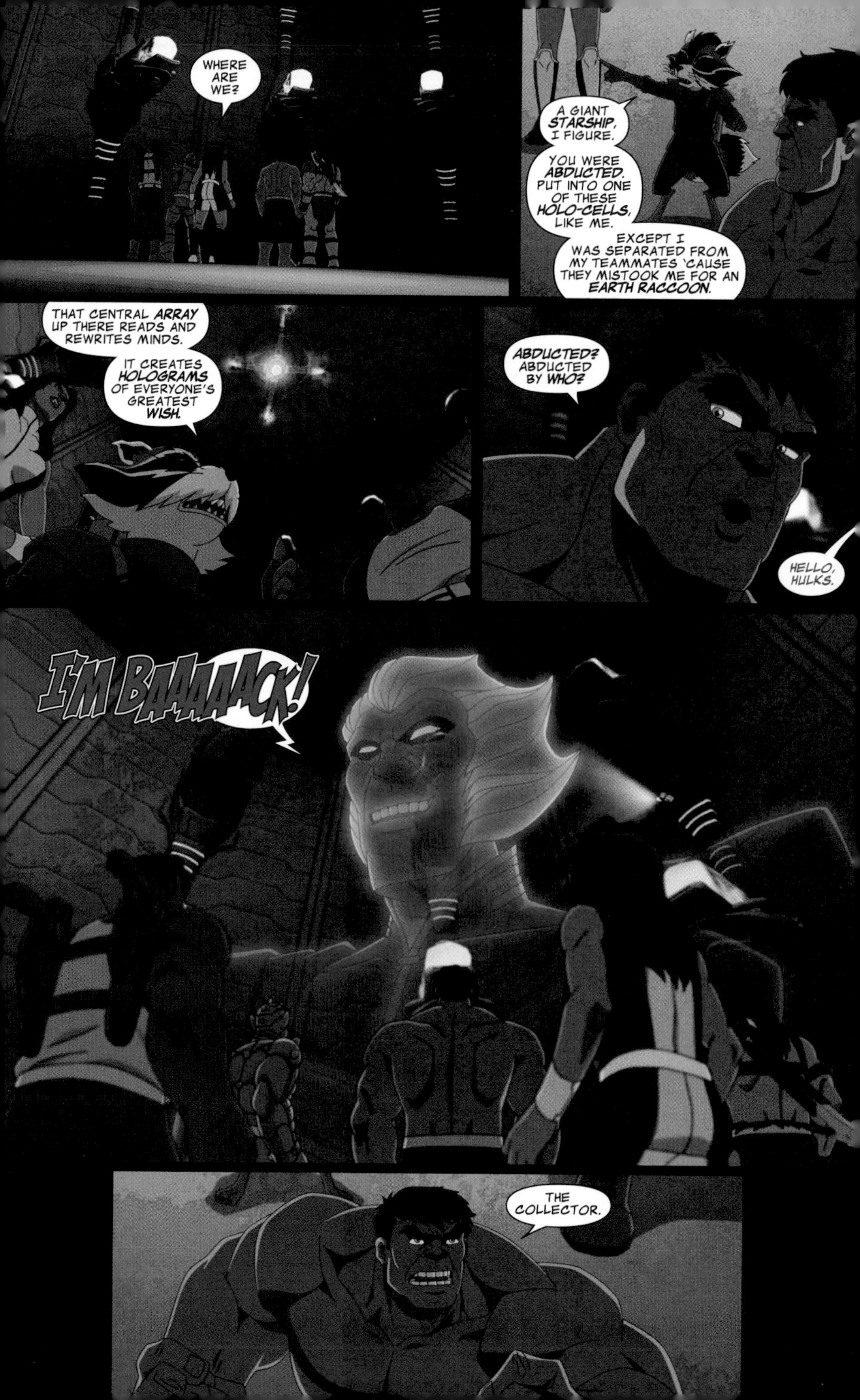
WHERE ARE WE?
A GIANT STARSHIP, I FIGURE.
YOU WERE ABDUCTED. PUT INTO ONE OF THESE HOLO-CELLS, LIKE ME.
EXCEPT I WAS SEPARATED FROM MY TEAMMATES 'CAUSE THEY MISTOOK ME FOR AN EARTH RACCOON.
THAT CENTRAL ARRAY UP THERE READS AND REWRITES MINDS.
IT CREATES HOLOGRAMS OF EVERYONE'S GREATEST WISH.
ABDUCTED? ABDUCTED BY WHO?
HELLO, HULKS.
I'M BAAAAACK!
THE COLLECTOR.

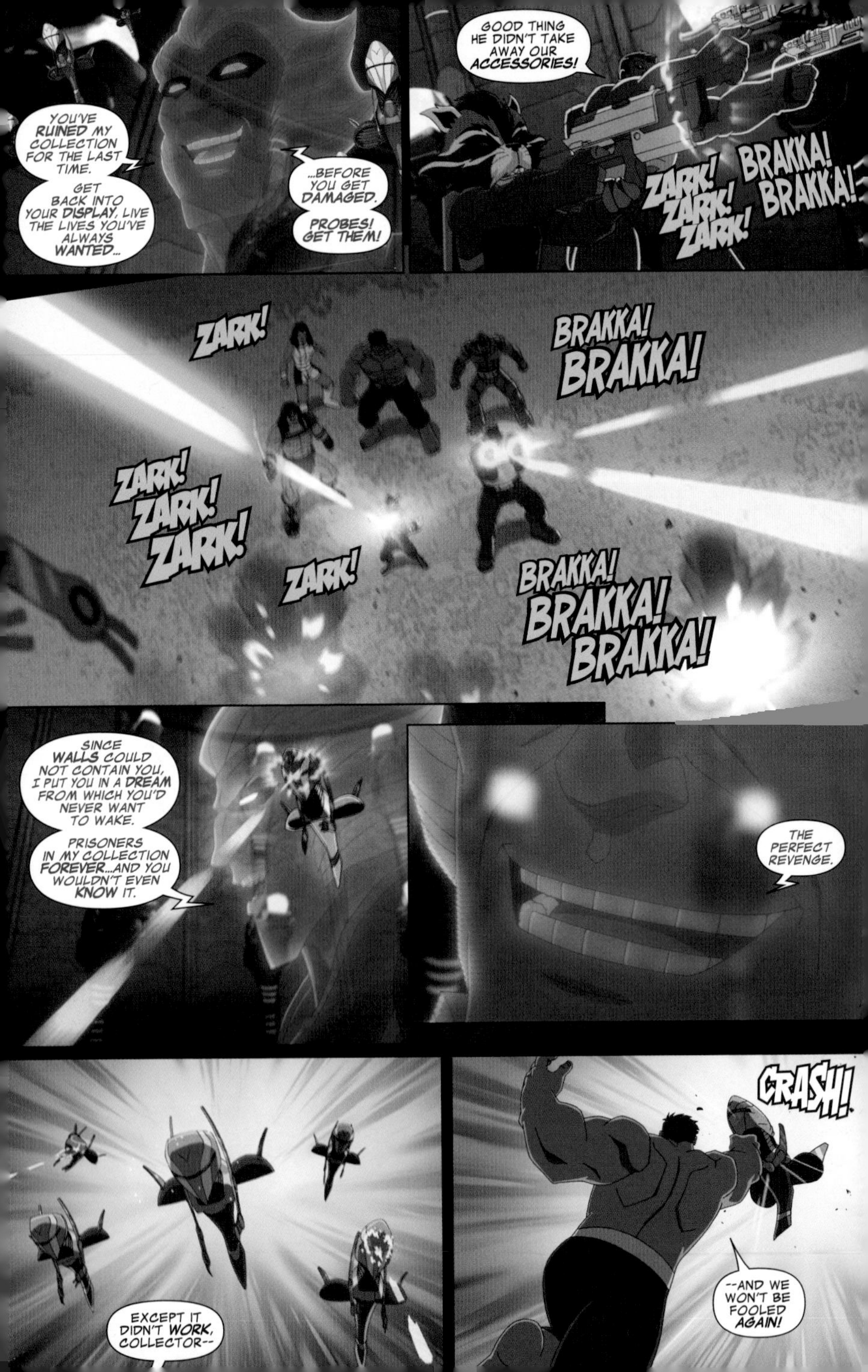
YOU'VE RUINED MY COLLECTION FOR THE LAST TIME.
GET BACK INTO YOUR DISPLAY, LIVE THE LIVES YOU'VE ALWAYS WANTED...
...BEFORE YOU GET DAMAGED.
PROBES! GET THEM!
GOOD THING HE DIDN'T TAKE AWAY OUR ACCESSORIES!
ZARK! ZARK! ZARK!
BRAKKA! BRAKKA!
ZARK!
BRAKKA! BRAKKA!
ZARK! ZARK! ZARK!
ZARK!
BRAKKA! BRAKKA! BRAKKA!
SINCE WALLS COULD NOT CONTAIN YOU, I PUT YOU IN A DREAM FROM WHICH YOU'D NEVER WANT TO WAKE.
PRISONERS IN MY COLLECTION FOREVER...AND YOU WOULDN'T EVEN KNOW IT.
THE PERFECT REVENGE.
EXCEPT IT DIDN'T WORK, COLLECTOR--
CRASH!
--AND WE WON'T BE FOOLED AGAIN!

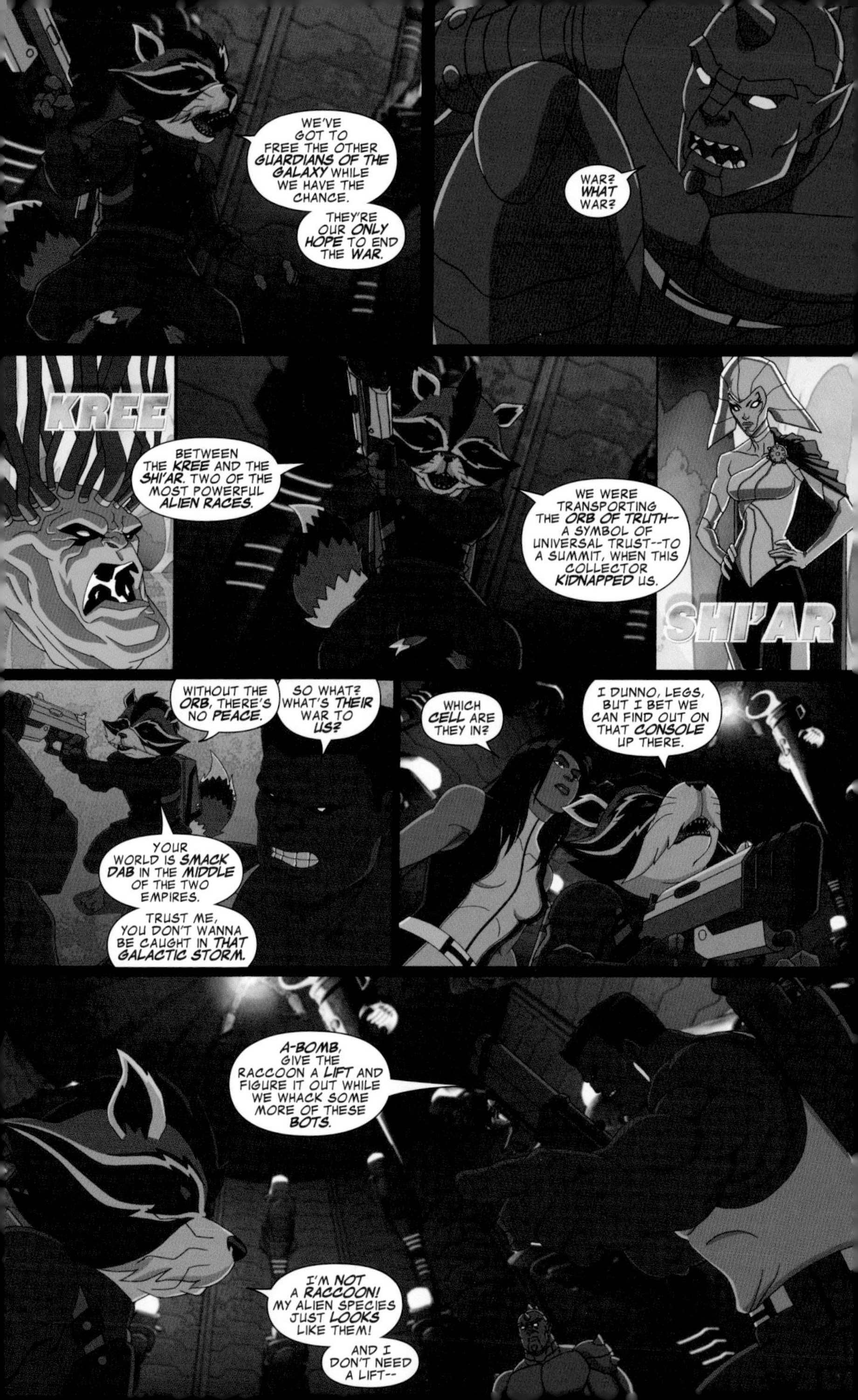
WE'VE GOT TO FREE THE OTHER GUARDIANS OF THE GALAXY WHILE WE HAVE THE CHANCE.
THEY'RE OUR ONLY HOPE TO END THE WAR.
WAR? WHAT WAR?
KREE
BETWEEN THE KREE AND THE SHI'AR. TWO OF THE MOST POWERFUL ALIEN RACES.
WE WERE TRANSPORTING THE ORB OF TRUTH-- A SYMBOL OF UNIVERSAL TRUST--TO A SUMMIT, WHEN THIS COLLECTOR KIDNAPPED US.
SHI'AR
WITHOUT THE ORB, THERE'S NO PEACE.
SO WHAT? WHAT'S THEIR WAR TO US?
YOUR WORLD IS SMACK DAB IN THE MIDDLE OF THE TWO EMPIRES.
TRUST ME, YOU DON'T WANNA BE CAUGHT IN THAT GALACTIC STORM.
WHICH CELL ARE THEY IN?
I DUNNO, LEGS, BUT I BET WE CAN FIND OUT ON THAT CONSOLE UP THERE.
A-BOMB, GIVE THE RACCOON A LIFT AND FIGURE IT OUT WHILE WE WHACK SOME MORE OF THESE BOTS.
I'M NOT A RACCOON! MY ALIEN SPECIES JUST LOOKS LIKE THEM!
AND I DON'T NEED A LIFT--

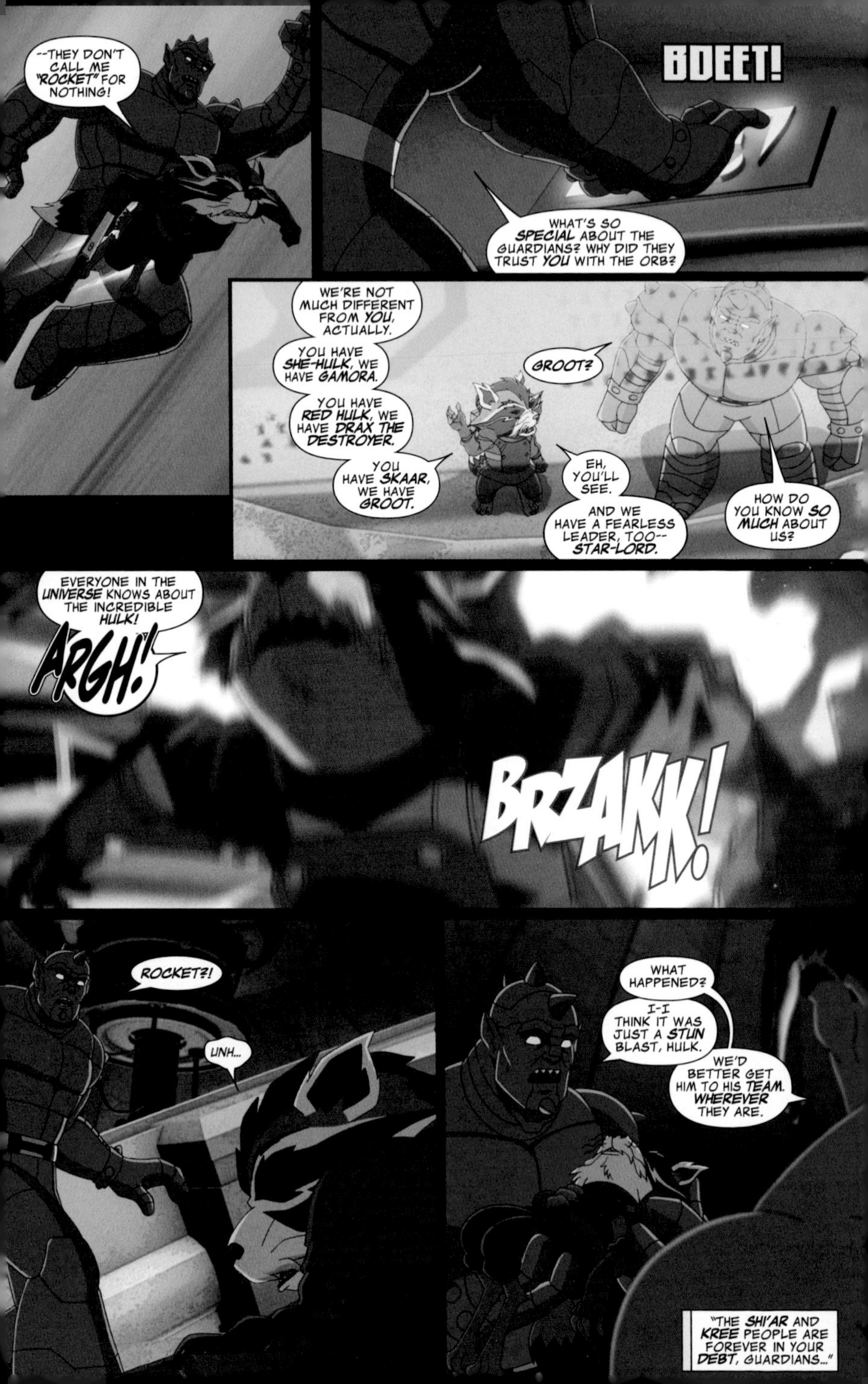

--THEY DON'T CALL ME "ROCKET" FOR NOTHING!
BDEET!
WHAT'S SO SPECIAL ABOUT THE GUARDIANS? WHY DID THEY TRUST YOU WITH THE ORB?
WE'RE NOT MUCH DIFFERENT FROM YOU, ACTUALLY.
YOU HAVE SHE-HULK, WE HAVE GAMORA.
YOU HAVE RED HULK, WE HAVE DRAX THE DESTROYER.
YOU HAVE SKAAR, WE HAVE GROOT.
GROOT?
EH, YOU'LL SEE.
AND WE HAVE A FEARLESS LEADER, TOO-- STAR-LORD.
HOW DO YOU KNOW SO MUCH ABOUT US?
EVERYONE IN THE UNIVERSE KNOWS ABOUT THE INCREDIBLE HULK!
ARGH!
BRZAKK!
ROCKET?!
UNH...
WHAT HAPPENED?
I-I THINK IT WAS JUST A STUN BLAST, HULK.
WE'D BETTER GET HIM TO HIS TEAM. WHEREVER THEY ARE.
"THE SHI'AR AND KREE PEOPLE ARE FOREVER IN YOUR DEBT, GUARDIANS..."

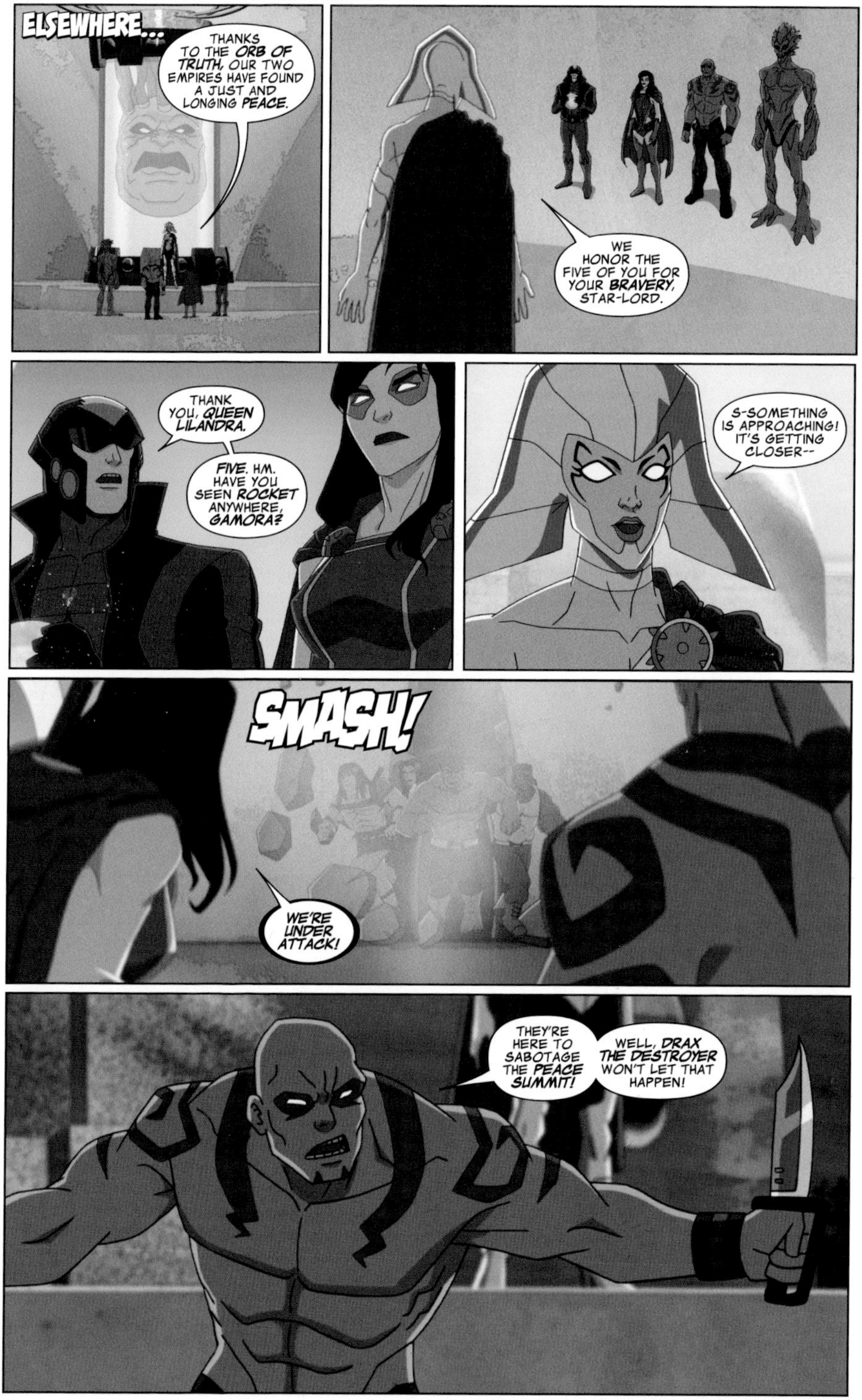
ELSEWHERE...
THANKS TO THE ORB OF TRUTH, OUR TWO EMPIRES HAVE FOUND A JUST AND LONGING PEACE.
WE HONOR THE FIVE OF YOU FOR YOUR BRAVERY, STAR-LORD.
THANK YOU, QUEEN LILANDRA.
FIVE. HM. HAVE YOU SEEN ROCKET ANYWHERE, GAMORA?
S-SOMETHING IS APPROACHING! IT'S GETTING CLOSER--
SMASH!
WE'RE UNDER ATTACK!
THEY'RE HERE TO SABOTAGE THE PEACE SUMMIT!
WELL, DRAX THE DESTROYER WON'T LET THAT HAPPEN!

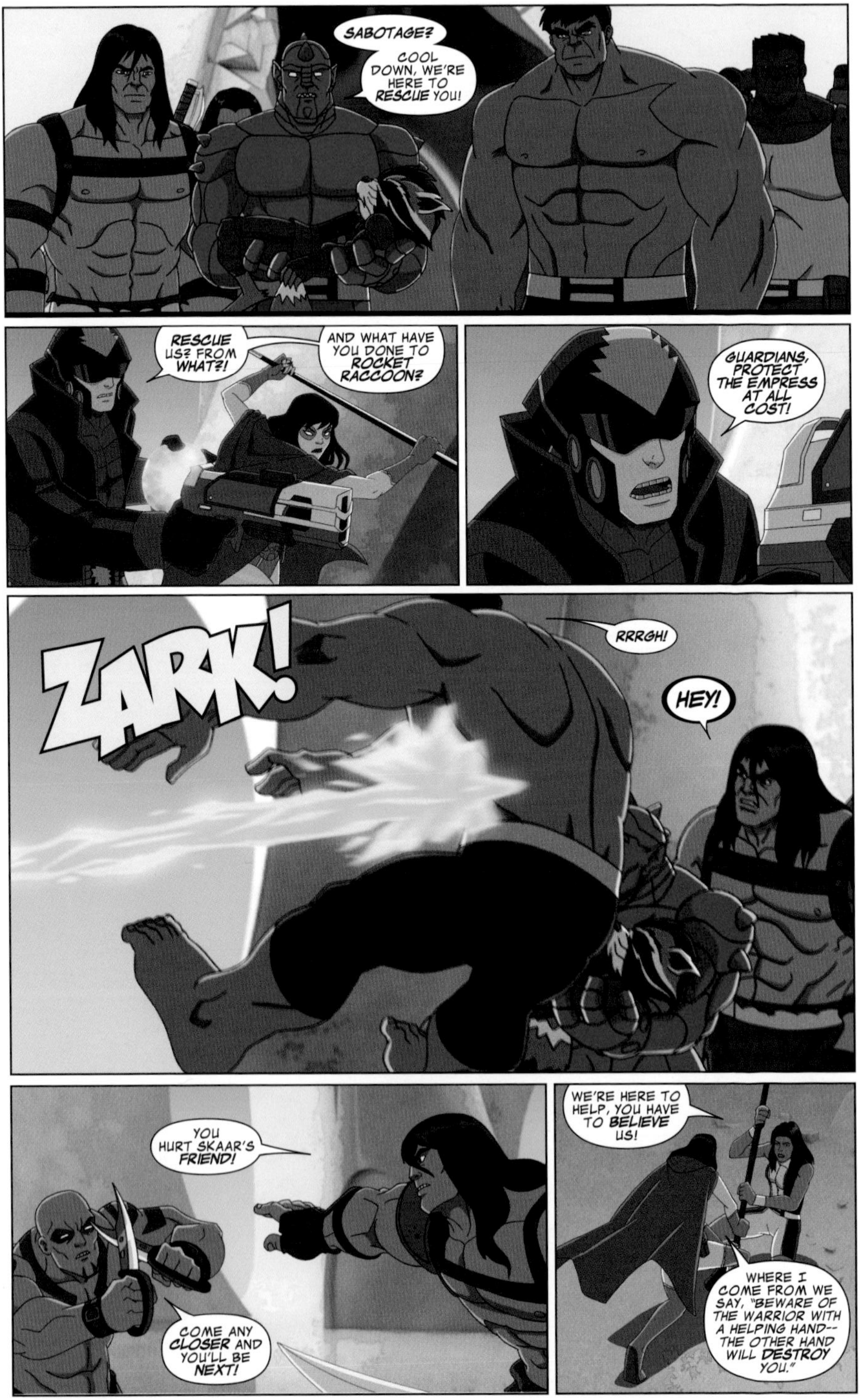
SABOTAGE?
COOL DOWN, WE'RE HERE TO RESCUE YOU!
RESCUE US? FROM WHAT?!
AND WHAT HAVE YOU DONE TO ROCKET RACCOON?
GUARDIANS, PROTECT THE EMPRESS AT ALL COST!
ZARK!
RRRGH!
HEY!
YOU HURT SKAAR'S FRIEND!
COME ANY CLOSER AND YOU'LL BE NEXT!
WE'RE HERE TO HELP, YOU HAVE TO BELIEVE US!
WHERE I COME FROM WE SAY, "BEWARE OF THE WARRIOR WITH A HELPING HAND-- THE OTHER HAND WILL DESTROY YOU."

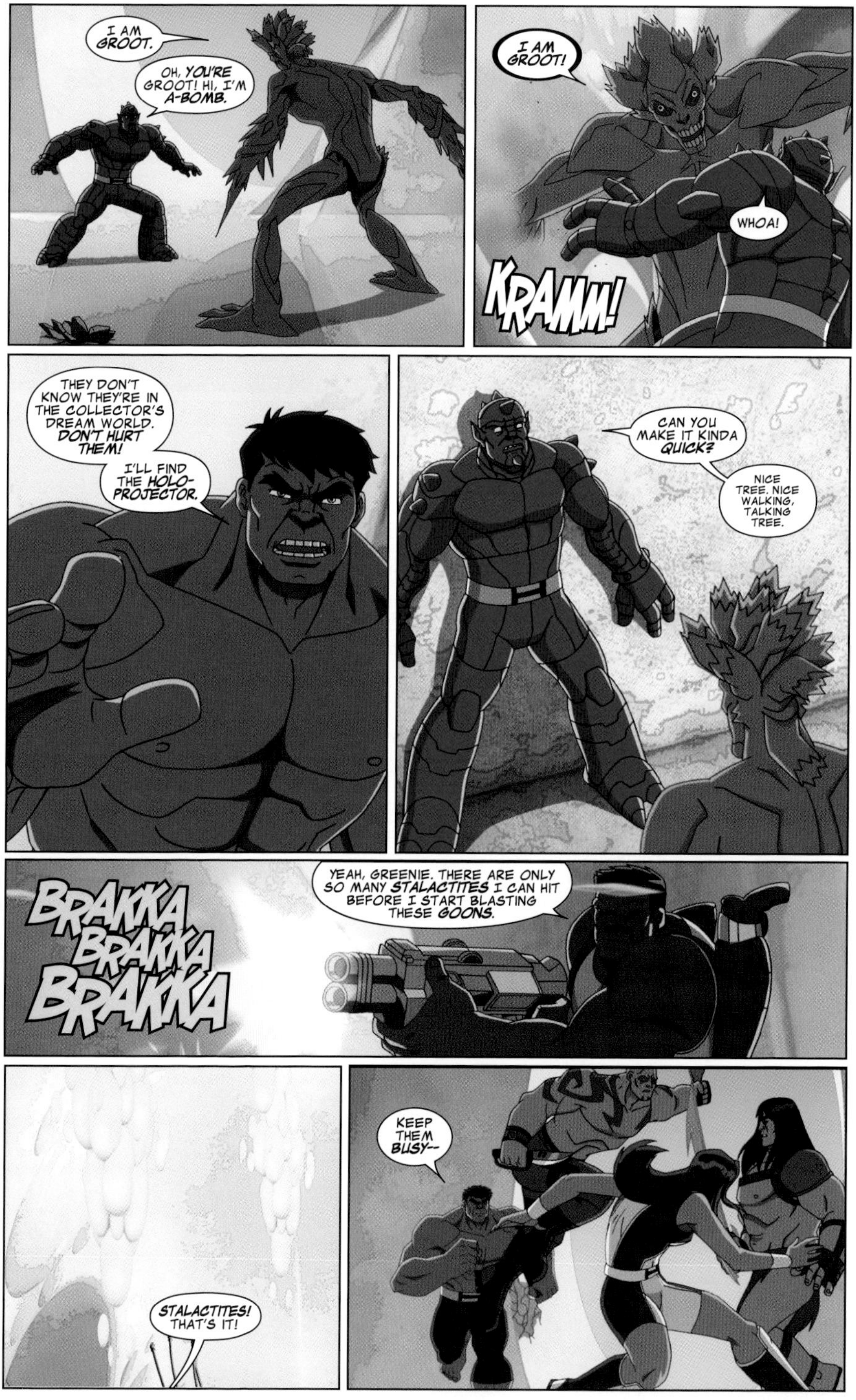
I AM GROOT.
OH, YOU'RE GROOT! HI, I'M A-BOMB.
I AM GROOT!
WHOA!
KRAMM!
THEY DON'T KNOW THEY'RE IN THE COLLECTOR'S DREAM WORLD. DON'T HURT THEM!
I'LL FIND THE HOLO-PROJECTOR.
CAN YOU MAKE IT KINDA QUICK?
NICE TREE. NICE WALKING, TALKING TREE.
BRAKKA BRAKKA BRAKKA
YEAH, GREENIE. THERE ARE ONLY SO MANY STALACTITES I CAN HIT BEFORE I START BLASTING THESE GOONS.
STALACTITES! THAT'S IT!
KEEP THEM BUSY--

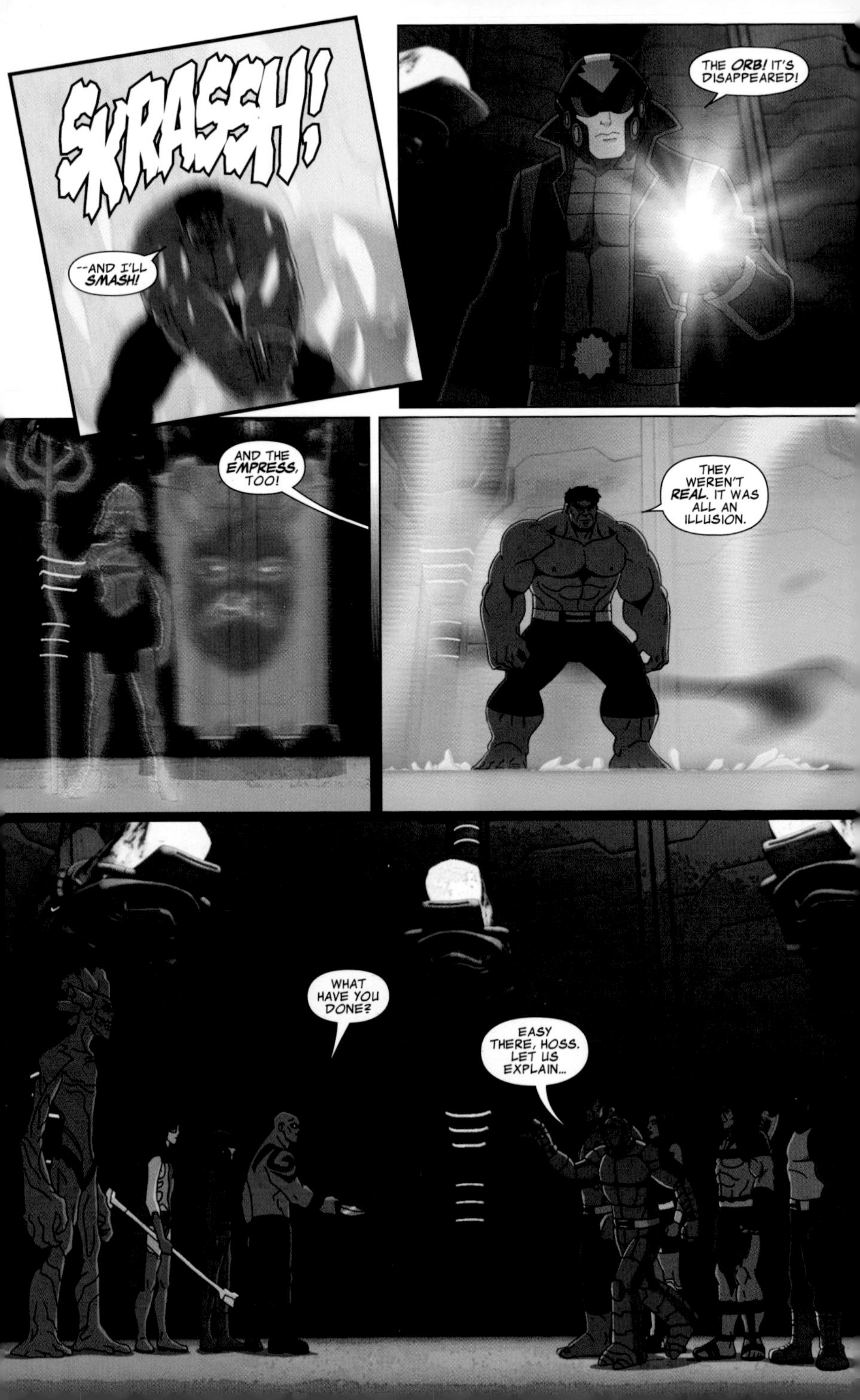
SKRASSH!
--AND I'LL SMASH!
THE ORB! IT'S DISAPPEARED!
AND THE EMPRESS, TOO!
THEY WEREN'T REAL. IT WAS ALL AN ILLUSION.
WHAT HAVE YOU DONE?
EASY THERE, HOSS. LET US EXPLAIN...

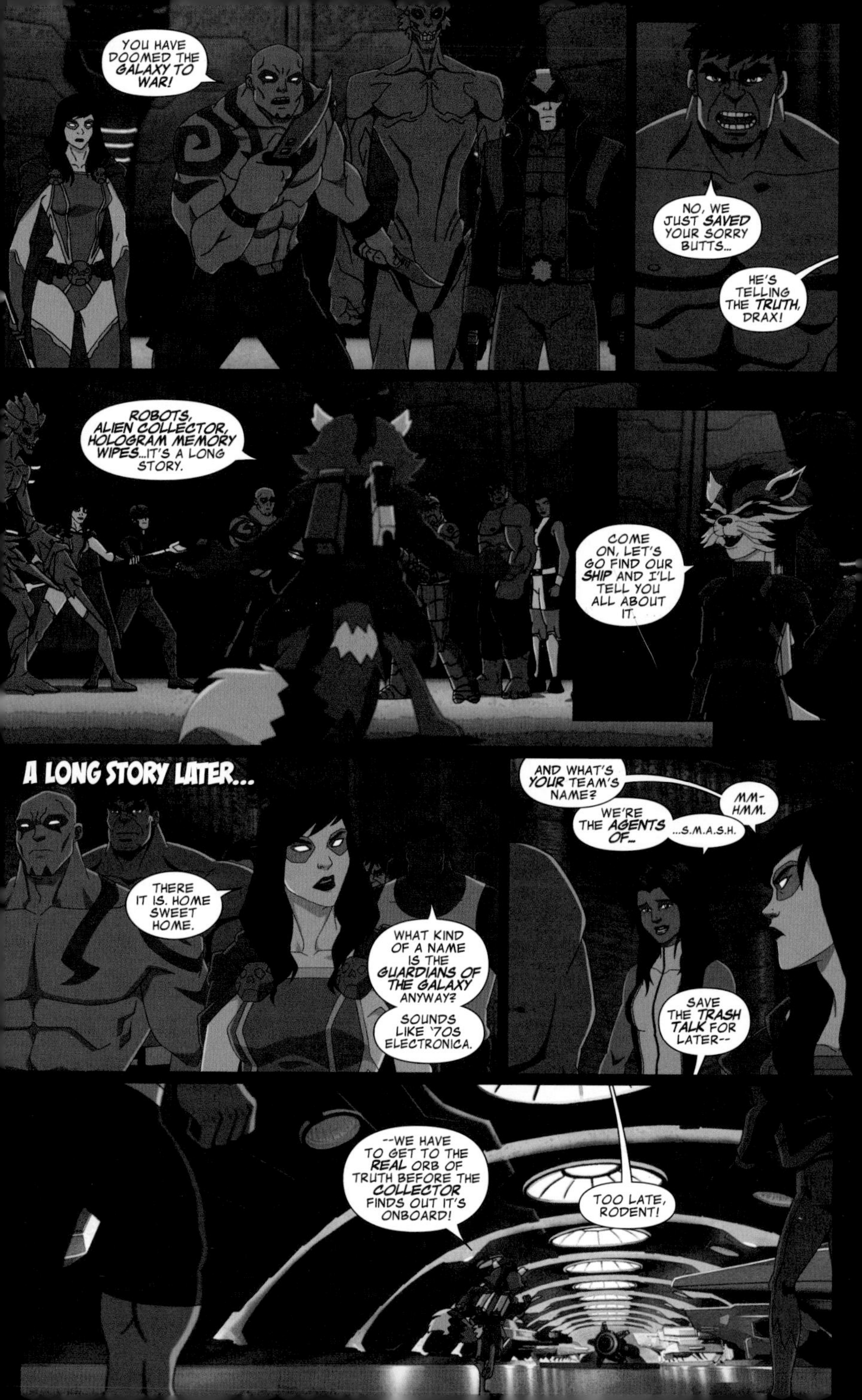
YOU HAVE DOOMED THE GALAXY TO WAR!
NO, WE JUST SAVED YOUR SORRY BUTTS...
HE'S TELLING THE TRUTH, DRAX!
ROBOTS, ALIEN COLLECTOR, HOLOGRAM MEMORY WIPES...IT'S A LONG STORY.
COME ON, LET'S GO FIND OUR SHIP AND I'LL TELL YOU ALL ABOUT IT.
A LONG STORY LATER...
THERE IT IS. HOME SWEET HOME.
WHAT KIND OF A NAME IS THE GUARDIANS OF THE GALAXY ANYWAY?
SOUNDS LIKE '70S ELECTRONICA.
AND WHAT'S YOUR TEAM'S NAME?
MM-HMM.
WE'RE THE AGENTS OF...
...S.M.A.S.H.
SAVE THE TRASH TALK FOR LATER--
--WE HAVE TO GET TO THE REAL ORB OF TRUTH BEFORE THE COLLECTOR FINDS OUT IT'S ONBOARD!
TOO LATE, RODENT!

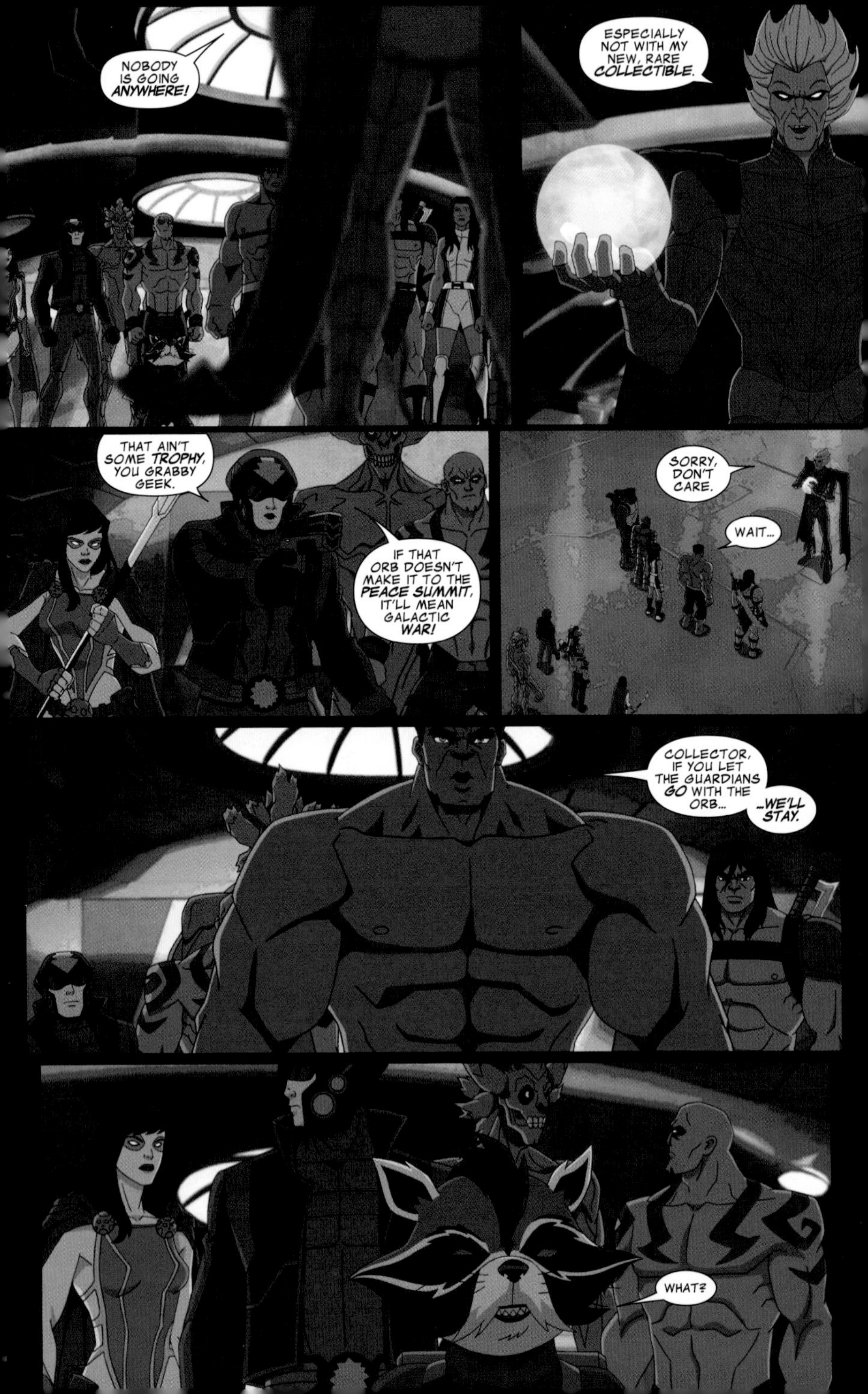
NOBODY IS GOING ANYWHERE!
ESPECIALLY NOT WITH MY NEW, RARE COLLECTIBLE.
THAT AIN'T SOME TROPHY, YOU GRABBY GEEK.
IF THAT ORB DOESN'T MAKE IT TO THE PEACE SUMMIT, IT'LL MEAN GALACTIC WAR!
SORRY, DON'T CARE.
WAIT...
COLLECTOR, IF YOU LET THE GUARDIANS GO WITH THE ORB...
...WE'LL STAY.
WHAT?

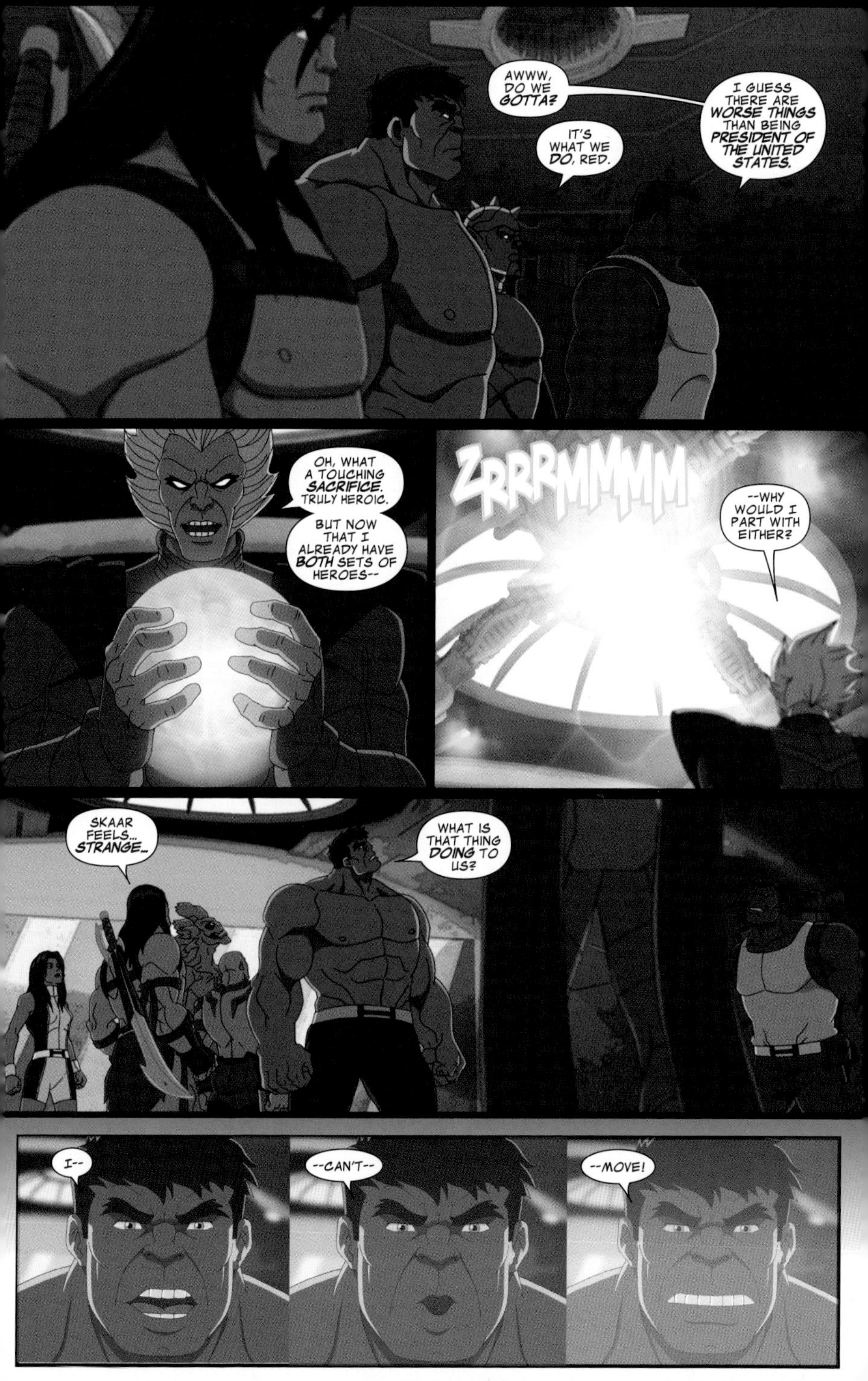

AWWW, DO WE GOTTA?
IT'S WHAT WE DO, RED.
I GUESS THERE ARE WORSE THINGS THAN BEING PRESIDENT OF THE UNITED STATES.
OH, WHAT A TOUCHING SACRIFICE. TRULY HEROIC.
BUT NOW THAT I ALREADY HAVE BOTH SETS OF HEROES--
ZRRRMMMM
--WHY WOULD I PART WITH EITHER?
SKAAR FEELS... STRANGE...
WHAT IS THAT THING DOING TO US?
I--
--CAN'T--
--MOVE!

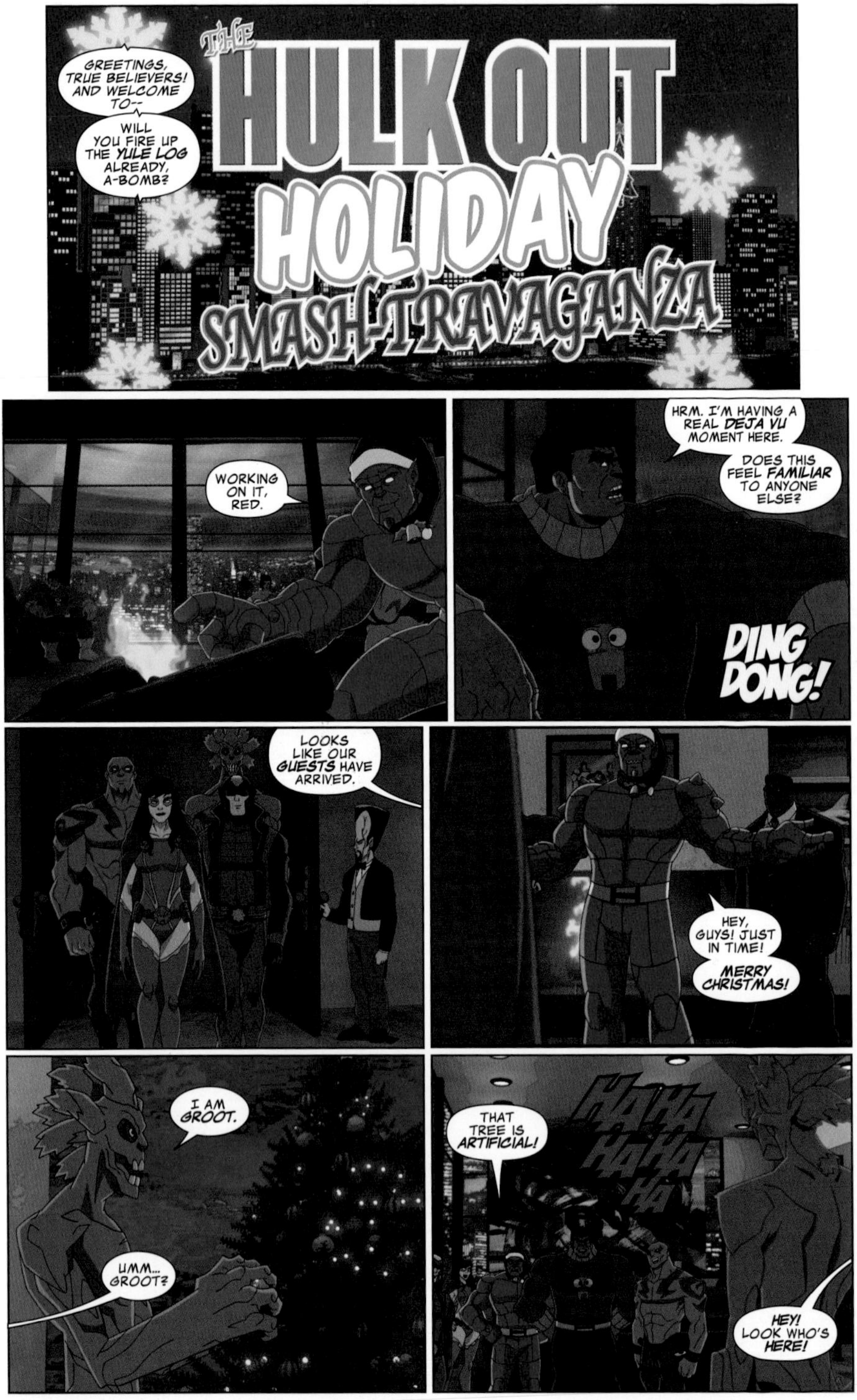
THE HULK OUT HOLIDAY SMASH-TRAVAGANZA
GREETINGS, TRUE BELIEVERS! AND WELCOME TO--
WILL YOU FIRE UP THE YULE LOG ALREADY, A-BOMB?
WORKING ON IT, RED.
HRM. I'M HAVING A REAL DEJA VU MOMENT HERE.
DOES THIS FEEL FAMILIAR TO ANYONE ELSE?
DING DONG!
LOOKS LIKE OUR GUESTS HAVE ARRIVED.
HEY, GUYS! JUST IN TIME!
MERRY CHRISTMAS!
I AM GROOT.
UMM... GROOT?
THAT TREE IS ARTIFICIAL!
HAHA HAHA HA
HEY! LOOK WHO'S HERE!

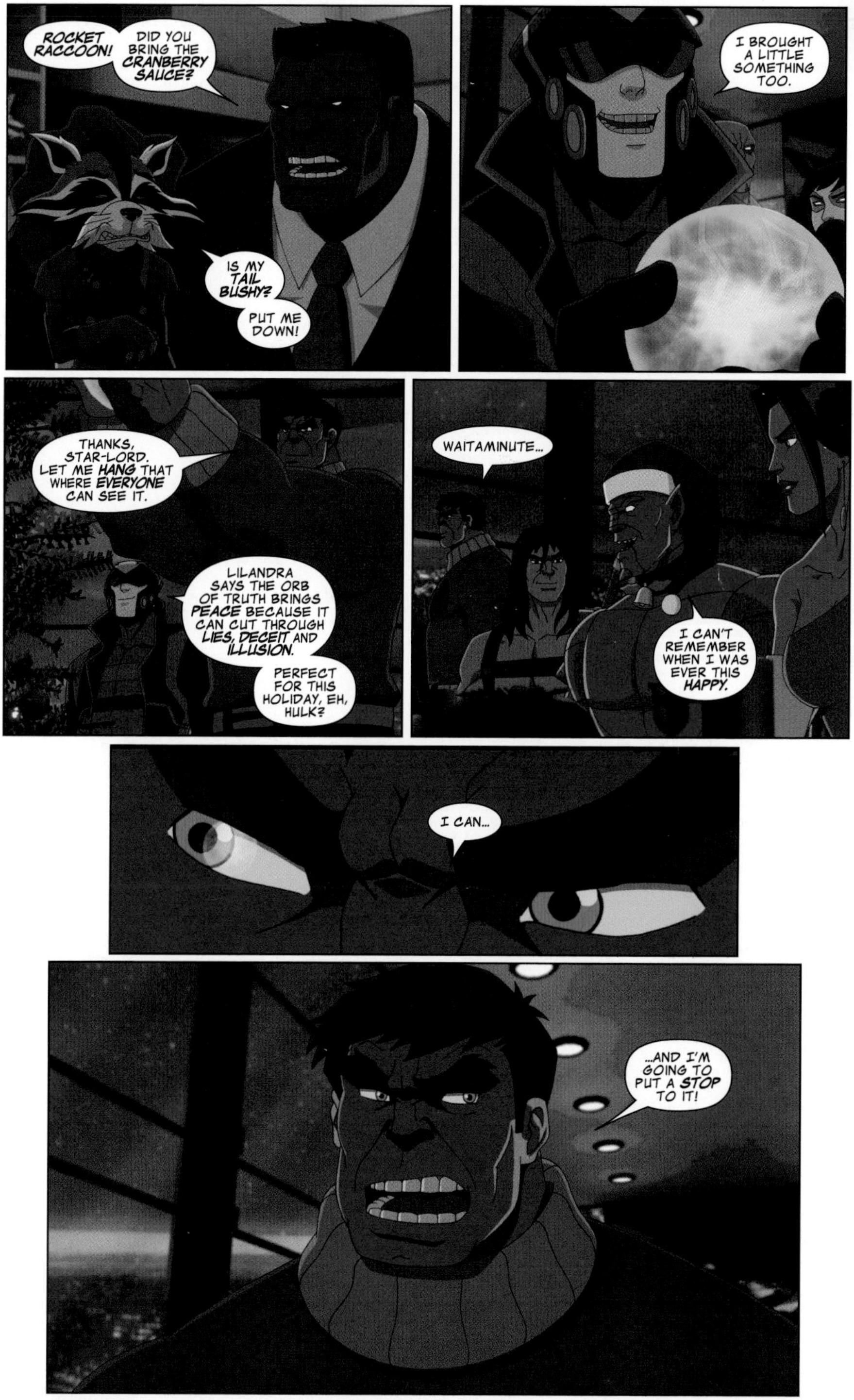
ROCKET RACCOON!
DID YOU BRING THE CRANBERRY SAUCE?
IS MY TAIL BUSHY?
PUT ME DOWN!
I BROUGHT A LITTLE SOMETHING TOO.
THANKS, STAR-LORD. LET ME HANG THAT WHERE EVERYONE CAN SEE IT.
LILANDRA SAYS THE ORB OF TRUTH BRINGS PEACE BECAUSE IT CAN CUT THROUGH LIES, DECEIT AND ILLUSION.
PERFECT FOR THIS HOLIDAY, EH, HULK?
WAITAMINUTE...
I CAN'T REMEMBER WHEN I WAS EVER THIS HAPPY.
I CAN...
...AND I'M GOING TO PUT A STOP TO IT!

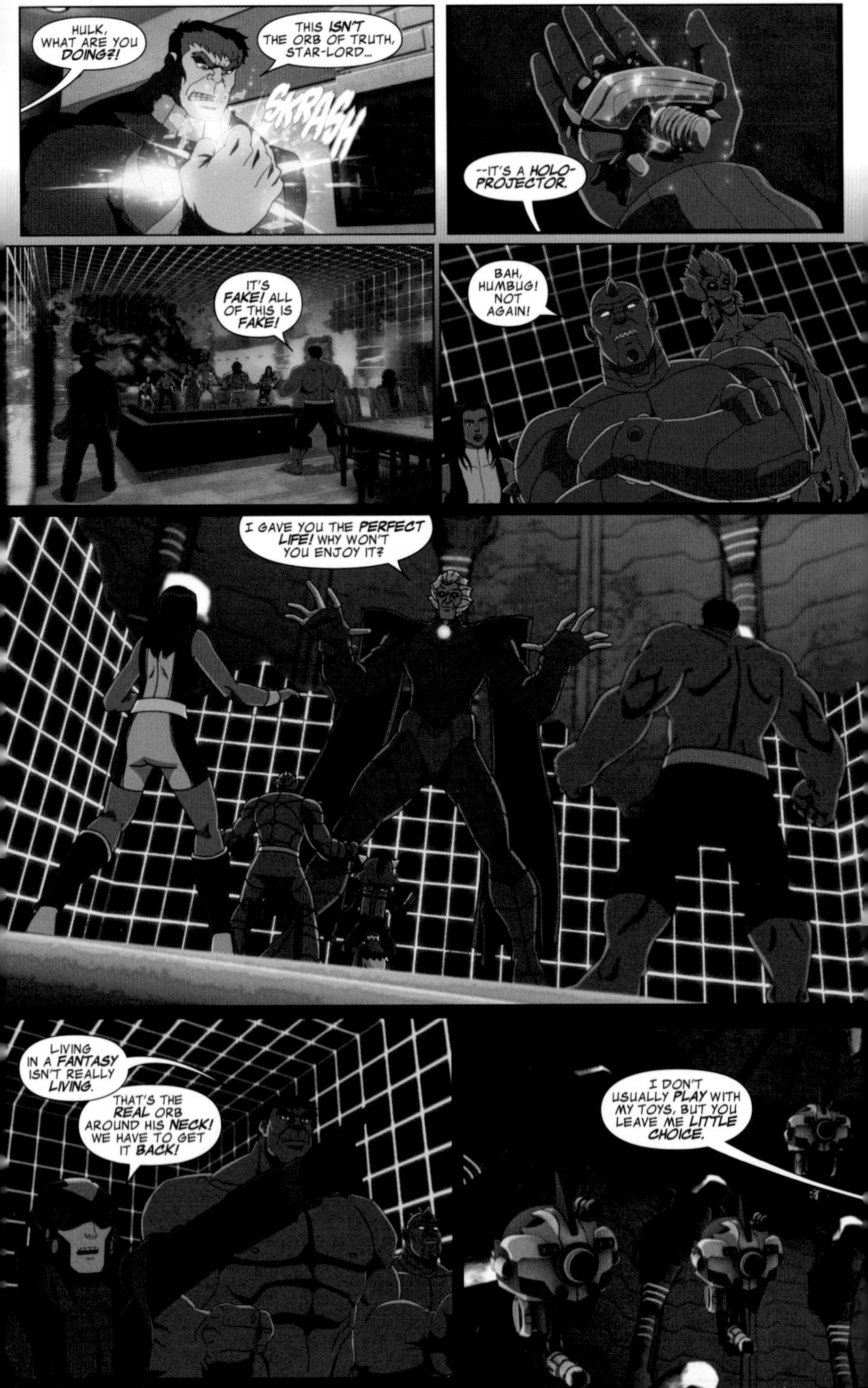
HULK, WHAT ARE YOU DOING?!
THIS ISN'T THE ORB OF TRUTH, STAR-LORD...
SKRASH
--IT'S A HOLO-PROJECTOR.
IT'S FAKE! ALL OF THIS IS FAKE!
BAH, HUMBUG! NOT AGAIN!
I GAVE YOU THE PERFECT LIFE! WHY WON'T YOU ENJOY IT?
LIVING IN A FANTASY ISN'T REALLY LIVING.
THAT'S THE REAL ORB AROUND HIS NECK! WE HAVE TO GET IT BACK!
I DON'T USUALLY PLAY WITH MY TOYS, BUT YOU LEAVE ME LITTLE CHOICE.

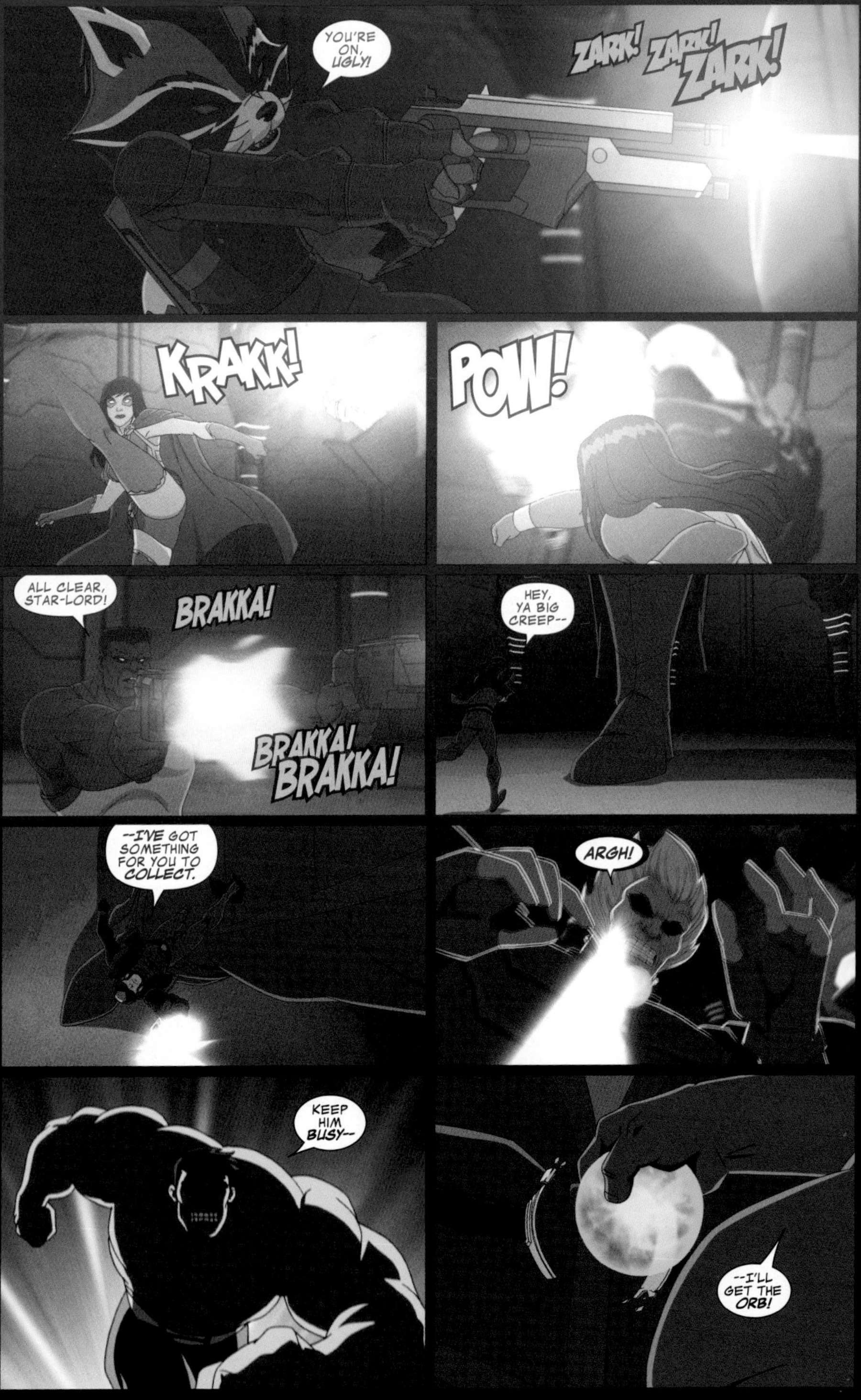
YOU'RE ON, UGLY!
ZARK! ZARK! ZARK!
KRAKK!
POW!
ALL CLEAR, STAR-LORD!
BRAKKA!
BRAKKA! BRAKKA!
HEY, YA BIG CREEP--
--I'VE GOT SOMETHING FOR YOU TO COLLECT.
ARGH!
KEEP HIM BUSY--
--I'LL GET THE ORB!

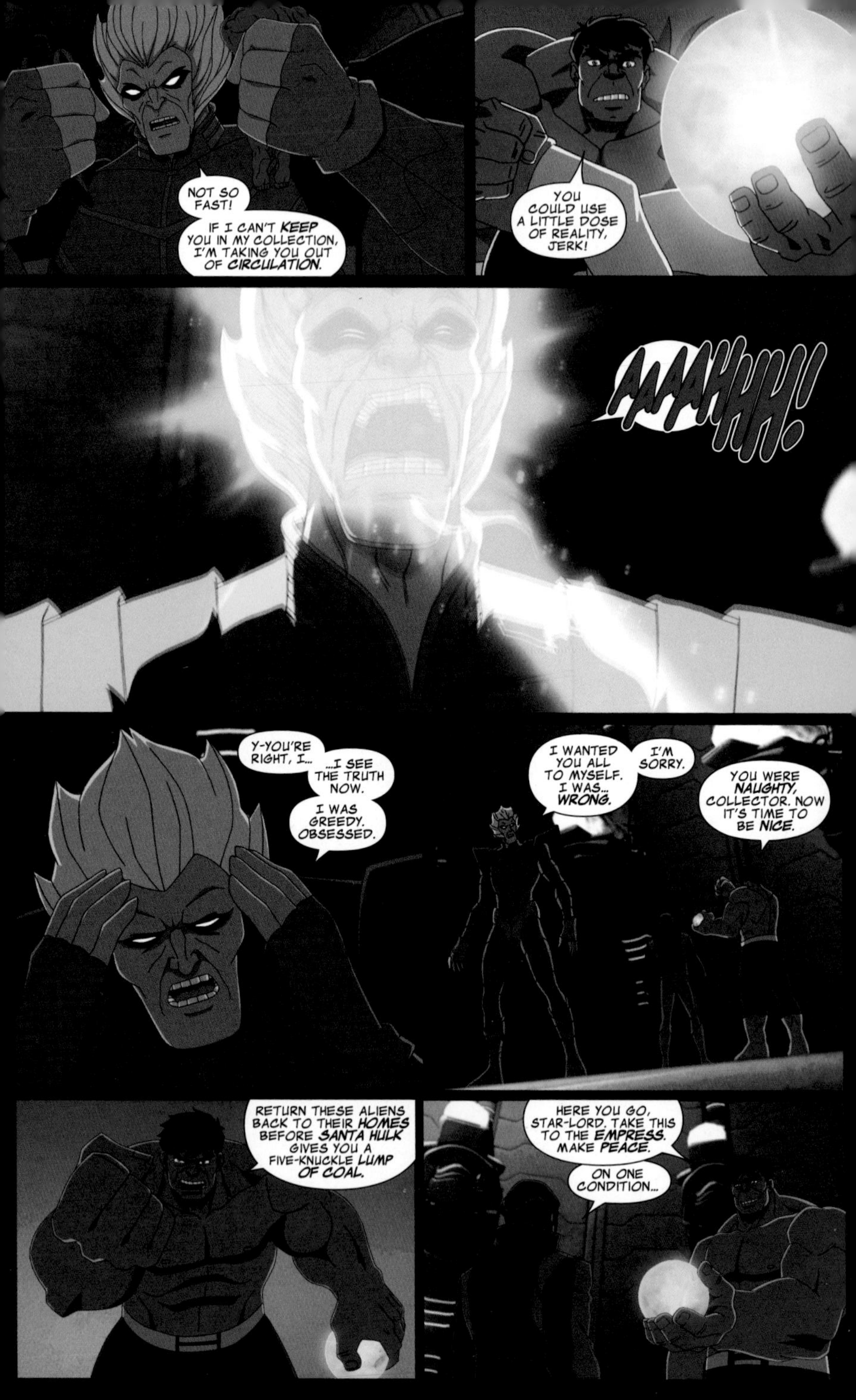
NOT SO FAST!
IF I CAN'T KEEP YOU IN MY COLLECTION, I'M TAKING YOU OUT OF CIRCULATION.
YOU COULD USE A LITTLE DOSE OF REALITY, JERK!
AAAAHHHH!
Y-YOU'RE RIGHT, I...
...I SEE THE TRUTH NOW.
I WAS GREEDY. OBSESSED.
I WANTED YOU ALL TO MYSELF. I WAS... WRONG.
I'M SORRY.
YOU WERE NAUGHTY, COLLECTOR. NOW IT'S TIME TO BE NICE.
RETURN THESE ALIENS BACK TO THEIR HOMES BEFORE SANTA HULK GIVES YOU A FIVE-KNUCKLE LUMP OF COAL.
HERE YOU GO, STAR-LORD. TAKE THIS TO THE EMPRESS. MAKE PEACE.
ON ONE CONDITION...

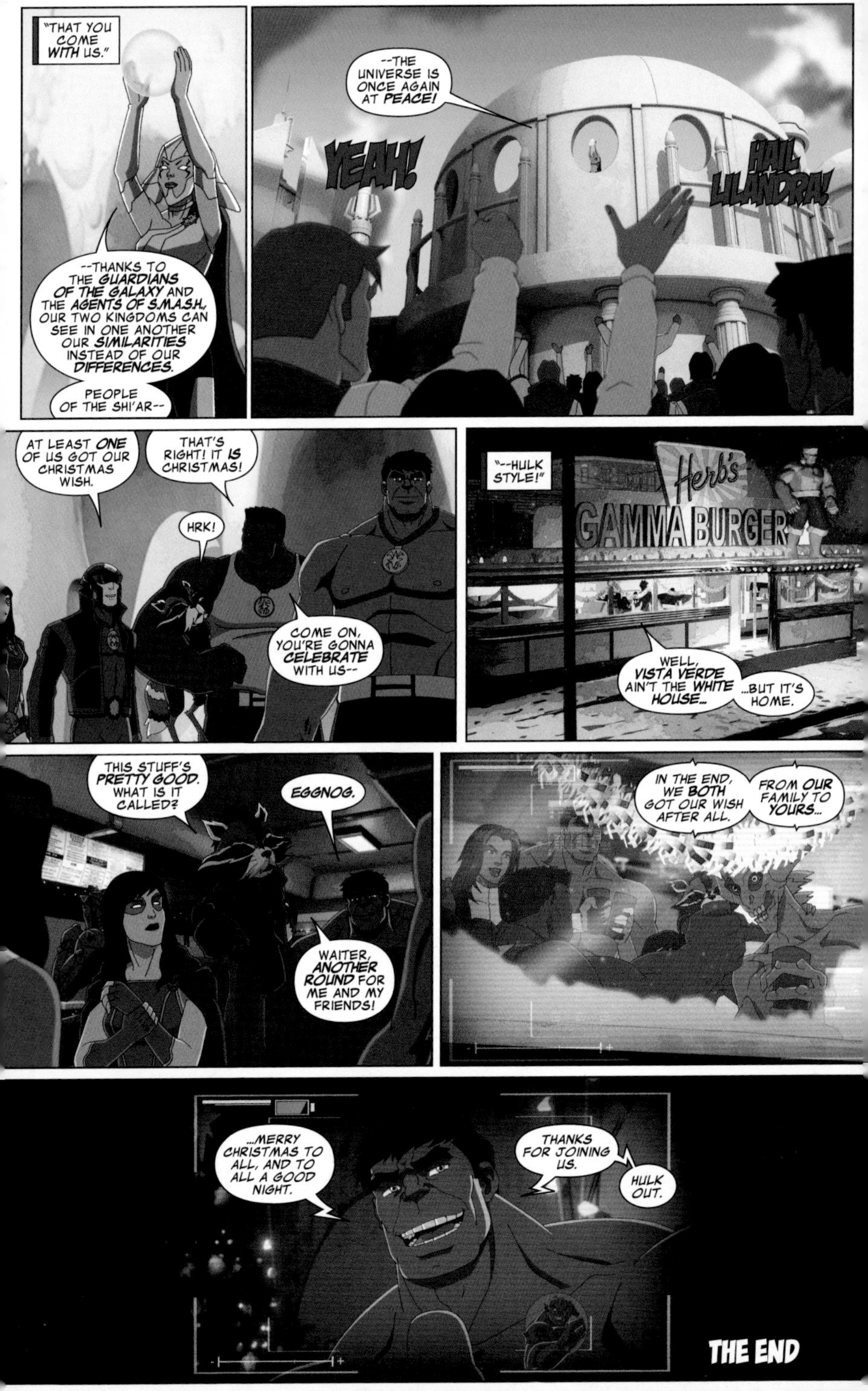
"THAT YOU COME WITH US."
--THANKS TO THE GUARDIANS OF THE GALAXY AND THE AGENTS OF S.M.A.S.H., OUR TWO KINGDOMS CAN SEE IN ONE ANOTHER OUR SIMILARITIES INSTEAD OF OUR DIFFERENCES.
PEOPLE OF THE SHI'AR--
--THE UNIVERSE IS ONCE AGAIN AT PEACE!
YEAH!
HAIL LILANDRA!
AT LEAST ONE OF US GOT OUR CHRISTMAS WISH.
THAT'S RIGHT! IT IS CHRISTMAS!
HRK!
COME ON, YOU'RE GONNA CELEBRATE WITH US--
"--HULK STYLE!"
Herb's
GAMMA BURGER
WELL, VISTA VERDE AIN'T THE WHITE HOUSE...
...BUT IT'S HOME.
THIS STUFF'S PRETTY GOOD. WHAT IS IT CALLED?
EGGNOG.
WAITER, ANOTHER ROUND FOR ME AND MY FRIENDS!
IN THE END, WE BOTH GOT OUR WISH AFTER ALL.
FROM OUR FAMILY TO YOURS...
...MERRY CHRISTMAS TO ALL, AND TO ALL A GOOD NIGHT.
THANKS FOR JOINING US.
HULK OUT.
THE END

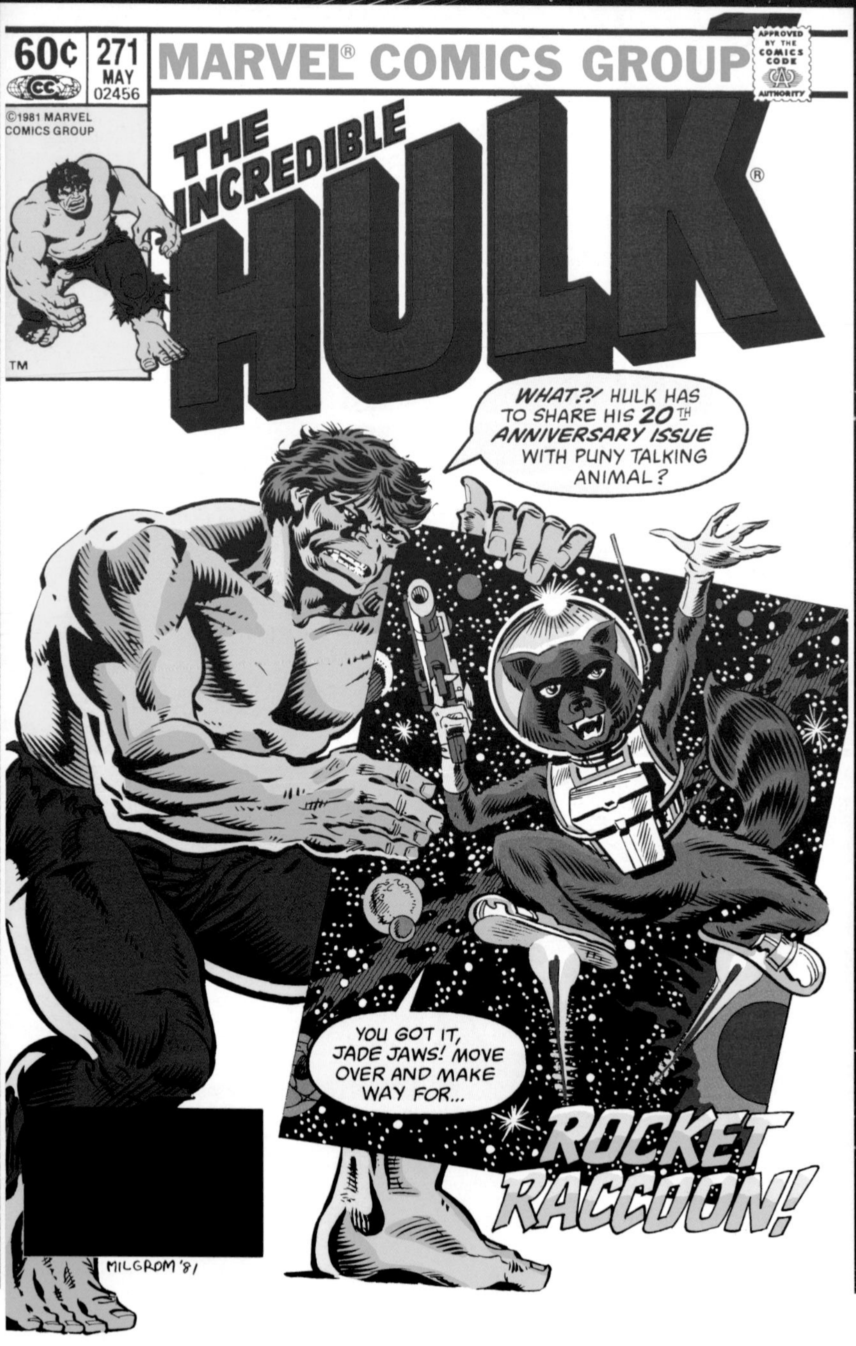
60¢
271
MAY
02456
MARVEL® COMICS GROUP
APPROVED BY THE COMICS CODE AUTHORITY
©1981 MARVEL COMICS GROUP
TM
THE INCREDIBLE HULK®
WHAT?!/ HULK HAS TO SHARE HIS 20TH ANNIVERSARY ISSUE WITH PUNY TALKING ANIMAL?
YOU GOT IT, JADE JAWS! MOVE OVER AND MAKE WAY FOR...
ROCKET RACCOON!
MILGROM '81

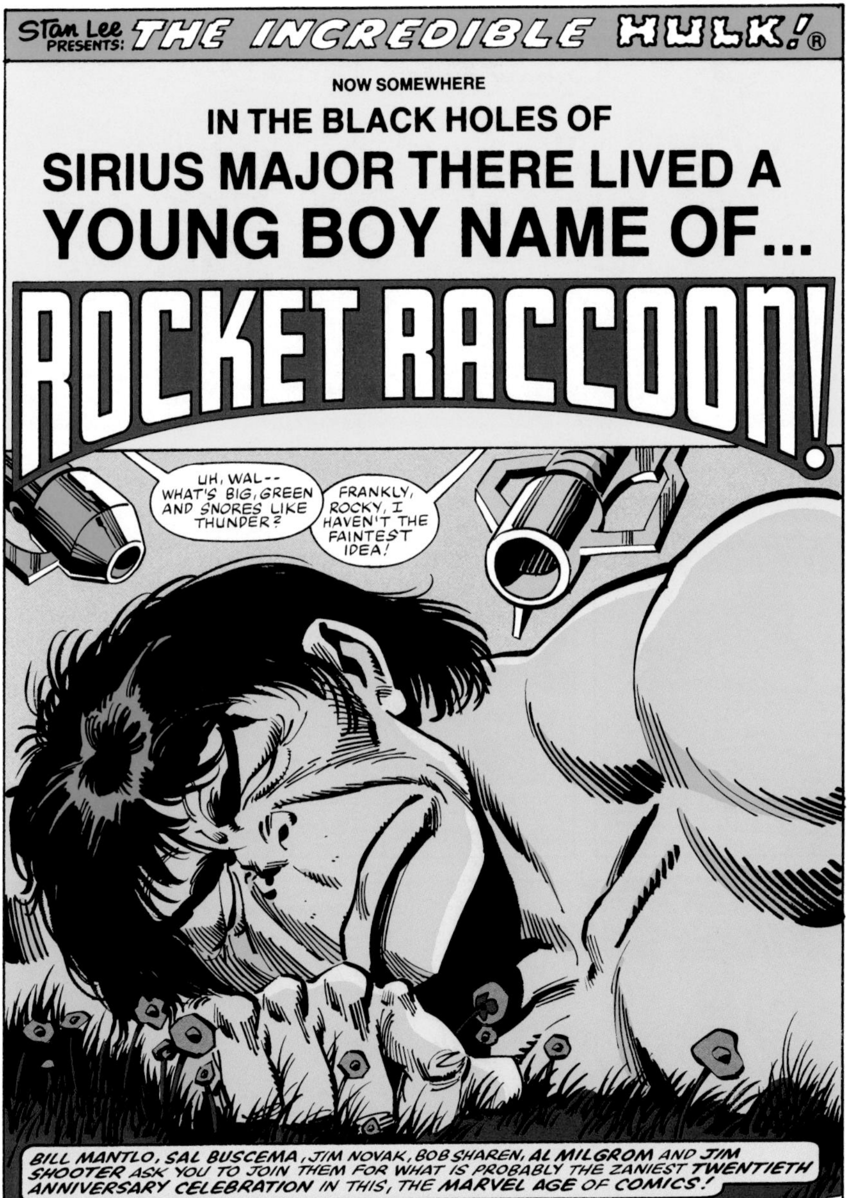

STAN LEE PRESENTS: THE INCREDIBLE HULK!®
NOW SOMEWHERE
IN THE BLACK HOLES OF
SIRIUS MAJOR THERE LIVED A
YOUNG BOY NAME OF...
ROCKET RACCOON!
UH, WAL-- WHAT'S BIG, GREEN AND SNORES LIKE THUNDER?
FRANKLY, ROCKY, I HAVEN'T THE FAINTEST IDEA!
BILL MANTLO, SAL BUSCEMA, JIM NOVAK, BOB SHAREN, AL MILGROM AND JIM SHOOTER ASK YOU TO JOIN THEM FOR WHAT IS PROBABLY THE ZANIEST TWENTIETH ANNIVERSARY CELEBRATION IN THIS, THE MARVEL AGE OF COMICS!
1

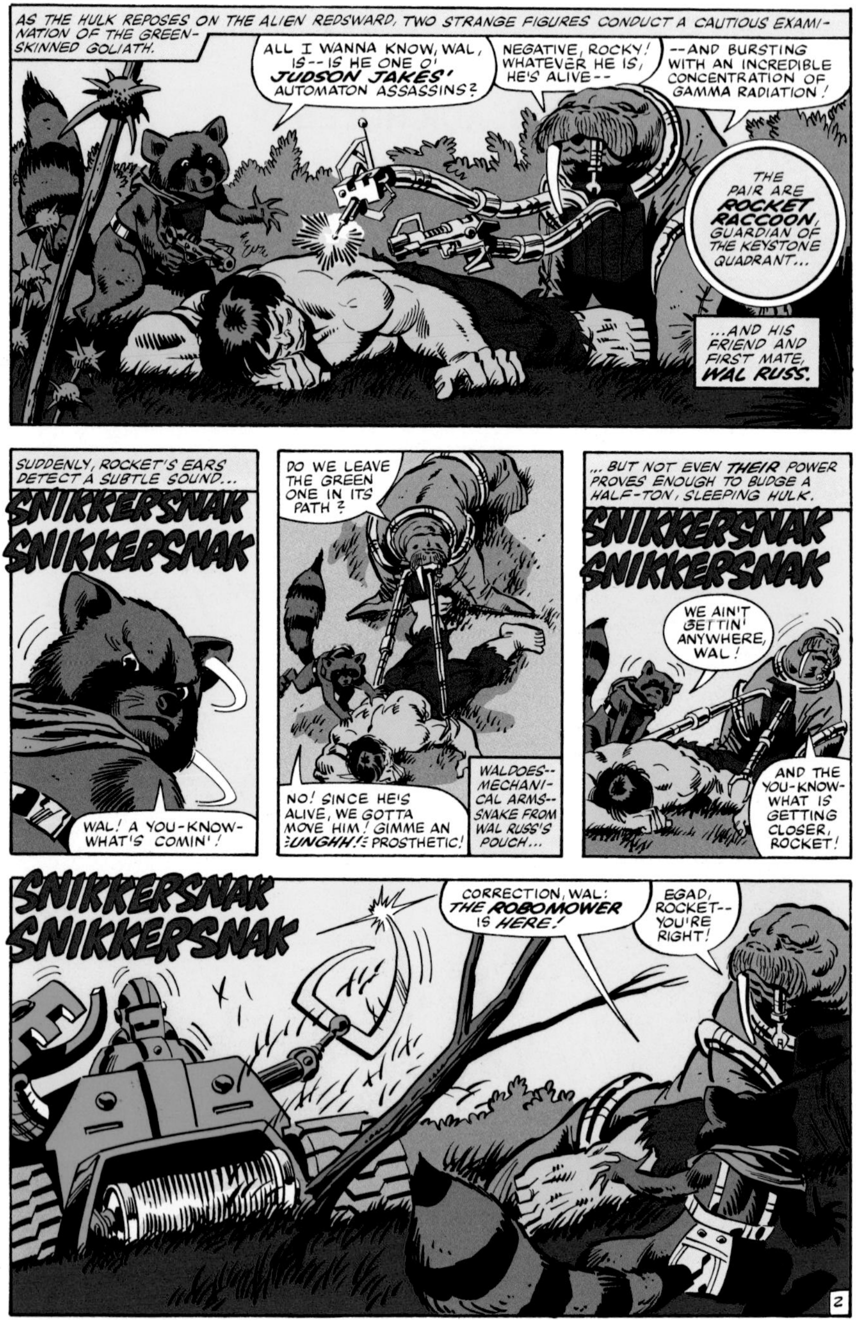

AS THE HULK REPOSES ON THE ALIEN REDSWARD, TWO STRANGE FIGURES CONDUCT A CAUTIOUS EXAMINATION OF THE GREEN-SKINNED GOLIATH.
ALL I WANNA KNOW, WAL, IS-- IS HE ONE O' JUDSON JAKES' AUTOMATON ASSASSINS?
NEGATIVE, ROCKY! WHATEVER HE IS, HE'S ALIVE--
--AND BURSTING WITH AN INCREDIBLE CONCENTRATION OF GAMMA RADIATION!
THE PAIR ARE ROCKET RACCOON, GUARDIAN OF THE KEYSTONE QUADRANT...
...AND HIS FRIEND AND FIRST MATE, WAL RUSS.
SUDDENLY, ROCKET'S EARS DETECT A SUBTLE SOUND...
SNIKKERSNAK SNIKKERSNAK
WAL! A YOU-KNOW-WHAT'S COMIN'!
DO WE LEAVE THE GREEN ONE IN ITS PATH?
NO! SINCE HE'S ALIVE, WE GOTTA MOVE HIM! GIMME AN UNGHH! PROSTHETIC!
WALDOES--MECHANICAL ARMS--SNAKE FROM WAL RUSS'S POUCH...
...BUT NOT EVEN THEIR POWER PROVES ENOUGH TO BUDGE A HALF-TON, SLEEPING HULK.
SNIKKERSNAK SNIKKERSNAK
WE AIN'T GETTIN' ANYWHERE, WAL!
AND THE YOU-KNOW-WHAT IS GETTING CLOSER, ROCKET!
SNIKKERSNAK SNIKKERSNAK
CORRECTION, WAL: THE ROBOMOWER IS HERE!
EGAD, ROCKET-- YOU'RE RIGHT!
2

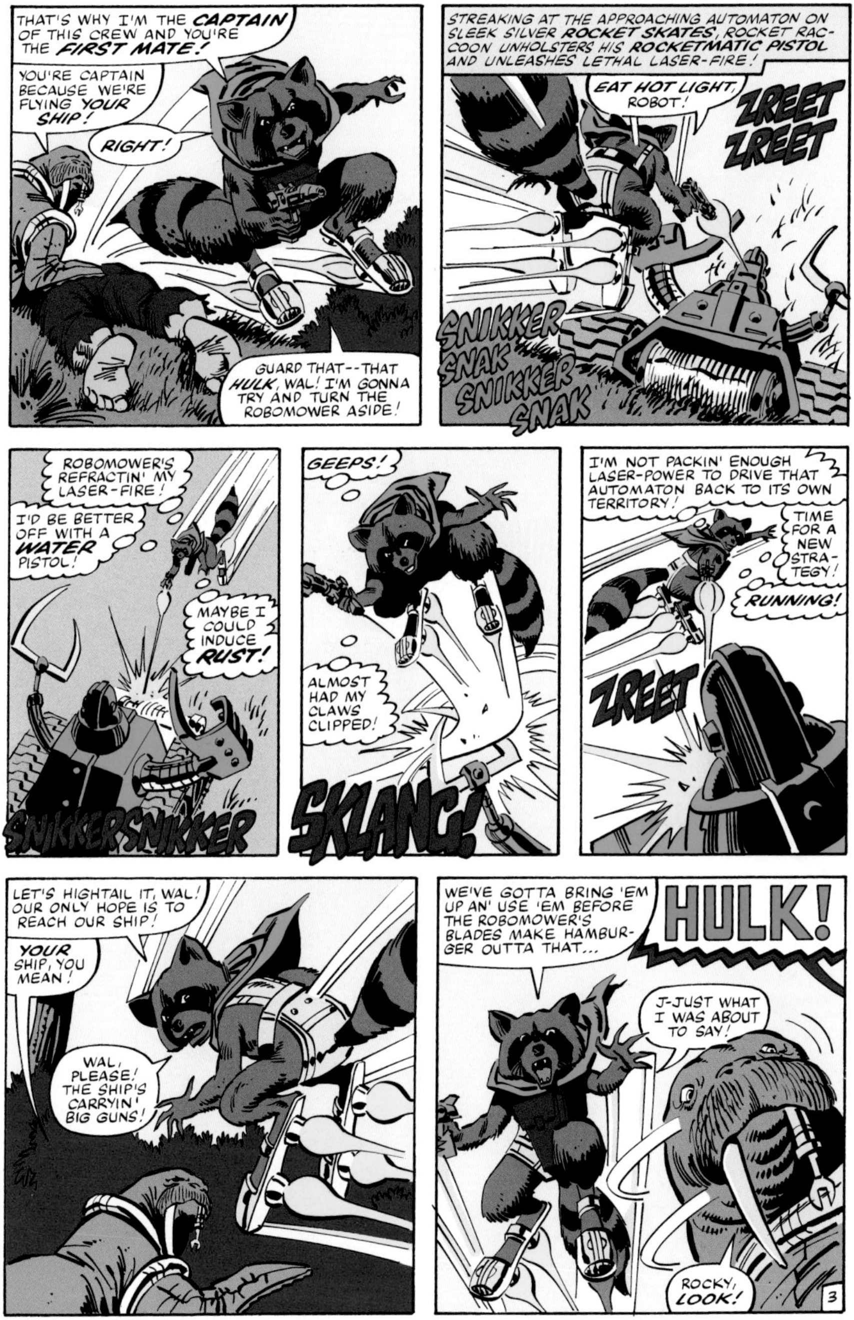
THAT'S WHY I'M THE CAPTAIN OF THIS CREW AND YOU'RE THE FIRST MATE!
YOU'RE CAPTAIN BECAUSE WE'RE FLYING YOUR SHIP!
RIGHT!
GUARD THAT--THAT HULK, WAL! I'M GONNA TRY AND TURN THE ROBOMOWER ASIDE!
STREAKING AT THE APPROACHING AUTOMATON ON SLEEK SILVER ROCKET SKATES, ROCKET RACCOON UNHOLSTERS HIS ROCKETMATIC PISTOL AND UNLEASHES LETHAL LASER-FIRE!
EAT HOT LIGHT, ROBOT!
ZREET ZREET
SNIKKER SNAK SNIKKER SNAK
ROBOMOWER'S REFRACTIN' MY LASER-FIRE!
I'D BE BETTER OFF WITH A WATER PISTOL!
MAYBE I COULD INDUCE RUST!
SNIKKERSNIKKER
GEEPS!
ALMOST HAD MY CLAWS CLIPPED!
SKLANG!
I'M NOT PACKIN' ENOUGH LASER-POWER TO DRIVE THAT AUTOMATON BACK TO ITS OWN TERRITORY!
TIME FOR A NEW STRATEGY!
RUNNING!
ZREET
LET'S HIGHTAIL IT, WAL! OUR ONLY HOPE IS TO REACH OUR SHIP!
YOUR SHIP, YOU MEAN!
WAL, PLEASE! THE SHIP'S CARRYIN' BIG GUNS!
WE'VE GOTTA BRING 'EM UP AN' USE 'EM BEFORE THE ROBOMOWER'S BLADES MAKE HAMBURGER OUTTA THAT...
HULK!
J-JUST WHAT I WAS ABOUT TO SAY!
ROCKY, LOOK!
3

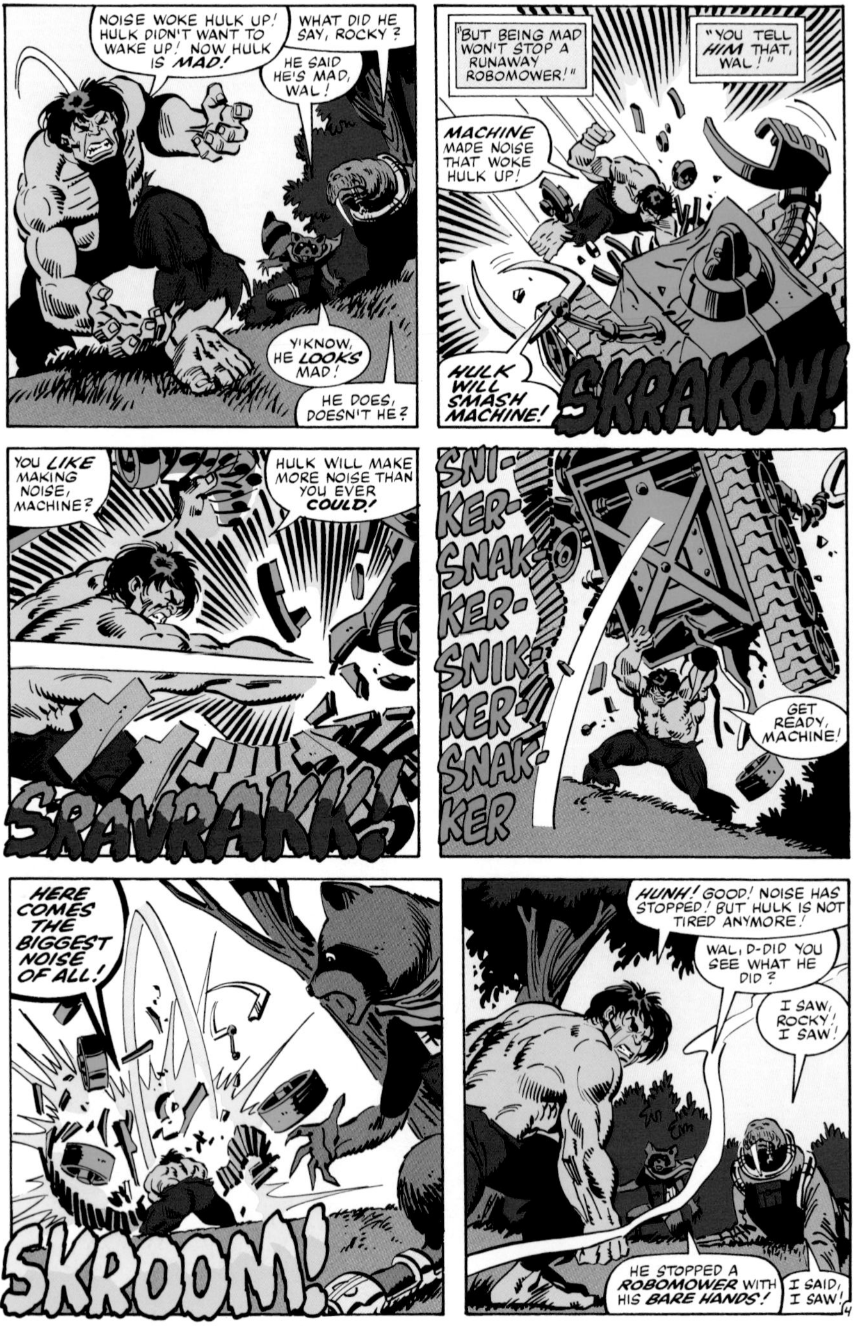
NOISE WOKE HULK UP! HULK DIDN'T WANT TO WAKE UP! NOW HULK IS MAD!
WHAT DID HE SAY, ROCKY?
HE SAID HE'S MAD, WAL!
Y'KNOW, HE LOOKS MAD!
HE DOES, DOESN'T HE?
"BUT BEING MAD WON'T STOP A RUNAWAY ROBOMOWER!"
"YOU TELL HIM THAT, WAL!"
MACHINE MADE NOISE THAT WOKE HULK UP!
HULK WILL SMASH MACHINE!
SKRAKOW!
YOU LIKE MAKING NOISE, MACHINE?
HULK WILL MAKE MORE NOISE THAN YOU EVER COULD!
SRAVRAKK!
SNI-KER-SNAK-KER-SNIK-KER-SNAK-KER
GET READY, MACHINE!
HERE COMES THE BIGGEST NOISE OF ALL!
SKROOM!
HUNH! GOOD! NOISE HAS STOPPED! BUT HULK IS NOT TIRED ANYMORE!
WAL, D-DID YOU SEE WHAT HE DID?
I SAW, ROCKY! I SAW!
HE STOPPED A ROBOMOWER WITH HIS BARE HANDS!
I SAID, I SAW!
4

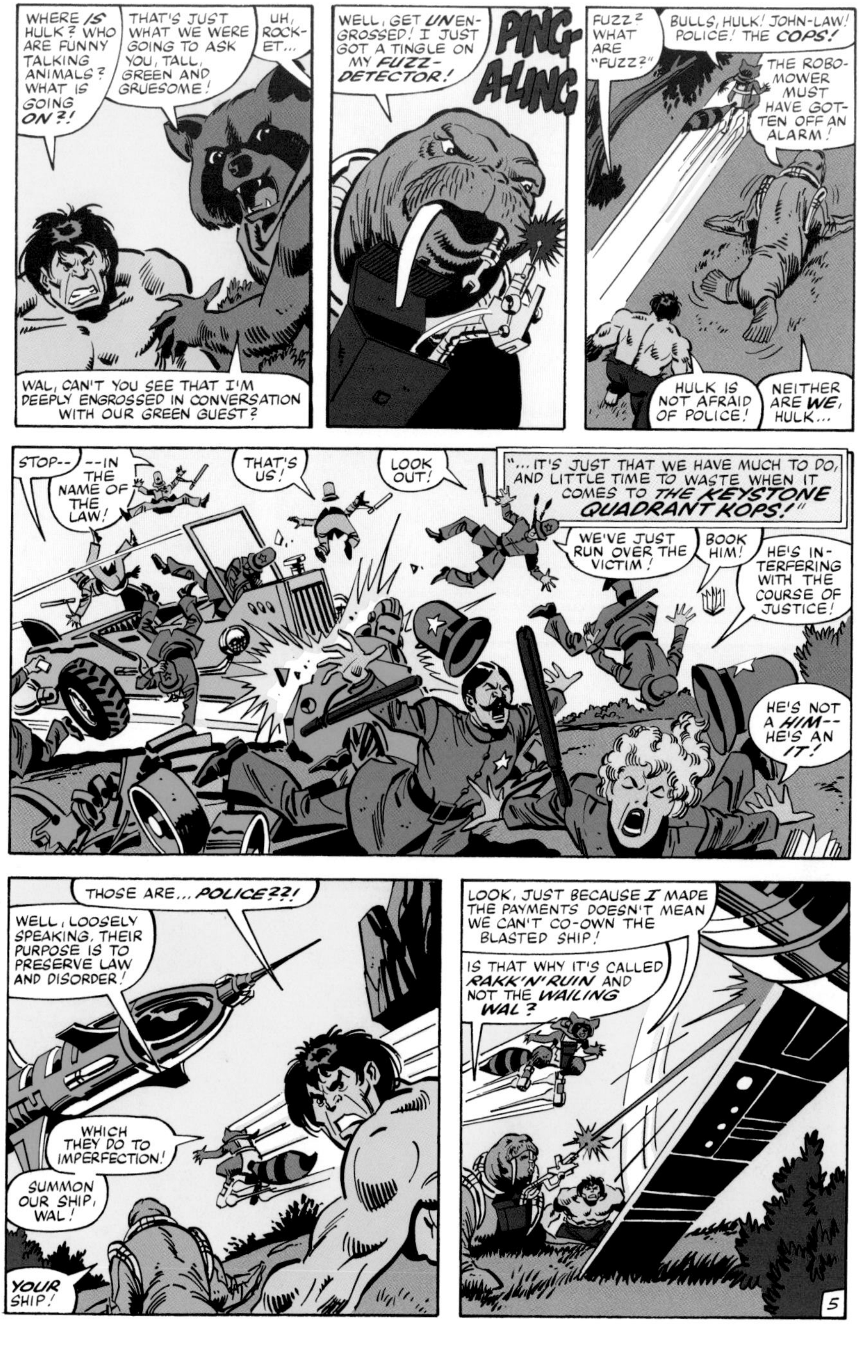
WHERE IS HULK? WHO ARE FUNNY TALKING ANIMALS? WHAT IS GOING ON?!
THAT'S JUST WHAT WE WERE GOING TO ASK YOU, TALL, GREEN AND GRUESOME!
UH, ROCKET...
WAL, CAN'T YOU SEE THAT I'M DEEPLY ENGROSSED IN CONVERSATION WITH OUR GREEN GUEST?
WELL, GET UNENGROSSED! I JUST GOT A TINGLE ON MY FUZZ-DETECTOR!
PING-A-LING
FUZZ? WHAT ARE "FUZZ?"
BULLS, HULK! JOHN-LAW! POLICE! THE COPS!
THE ROBO-MOWER MUST HAVE GOTTEN OFF AN ALARM!
HULK IS NOT AFRAID OF POLICE!
NEITHER ARE WE, HULK...
STOP--
--IN THE NAME OF THE LAW!
THAT'S US!
LOOK OUT!
"...IT'S JUST THAT WE HAVE MUCH TO DO, AND LITTLE TIME TO WASTE WHEN IT COMES TO THE KEYSTONE QUADRANT KOPS!"
WE'VE JUST RUN OVER THE VICTIM!
BOOK HIM!
HE'S INTERFERING WITH THE COURSE OF JUSTICE!
HE'S NOT A HIM-- HE'S AN IT!
THOSE ARE... POLICE??!
WELL, LOOSELY SPEAKING, THEIR PURPOSE IS TO PRESERVE LAW AND DISORDER!
WHICH THEY DO TO IMPERFECTION!
SUMMON OUR SHIP, WAL!
YOUR SHIP!
LOOK, JUST BECAUSE I MADE THE PAYMENTS DOESN'T MEAN WE CAN'T CO-OWN THE BLASTED SHIP!
IS THAT WHY IT'S CALLED RAKK'N'RUIN AND NOT THE WAILING WAL?
5

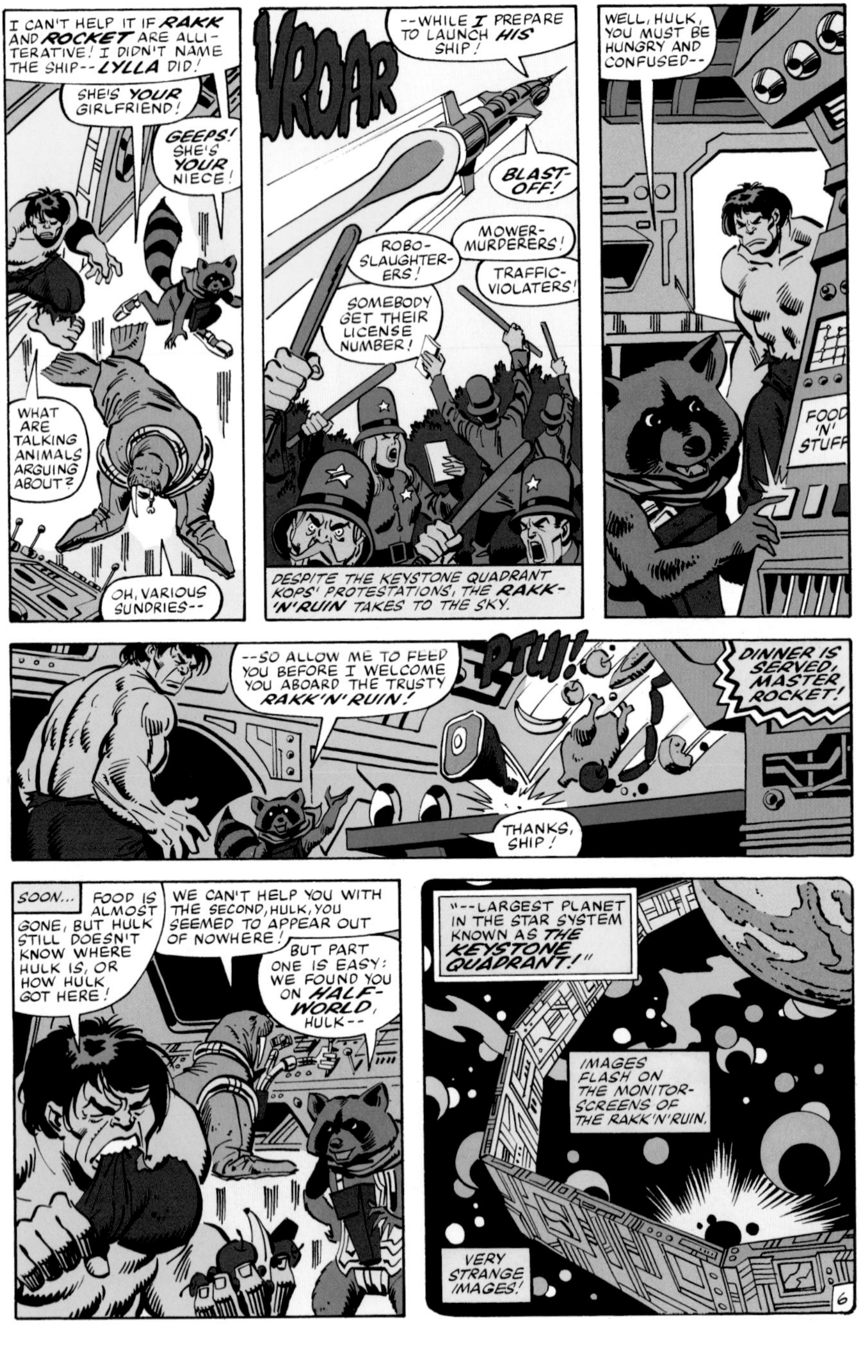
I CAN'T HELP IT IF RAKK AND ROCKET ARE ALLITERATIVE! I DIDN'T NAME THE SHIP--LYLLA DID!
SHE'S YOUR GIRLFRIEND!
GEEPS! SHE'S YOUR NIECE!
WHAT ARE TALKING ANIMALS ARGUING ABOUT?
OH, VARIOUS SUNDRIES--
VROAR
--WHILE I PREPARE TO LAUNCH HIS SHIP!
BLAST-OFF!
ROBO-SLAUGHTERERS!
MOWER-MURDERERS!
TRAFFIC-VIOLATERS!
SOMEBODY GET THEIR LICENSE NUMBER!
DESPITE THE KEYSTONE QUADRANT KOPS' PROTESTATIONS, THE RAKK-'N'RUIN TAKES TO THE SKY.
WELL, HULK, YOU MUST BE HUNGRY AND CONFUSED--
FOOD 'N' STUFF
--SO ALLOW ME TO FEED YOU BEFORE I WELCOME YOU ABOARD THE TRUSTY RAKK'N'RUIN!
PTUI!
DINNER IS SERVED, MASTER ROCKET!
THANKS, SHIP!
SOON...
FOOD IS ALMOST GONE, BUT HULK STILL DOESN'T KNOW WHERE HULK IS, OR HOW HULK GOT HERE!
WE CAN'T HELP YOU WITH THE SECOND, HULK, YOU SEEMED TO APPEAR OUT OF NOWHERE!
BUT PART ONE IS EASY: WE FOUND YOU ON HALF-WORLD, HULK--
"--LARGEST PLANET IN THE STAR SYSTEM KNOWN AS THE KEYSTONE QUADRANT!"
IMAGES FLASH ON THE MONITOR-SCREENS OF THE RAKK'N'RUIN.
VERY STRANGE IMAGES!
6

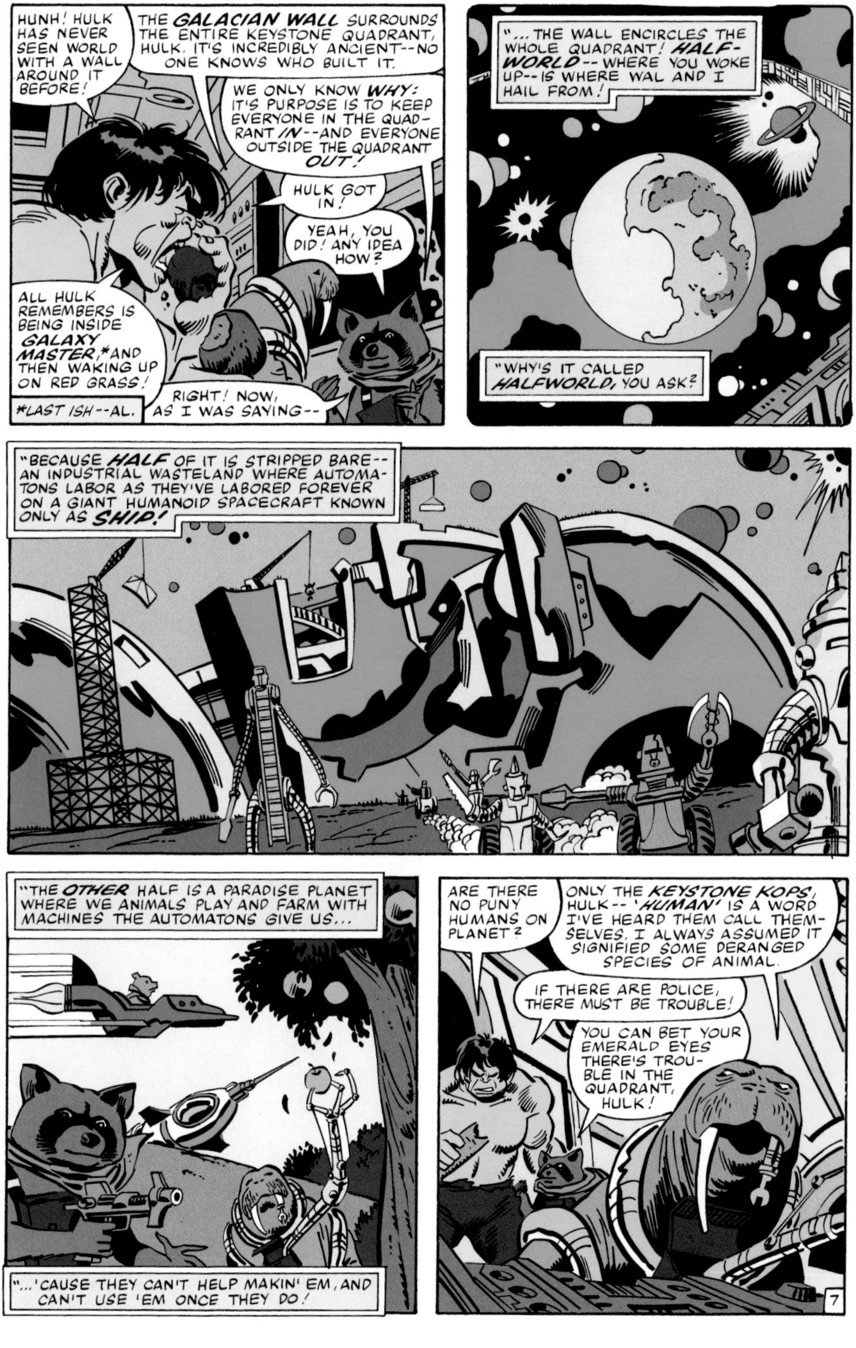
HUNH! HULK HAS NEVER SEEN WORLD WITH A WALL AROUND IT BEFORE!
THE GALACIAN WALL SURROUNDS THE ENTIRE KEYSTONE QUADRANT, HULK. IT'S INCREDIBLY ANCIENT--NO ONE KNOWS WHO BUILT IT.
WE ONLY KNOW WHY: IT'S PURPOSE IS TO KEEP EVERYONE IN THE QUADRANT IN--AND EVERYONE OUTSIDE THE QUADRANT OUT!
HULK GOT IN!
YEAH, YOU DID! ANY IDEA HOW?
ALL HULK REMEMBERS IS BEING INSIDE GALAXY MASTER,*AND THEN WAKING UP ON RED GRASS!
*LAST ISH--AL.
RIGHT! NOW, AS I WAS SAYING--
"...THE WALL ENCIRCLES THE WHOLE QUADRANT! HALF-WORLD--WHERE YOU WOKE UP--IS WHERE WAL AND I HAIL FROM!
"WHY'S IT CALLED HALFWORLD, YOU ASK?
"BECAUSE HALF OF IT IS STRIPPED BARE--AN INDUSTRIAL WASTELAND WHERE AUTOMATONS LABOR AS THEY'VE LABORED FOREVER ON A GIANT HUMANOID SPACECRAFT KNOWN ONLY AS SHIP!
"THE OTHER HALF IS A PARADISE PLANET WHERE WE ANIMALS PLAY AND FARM WITH MACHINES THE AUTOMATONS GIVE US...
"...'CAUSE THEY CAN'T HELP MAKIN' EM, AND CAN'T USE 'EM ONCE THEY DO!
ARE THERE NO PUNY HUMANS ON PLANET?
ONLY THE KEYSTONE KOPS, HULK--'HUMAN' IS A WORD I'VE HEARD THEM CALL THEMSELVES. I ALWAYS ASSUMED IT SIGNIFIED SOME DERANGED SPECIES OF ANIMAL.
IF THERE ARE POLICE, THERE MUST BE TROUBLE!
YOU CAN BET YOUR EMERALD EYES THERE'S TROUBLE IN THE QUADRANT, HULK!
7

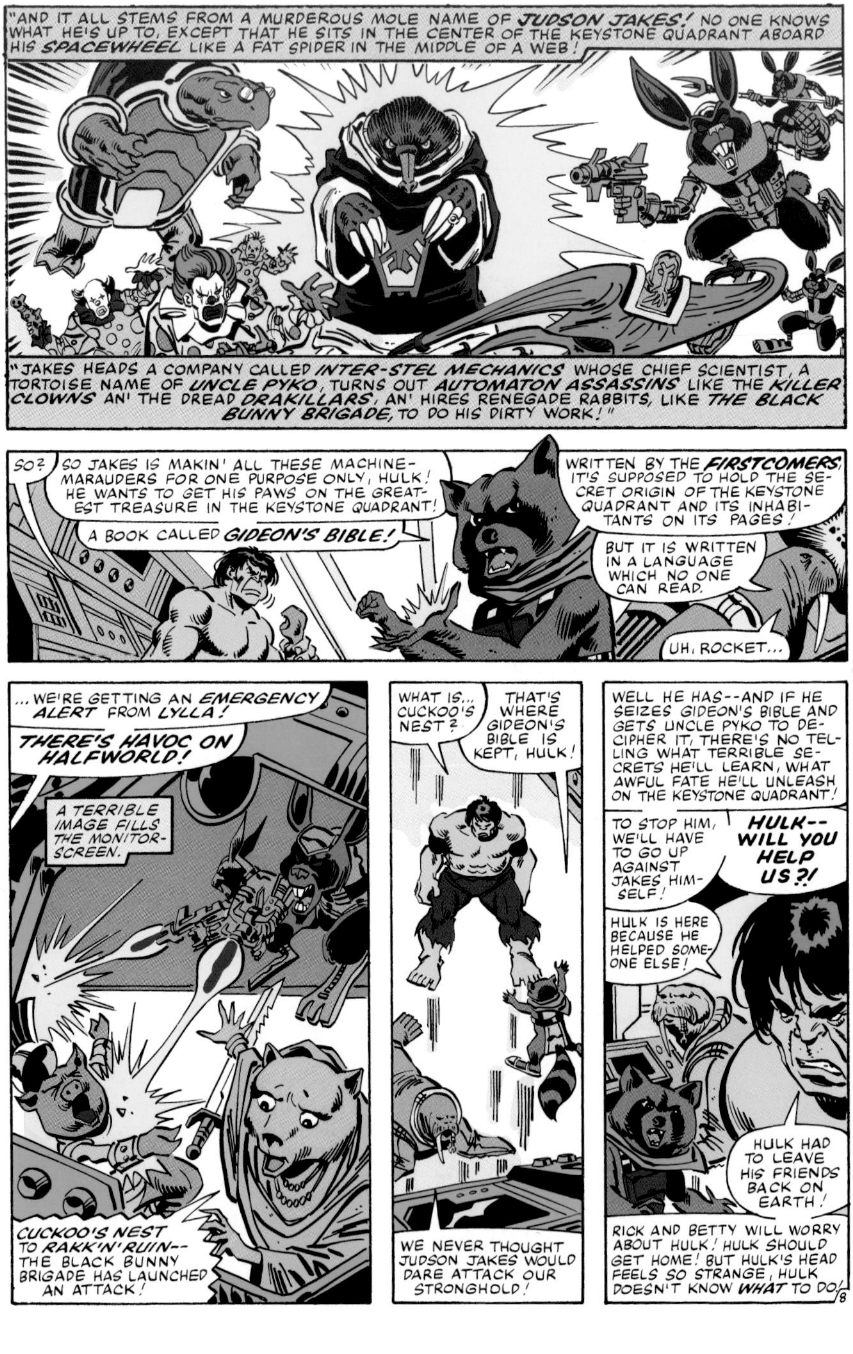
"AND IT ALL STEMS FROM A MURDEROUS MOLE NAME OF JUDSON JAKES! NO ONE KNOWS WHAT HE'S UP TO, EXCEPT THAT HE SITS IN THE CENTER OF THE KEYSTONE QUADRANT ABOARD HIS SPACEWHEEL LIKE A FAT SPIDER IN THE MIDDLE OF A WEB!
"JAKES HEADS A COMPANY CALLED INTER-STEL MECHANICS WHOSE CHIEF SCIENTIST, A TORTOISE NAME OF UNCLE PYKO, TURNS OUT AUTOMATON ASSASSINS LIKE THE KILLER CLOWNS AN' THE DREAD DRAKILLARS, AN' HIRES RENEGADE RABBITS, LIKE THE BLACK BUNNY BRIGADE, TO DO HIS DIRTY WORK!"
SO?
SO JAKES IS MAKIN' ALL THESE MACHINE-MARAUDERS FOR ONE PURPOSE ONLY, HULK! HE WANTS TO GET HIS PAWS ON THE GREATEST TREASURE IN THE KEYSTONE QUADRANT!
A BOOK CALLED GIDEON'S BIBLE!
WRITTEN BY THE FIRSTCOMERS, IT'S SUPPOSED TO HOLD THE SECRET ORIGIN OF THE KEYSTONE QUADRANT AND ITS INHABITANTS ON ITS PAGES!
BUT IT IS WRITTEN IN A LANGUAGE WHICH NO ONE CAN READ.
UH, ROCKET...
...WE'RE GETTING AN EMERGENCY ALERT FROM LYLLA!
THERE'S HAVOC ON HALFWORLD!
A TERRIBLE IMAGE FILLS THE MONITOR-SCREEN.
CUCKOO'S NEST TO RAKK'N'RUIN-- THE BLACK BUNNY BRIGADE HAS LAUNCHED AN ATTACK!
WHAT IS... CUCKOO'S NEST?
THAT'S WHERE GIDEON'S BIBLE IS KEPT, HULK!
WE NEVER THOUGHT JUDSON JAKES WOULD DARE ATTACK OUR STRONGHOLD!
WELL HE HAS--AND IF HE SEIZES GIDEON'S BIBLE AND GETS UNCLE PYKO TO DECIPHER IT, THERE'S NO TELLING WHAT TERRIBLE SECRETS HE'LL LEARN, WHAT AWFUL FATE HE'LL UNLEASH ON THE KEYSTONE QUADRANT!
TO STOP HIM, WE'LL HAVE TO GO UP AGAINST JAKES HIMSELF!
HULK-- WILL YOU HELP US?!
HULK IS HERE BECAUSE HE HELPED SOMEONE ELSE!
HULK HAD TO LEAVE HIS FRIENDS BACK ON EARTH!
RICK AND BETTY WILL WORRY ABOUT HULK! HULK SHOULD GET HOME! BUT HULK'S HEAD FEELS SO STRANGE, HULK DOESN'T KNOW WHAT TO DO!
8

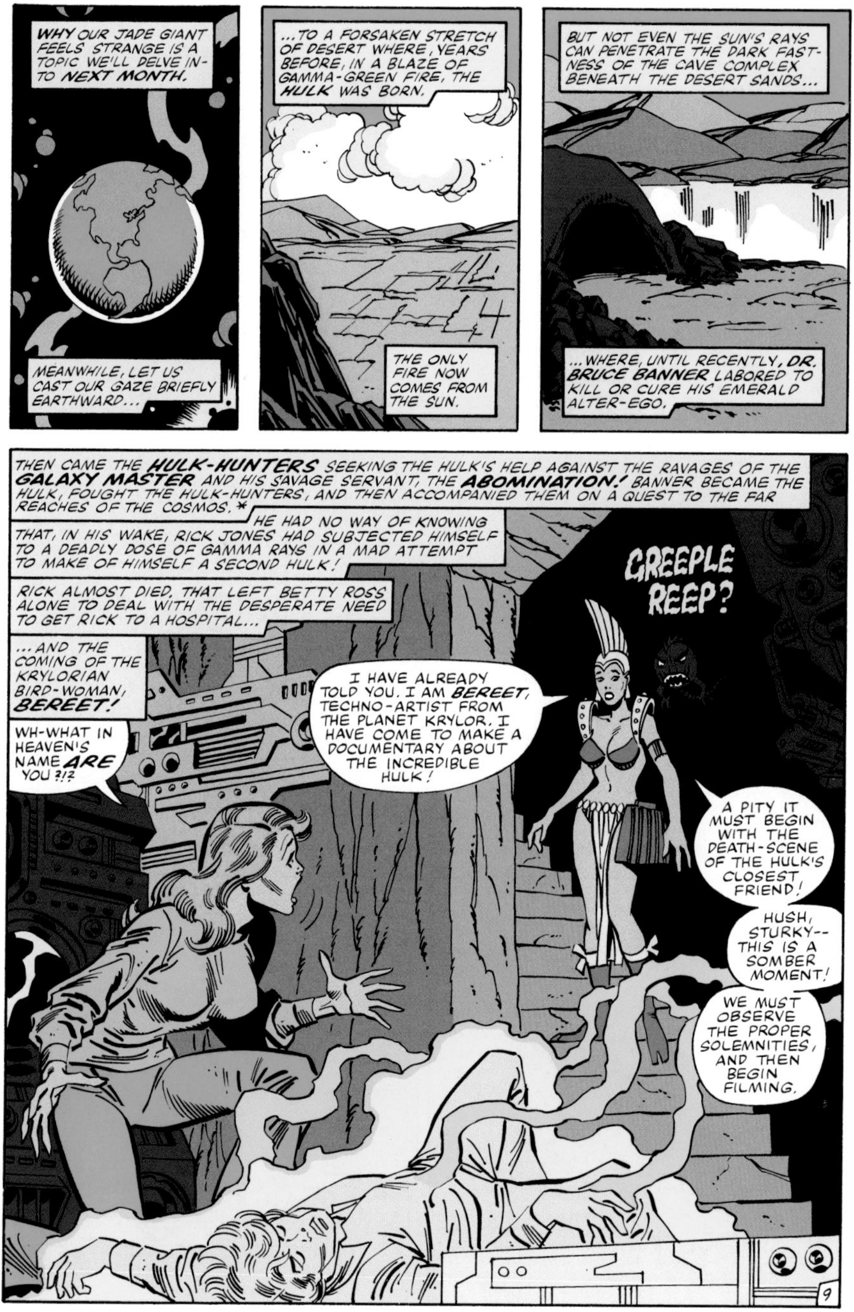
WHY OUR JADE GIANT FEELS STRANGE IS A TOPIC WE'LL DELVE INTO NEXT MONTH.
MEANWHILE, LET US CAST OUR GAZE BRIEFLY EARTHWARD...
...TO A FORSAKEN STRETCH OF DESERT WHERE, YEARS BEFORE, IN A BLAZE OF GAMMA-GREEN FIRE, THE HULK WAS BORN.
THE ONLY FIRE NOW COMES FROM THE SUN.
BUT NOT EVEN THE SUN'S RAYS CAN PENETRATE THE DARK FASTNESS OF THE CAVE COMPLEX BENEATH THE DESERT SANDS...
...WHERE, UNTIL RECENTLY, DR. BRUCE BANNER LABORED TO KILL OR CURE HIS EMERALD ALTER-EGO.
THEN CAME THE HULK-HUNTERS SEEKING THE HULK'S HELP AGAINST THE RAVAGES OF THE GALAXY MASTER AND HIS SAVAGE SERVANT, THE ABOMINATION! BANNER BECAME THE HULK, FOUGHT THE HULK-HUNTERS, AND THEN ACCOMPANIED THEM ON A QUEST TO THE FAR REACHES OF THE COSMOS.*
HE HAD NO WAY OF KNOWING THAT, IN HIS WAKE, RICK JONES HAD SUBJECTED HIMSELF TO A DEADLY DOSE OF GAMMA RAYS IN A MAD ATTEMPT TO MAKE OF HIMSELF A SECOND HULK!
RICK ALMOST DIED. THAT LEFT BETTY ROSS ALONE TO DEAL WITH THE DESPERATE NEED TO GET RICK TO A HOSPITAL...
...AND THE COMING OF THE KRYLORIAN BIRD-WOMAN, BEREET!
GREEPLE REEP?
WH-WHAT IN HEAVEN'S NAME ARE YOU?!?
I HAVE ALREADY TOLD YOU. I AM BEREET, TECHNO-ARTIST FROM THE PLANET KRYLOR. I HAVE COME TO MAKE A DOCUMENTARY ABOUT THE INCREDIBLE HULK!
A PITY IT MUST BEGIN WITH THE DEATH-SCENE OF THE HULK'S CLOSEST FRIEND!
HUSH, STURKY-- THIS IS A SOMBER MOMENT!
WE MUST OBSERVE THE PROPER SOLEMNITIES, AND THEN BEGIN FILMING.
9

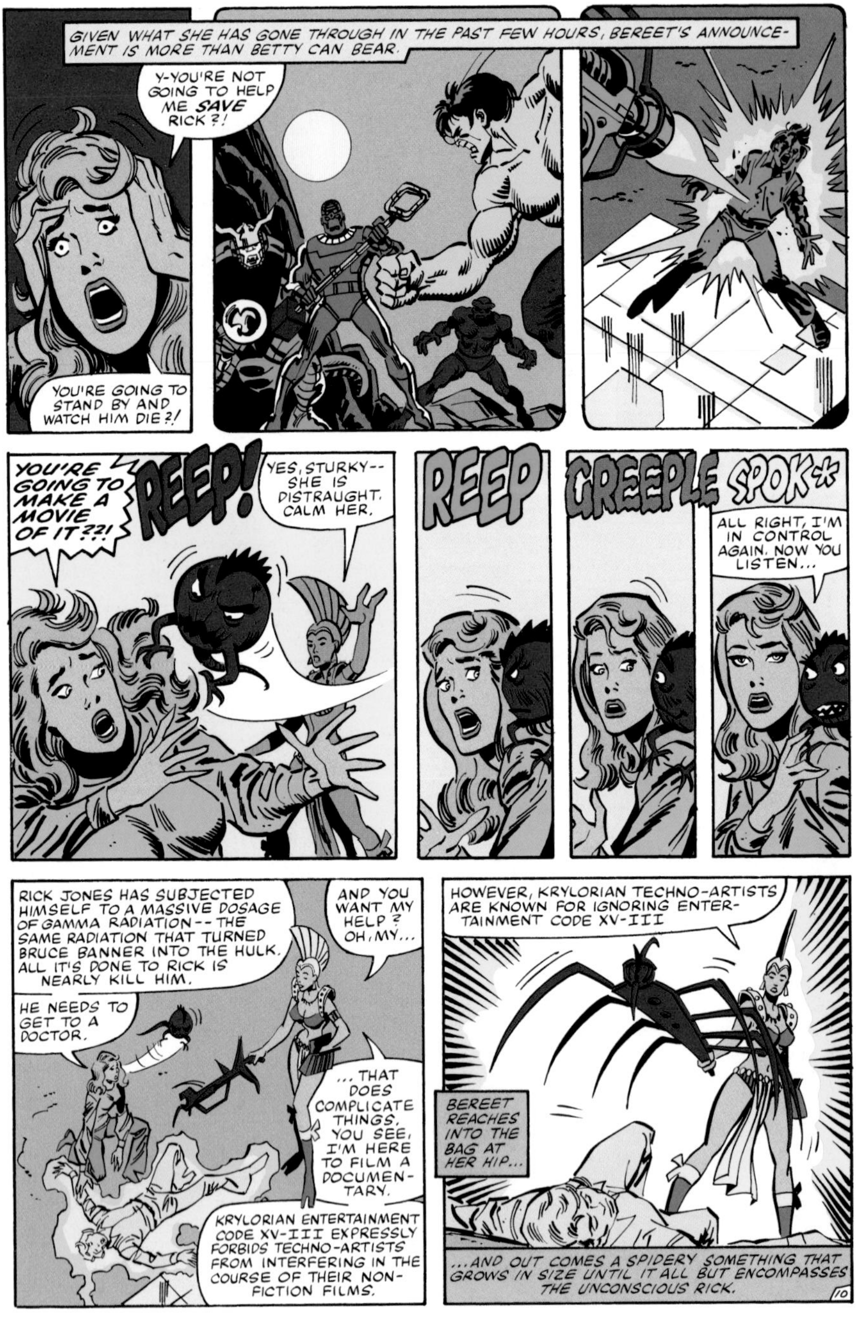

GIVEN WHAT SHE HAS GONE THROUGH IN THE PAST FEW HOURS, BEREET'S ANNOUNCEMENT IS MORE THAN BETTY CAN BEAR.
Y-YOU'RE NOT GOING TO HELP ME SAVE RICK?!
YOU'RE GOING TO STAND BY AND WATCH HIM DIE?!
YOU'RE GOING TO MAKE A MOVIE OF IT??!
REEP!
YES, STURKY-- SHE IS DISTRAUGHT. CALM HER.
REEP
GREEPLE
SPOK*
ALL RIGHT, I'M IN CONTROL AGAIN. NOW YOU LISTEN...
RICK JONES HAS SUBJECTED HIMSELF TO A MASSIVE DOSAGE OF GAMMA RADIATION--THE SAME RADIATION THAT TURNED BRUCE BANNER INTO THE HULK. ALL IT'S DONE TO RICK IS NEARLY KILL HIM.
HE NEEDS TO GET TO A DOCTOR.
AND YOU WANT MY HELP? OH, MY...
...THAT DOES COMPLICATE THINGS, YOU SEE, I'M HERE TO FILM A DOCUMENTARY.
KRYLORIAN ENTERTAINMENT CODE XV-III EXPRESSLY FORBIDS TECHNO-ARTISTS FROM INTERFERING IN THE COURSE OF THEIR NON-FICTION FILMS.
HOWEVER, KRYLORIAN TECHNO-ARTISTS ARE KNOWN FOR IGNORING ENTERTAINMENT CODE XV-III
BEREET REACHES INTO THE BAG AT HER HIP...
...AND OUT COMES A SPIDERY SOMETHING THAT GROWS IN SIZE UNTIL IT ALL BUT ENCOMPASSES THE UNCONSCIOUS RICK.
10

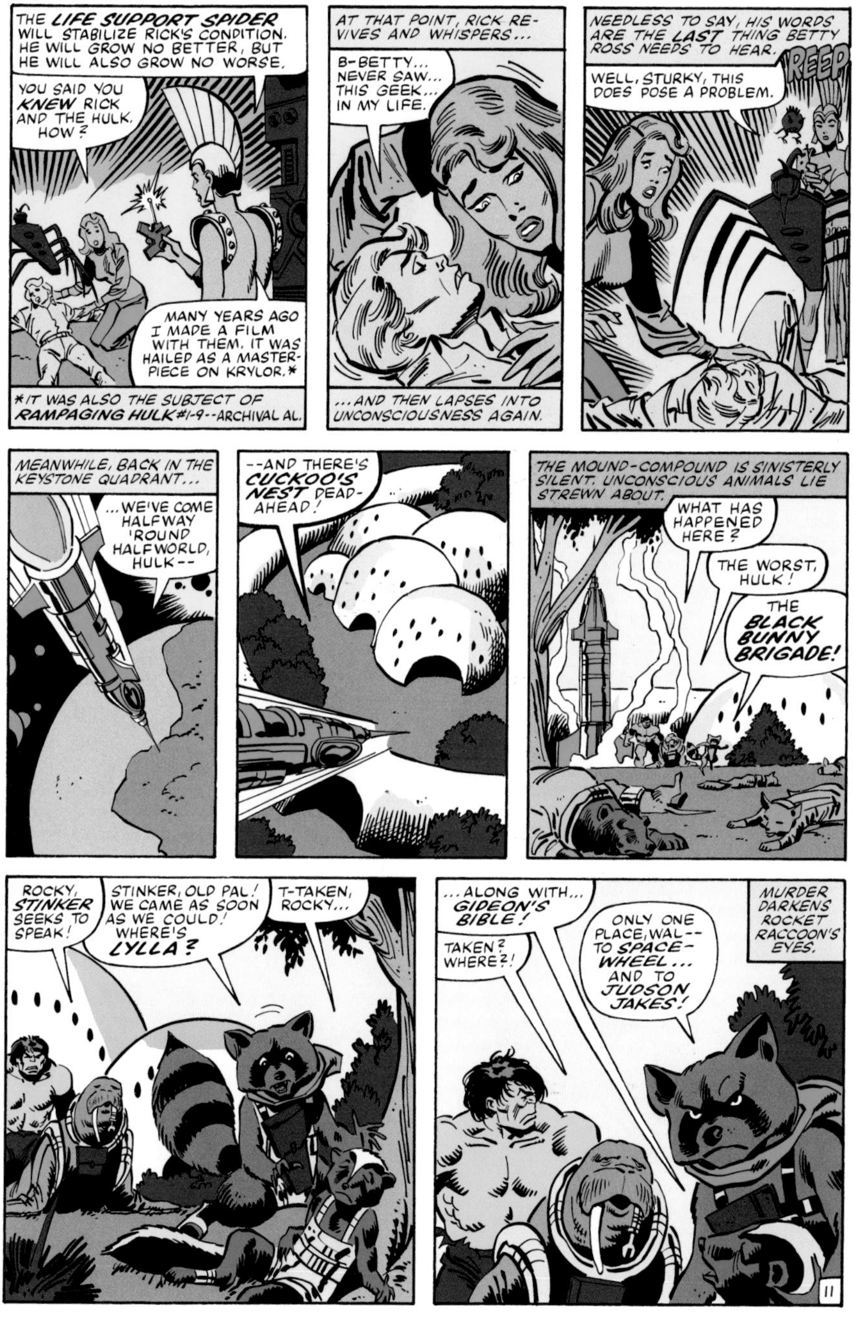
THE LIFE SUPPORT SPIDER WILL STABILIZE RICK'S CONDITION. HE WILL GROW NO BETTER, BUT HE WILL ALSO GROW NO WORSE.
YOU SAID YOU KNEW RICK AND THE HULK. HOW?
MANY YEARS AGO I MADE A FILM WITH THEM. IT WAS HAILED AS A MASTERPIECE ON KRYLOR.*
*IT WAS ALSO THE SUBJECT OF RAMPAGING HULK #1-9--ARCHIVAL AL.
AT THAT POINT, RICK REVIVES AND WHISPERS...
B-BETTY... NEVER SAW... THIS GEEK... IN MY LIFE.
...AND THEN LAPSES INTO UNCONSCIOUSNESS AGAIN.
NEEDLESS TO SAY, HIS WORDS ARE THE LAST THING BETTY ROSS NEEDS TO HEAR.
REEP
WELL, STURKY, THIS DOES POSE A PROBLEM.
MEANWHILE, BACK IN THE KEYSTONE QUADRANT...
...WE'VE COME HALFWAY 'ROUND HALFWORLD, HULK--
--AND THERE'S CUCKOO'S NEST DEAD-AHEAD!
THE MOUND-COMPOUND IS SINISTERLY SILENT. UNCONSCIOUS ANIMALS LIE STREWN ABOUT.
WHAT HAS HAPPENED HERE?
THE WORST, HULK!
THE BLACK BUNNY BRIGADE!
ROCKY, STINKER SEEKS TO SPEAK!
STINKER, OLD PAL! WE CAME AS SOON AS WE COULD! WHERE'S LYLLA?
T-TAKEN, ROCKY...
...ALONG WITH... GIDEON'S BIBLE!
TAKEN? WHERE?!
ONLY ONE PLACE, WAL--TO SPACE-WHEEL... AND TO JUDSON JAKES!
MURDER DARKENS ROCKET RACCOON'S EYES.

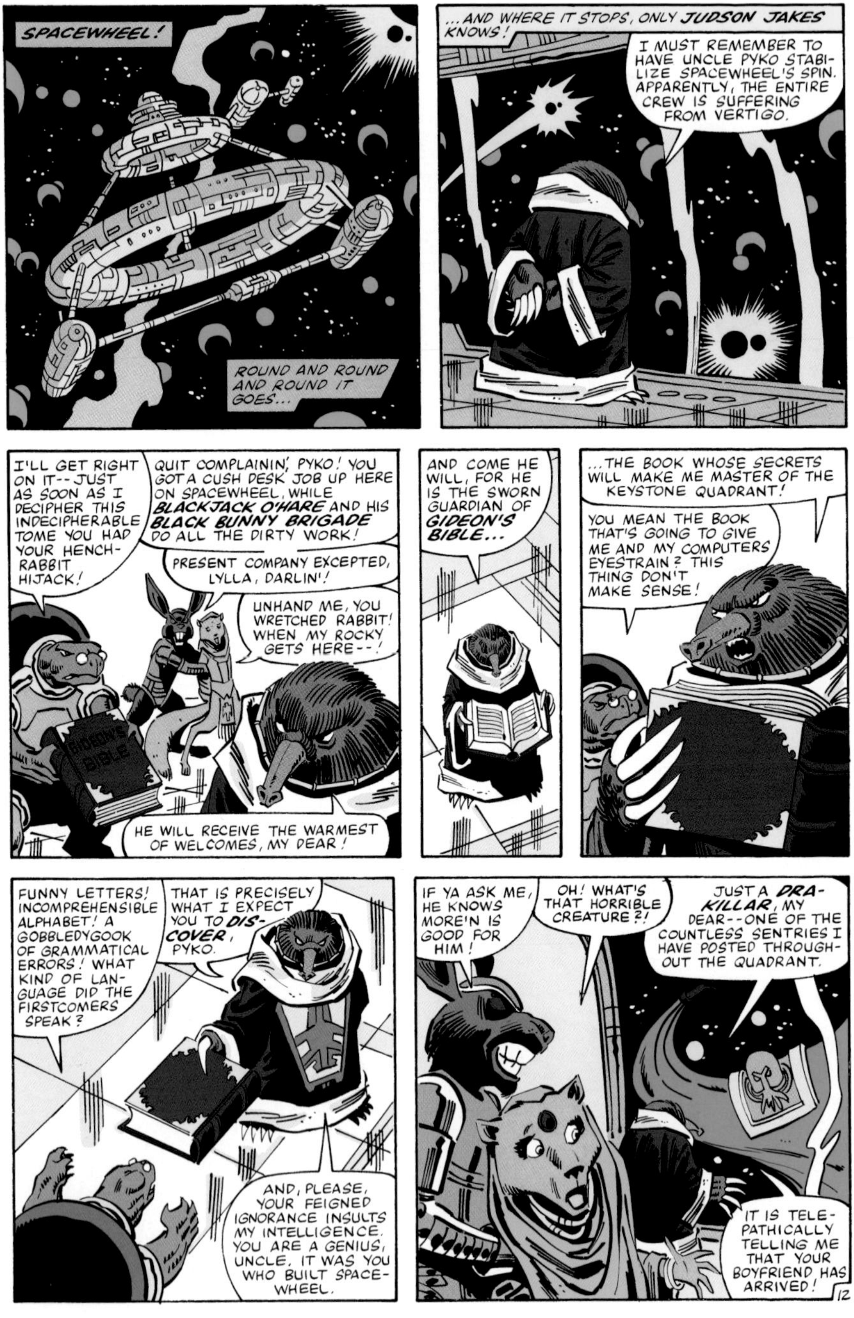
SPACEWHEEL!
ROUND AND ROUND AND ROUND IT GOES...
...AND WHERE IT STOPS, ONLY JUDSON JAKES KNOWS!
I MUST REMEMBER TO HAVE UNCLE PYKO STABILIZE SPACEWHEEL'S SPIN. APPARENTLY, THE ENTIRE CREW IS SUFFERING FROM VERTIGO.
I'LL GET RIGHT ON IT--JUST AS SOON AS I DECIPHER THIS INDECIPHERABLE TOME YOU HAD YOUR HENCH-RABBIT HIJACK!
QUIT COMPLAININ', PYKO! YOU GOT A CUSH DESK JOB UP HERE ON SPACEWHEEL, WHILE BLACKJACK O'HARE AND HIS BLACK BUNNY BRIGADE DO ALL THE DIRTY WORK!
PRESENT COMPANY EXCEPTED, LYLLA, DARLIN'!
UNHAND ME, YOU WRETCHED RABBIT! WHEN MY ROCKY GETS HERE--!
HE WILL RECEIVE THE WARMEST OF WELCOMES, MY DEAR!
GIDEON'S BIBLE
AND COME HE WILL, FOR HE IS THE SWORN GUARDIAN OF GIDEON'S BIBLE...
...THE BOOK WHOSE SECRETS WILL MAKE ME MASTER OF THE KEYSTONE QUADRANT!
YOU MEAN THE BOOK THAT'S GOING TO GIVE ME AND MY COMPUTERS EYESTRAIN? THIS THING DON'T MAKE SENSE!
FUNNY LETTERS! INCOMPREHENSIBLE ALPHABET! A GOBBLEDYGOOK OF GRAMMATICAL ERRORS! WHAT KIND OF LANGUAGE DID THE FIRSTCOMERS SPEAK?
THAT IS PRECISELY WHAT I EXPECT YOU TO DISCOVER, PYKO.
AND, PLEASE, YOUR FEIGNED IGNORANCE INSULTS MY INTELLIGENCE. YOU ARE A GENIUS, UNCLE. IT WAS YOU WHO BUILT SPACEWHEEL.
IF YA ASK ME, HE KNOWS MORE'N IS GOOD FOR HIM!
OH! WHAT'S THAT HORRIBLE CREATURE?!
JUST A DRAKILLAR, MY DEAR--ONE OF THE COUNTLESS SENTRIES I HAVE POSTED THROUGHOUT THE QUADRANT.
IT IS TELEPATHICALLY TELLING ME THAT YOUR BOYFRIEND HAS ARRIVED!

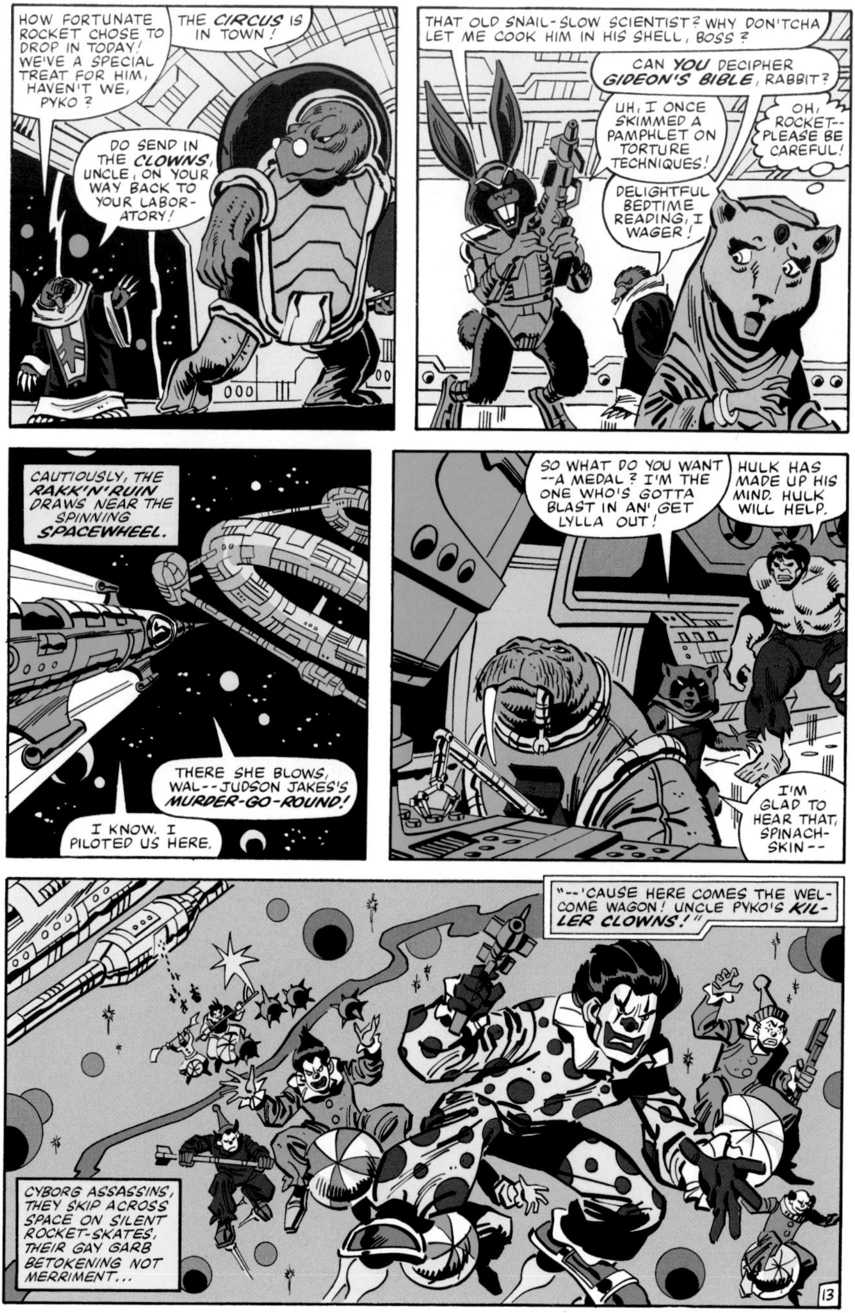

HOW FORTUNATE ROCKET CHOSE TO DROP IN TODAY! WE'VE A SPECIAL TREAT FOR HIM, HAVEN'T WE, PYKO?
THE CIRCUS IS IN TOWN!
DO SEND IN THE CLOWNS, UNCLE, ON YOUR WAY BACK TO YOUR LABOR-ATORY!
THAT OLD SNAIL-SLOW SCIENTIST? WHY DON'TCHA LET ME COOK HIM IN HIS SHELL, BOSS?
CAN YOU DECIPHER GIDEON'S BIBLE, RABBIT?
UH, I ONCE SKIMMED A PAMPHLET ON TORTURE TECHNIQUES!
DELIGHTFUL BEDTIME READING, I WAGER!
OH, ROCKET-- PLEASE BE CAREFUL!
CAUTIOUSLY, THE RAKK'N'RUIN DRAWS NEAR THE SPINNING SPACEWHEEL.
THERE SHE BLOWS, WAL--JUDSON JAKES'S MURDER-GO-ROUND!
I KNOW. I PILOTED US HERE.
SO WHAT DO YOU WANT --A MEDAL? I'M THE ONE WHO'S GOTTA BLAST IN AN' GET LYLLA OUT!
HULK HAS MADE UP HIS MIND. HULK WILL HELP.
I'M GLAD TO HEAR THAT, SPINACH-SKIN--
"--'CAUSE HERE COMES THE WEL-COME WAGON! UNCLE PYKO'S KIL-LER CLOWNS!"
CYBORG ASSASSINS, THEY SKIP ACROSS SPACE ON SILENT ROCKET-SKATES, THEIR GAY GARB BETOKENING NOT MERRIMENT...

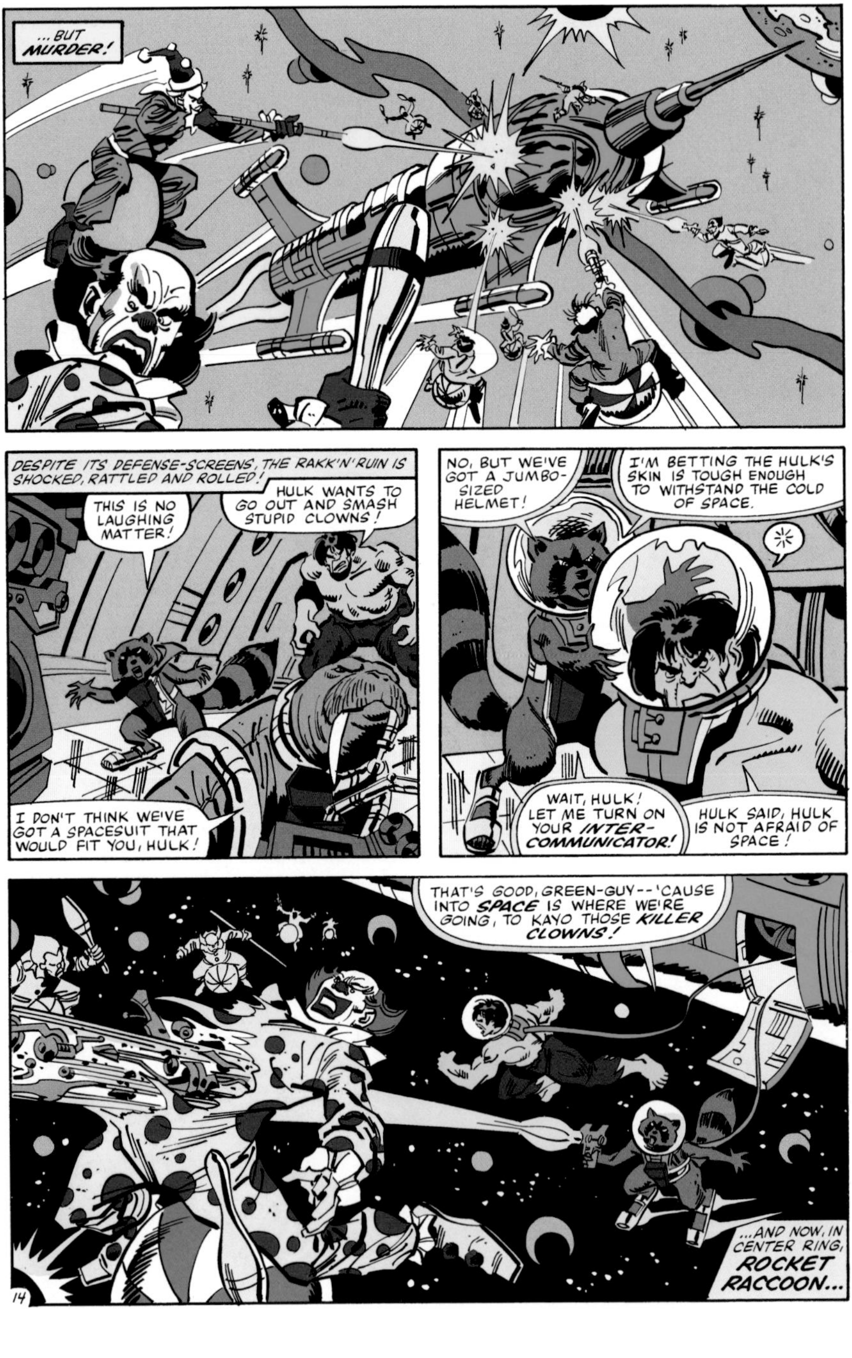
...BUT MURDER!
DESPITE ITS DEFENSE-SCREENS, THE RAKK'N'RUIN IS SHOCKED, RATTLED AND ROLLED!
THIS IS NO LAUGHING MATTER!
HULK WANTS TO GO OUT AND SMASH STUPID CLOWNS!
I DON'T THINK WE'VE GOT A SPACESUIT THAT WOULD FIT YOU, HULK!
NO, BUT WE'VE GOT A JUMBO-SIZED HELMET!
I'M BETTING THE HULK'S SKIN IS TOUGH ENOUGH TO WITHSTAND THE COLD OF SPACE.
WAIT, HULK! LET ME TURN ON YOUR INTER-COMMUNICATOR!
HULK SAID, HULK IS NOT AFRAID OF SPACE!
THAT'S GOOD, GREEN-GUY--'CAUSE INTO SPACE IS WHERE WE'RE GOING, TO KAYO THOSE KILLER CLOWNS!
...AND NOW, IN CENTER RING, ROCKET RACCOON...

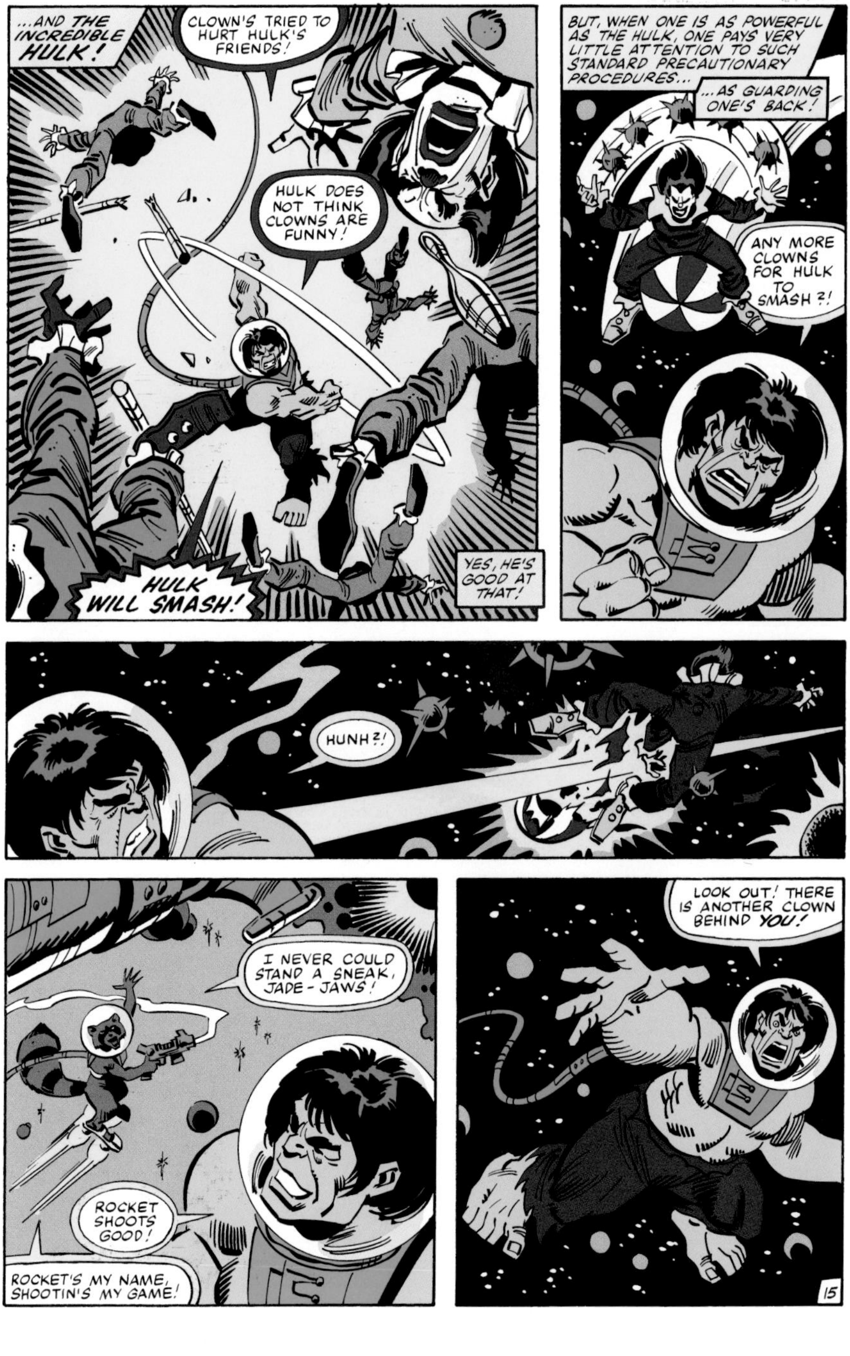
...AND THE INCREDIBLE HULK!
CLOWN'S TRIED TO HURT HULK'S FRIENDS!
HULK DOES NOT THINK CLOWNS ARE FUNNY!
HULK WILL SMASH!
YES, HE'S GOOD AT THAT!
BUT, WHEN ONE IS AS POWERFUL AS THE HULK, ONE PAYS VERY LITTLE ATTENTION TO SUCH STANDARD PRECAUTIONARY PROCEDURES...
...AS GUARDING ONE'S BACK!
ANY MORE CLOWNS FOR HULK TO SMASH ?!
HUNH ?!
I NEVER COULD STAND A SNEAK, JADE-JAWS!
ROCKET SHOOTS GOOD!
ROCKET'S MY NAME, SHOOTIN'S MY GAME!
LOOK OUT! THERE IS ANOTHER CLOWN BEHIND YOU!
15

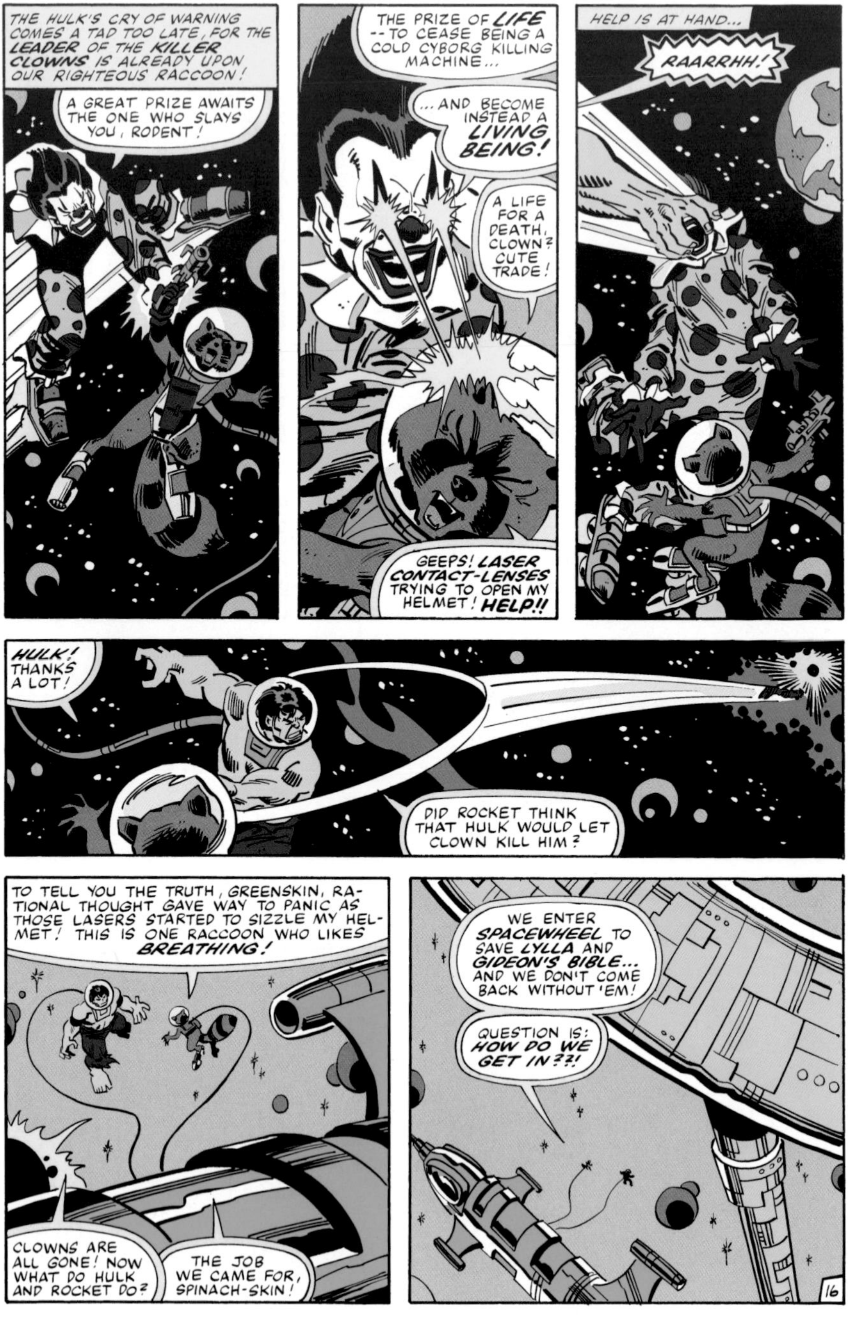
THE HULK'S CRY OF WARNING COMES A TAD TOO LATE, FOR THE LEADER OF THE KILLER CLOWNS IS ALREADY UPON OUR RIGHTEOUS RACCOON!
A GREAT PRIZE AWAITS THE ONE WHO SLAYS YOU, RODENT!
THE PRIZE OF LIFE --TO CEASE BEING A COLD CYBORG KILLING MACHINE...
...AND BECOME INSTEAD A LIVING BEING!
A LIFE FOR A DEATH, CLOWN? CUTE TRADE!
GEEPS! LASER CONTACT-LENSES TRYING TO OPEN MY HELMET! HELP!!
HELP IS AT HAND...
RAARRHH!
HULK! THANKS A LOT!
DID ROCKET THINK THAT HULK WOULD LET CLOWN KILL HIM?
TO TELL YOU THE TRUTH, GREENSKIN, RATIONAL THOUGHT GAVE WAY TO PANIC AS THOSE LASERS STARTED TO SIZZLE MY HELMET! THIS IS ONE RACCOON WHO LIKES BREATHING!
CLOWNS ARE ALL GONE! NOW WHAT DO HULK AND ROCKET DO?
THE JOB WE CAME FOR, SPINACH-SKIN!
WE ENTER SPACEWHEEL TO SAVE LYLLA AND GIDEON'S BIBLE... AND WE DON'T COME BACK WITHOUT 'EM!
QUESTION IS: HOW DO WE GET IN??!
16

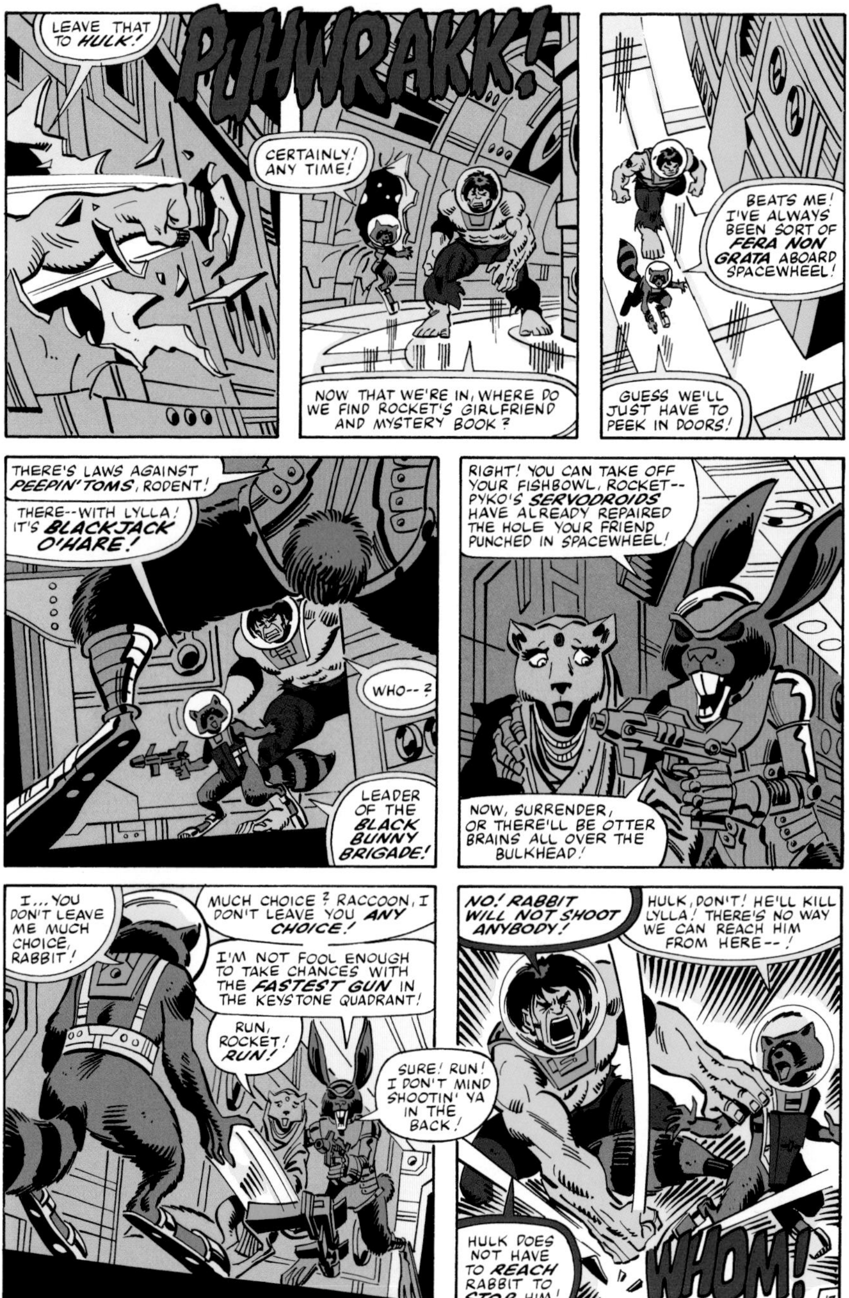

LEAVE THAT TO HULK!
PUHWRAKK!
CERTAINLY! ANY TIME!
NOW THAT WE'RE IN, WHERE DO WE FIND ROCKET'S GIRLFRIEND AND MYSTERY BOOK?
BEATS ME! I'VE ALWAYS BEEN SORT OF FERA NON GRATA ABOARD SPACEWHEEL!
GUESS WE'LL JUST HAVE TO PEEK IN DOORS!
THERE'S LAWS AGAINST PEEPIN' TOMS, RODENT!
THERE--WITH LYLLA! IT'S BLACKJACK O'HARE!
WHO--?
LEADER OF THE BLACK BUNNY BRIGADE!
RIGHT! YOU CAN TAKE OFF YOUR FISHBOWL, ROCKET-- PYKO'S SERVODROIDS HAVE ALREADY REPAIRED THE HOLE YOUR FRIEND PUNCHED IN SPACEWHEEL!
NOW, SURRENDER, OR THERE'LL BE OTTER BRAINS ALL OVER THE BULKHEAD!
I... YOU DON'T LEAVE ME MUCH CHOICE, RABBIT!
MUCH CHOICE? RACCOON, I DON'T LEAVE YOU ANY CHOICE!
I'M NOT FOOL ENOUGH TO TAKE CHANCES WITH THE FASTEST GUN IN THE KEYSTONE QUADRANT!
RUN, ROCKET! RUN!
SURE! RUN! I DON'T MIND SHOOTIN' YA IN THE BACK!
NO! RABBIT WILL NOT SHOOT ANYBODY!
HULK, DON'T! HE'LL KILL LYLLA! THERE'S NO WAY WE CAN REACH HIM FROM HERE--!
HULK DOES NOT HAVE TO REACH RABBIT TO STOP HIM!
WHOM!

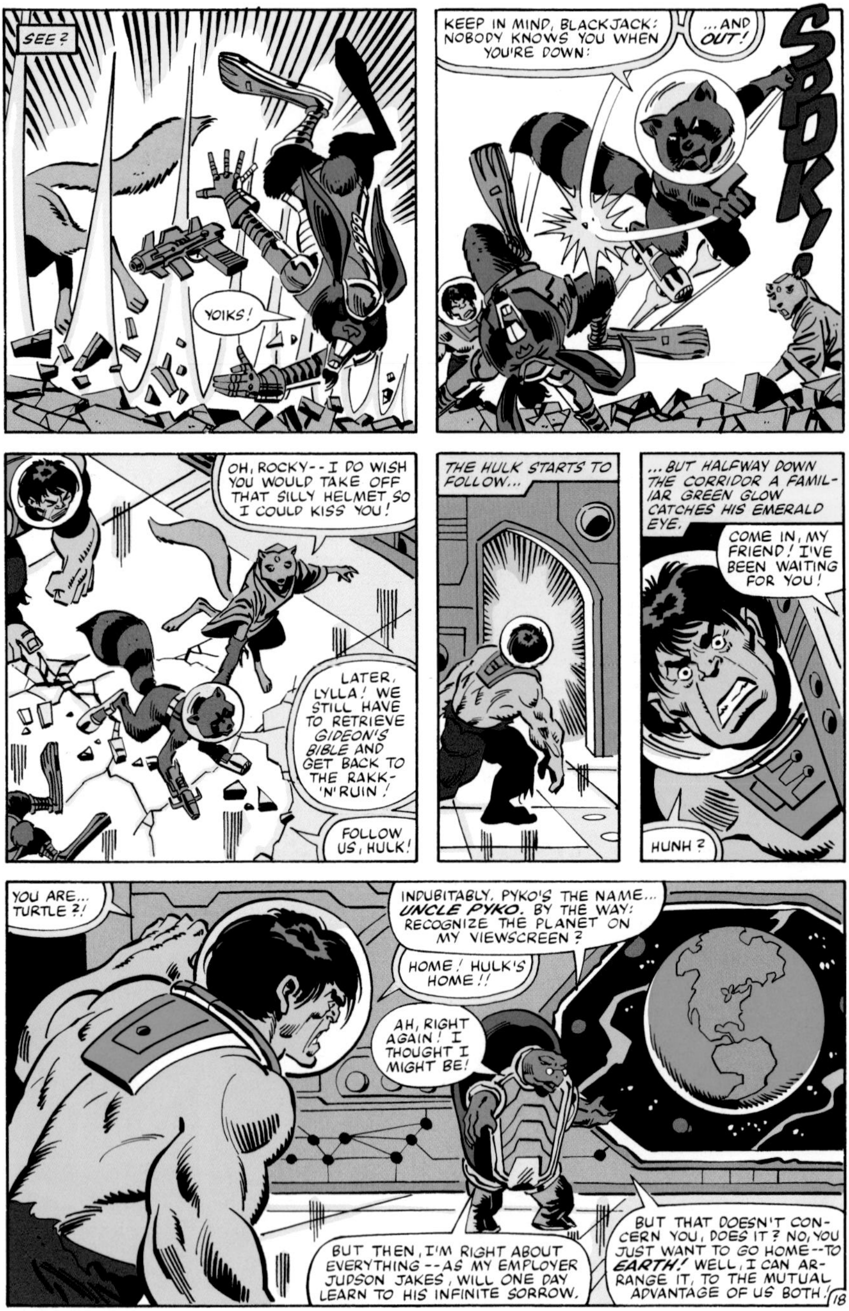
SEE?
YOIKS!
KEEP IN MIND, BLACKJACK: NOBODY KNOWS YOU WHEN YOU'RE DOWN:
...AND OUT!
SPOK!
OH, ROCKY--I DO WISH YOU WOULD TAKE OFF THAT SILLY HELMET SO I COULD KISS YOU!
LATER, LYLLA! WE STILL HAVE TO RETRIEVE GIDEON'S BIBLE AND GET BACK TO THE RAKK-'N'RUIN!
FOLLOW US, HULK!
THE HULK STARTS TO FOLLOW...
...BUT HALFWAY DOWN THE CORRIDOR A FAMILIAR GREEN GLOW CATCHES HIS EMERALD EYE.
COME IN, MY FRIEND! I'VE BEEN WAITING FOR YOU!
HUNH?
YOU ARE... TURTLE?!
INDUBITABLY. PYKO'S THE NAME... UNCLE PYKO. BY THE WAY: RECOGNIZE THE PLANET ON MY VIEWSCREEN?
HOME! HULK'S HOME!!
AH, RIGHT AGAIN! I THOUGHT I MIGHT BE!
BUT THEN, I'M RIGHT ABOUT EVERYTHING--AS MY EMPLOYER JUDSON JAKES, WILL ONE DAY LEARN TO HIS INFINITE SORROW.
BUT THAT DOESN'T CONCERN YOU, DOES IT? NO, YOU JUST WANT TO GO HOME--TO EARTH! WELL, I CAN ARRANGE IT, TO THE MUTUAL ADVANTAGE OF US BOTH!
18

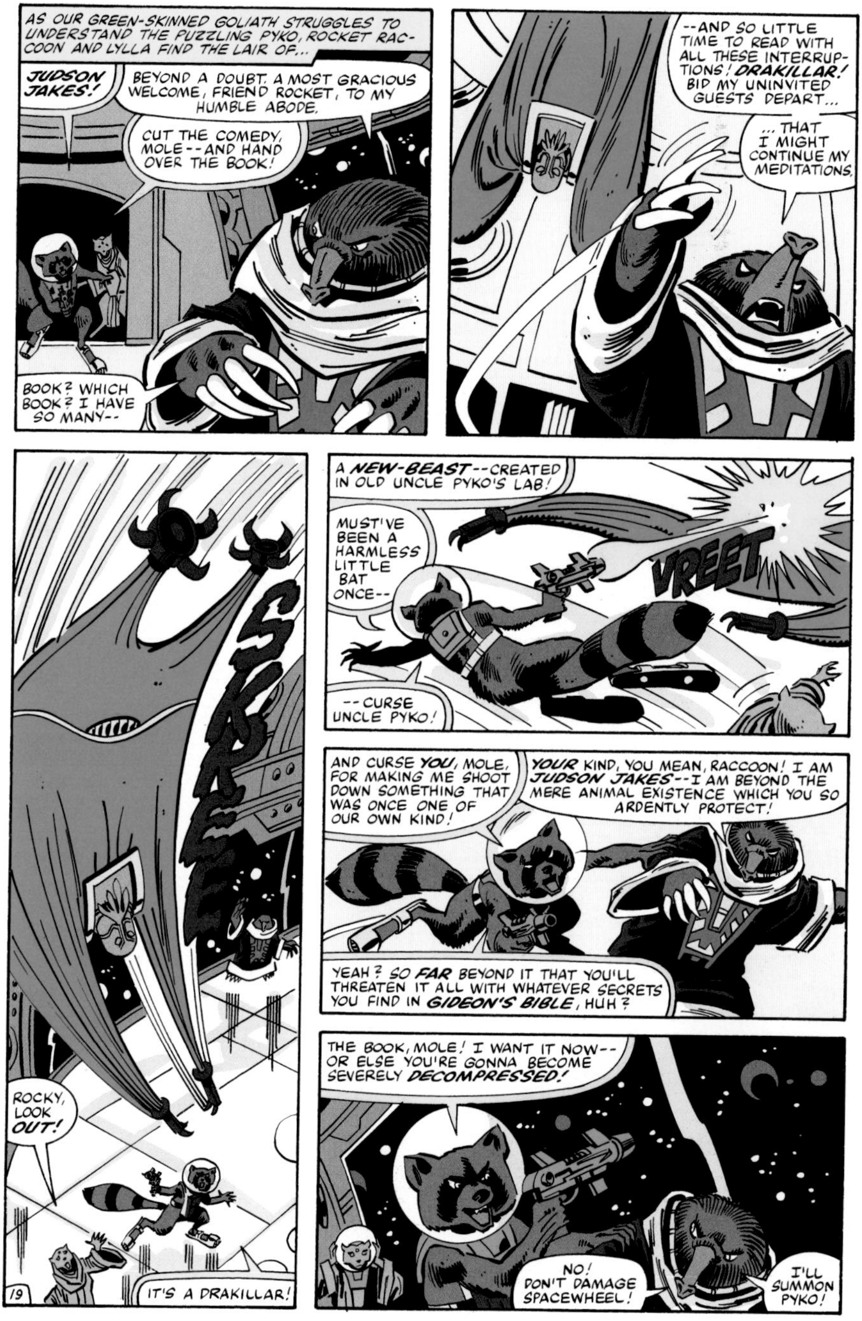
AS OUR GREEN-SKINNED GOLIATH STRUGGLES TO UNDERSTAND THE PUZZLING PYKO, ROCKET RACCOON AND LYLLA FIND THE LAIR OF...
JUDSON JAKES!
BEYOND A DOUBT. A MOST GRACIOUS WELCOME, FRIEND ROCKET, TO MY HUMBLE ABODE.
CUT THE COMEDY, MOLE--AND HAND OVER THE BOOK!
BOOK? WHICH BOOK? I HAVE SO MANY--
--AND SO LITTLE TIME TO READ WITH ALL THESE INTERRUPTIONS! DRAKILLAR! BID MY UNINVITED GUESTS DEPART...
...THAT I MIGHT CONTINUE MY MEDITATIONS.
SKREEE
ROCKY, LOOK OUT!
IT'S A DRAKILLAR!
A NEW-BEAST--CREATED IN OLD UNCLE PYKO'S LAB!
MUST'VE BEEN A HARMLESS LITTLE BAT ONCE--
VREET
--CURSE UNCLE PYKO!
AND CURSE YOU, MOLE, FOR MAKING ME SHOOT DOWN SOMETHING THAT WAS ONCE ONE OF OUR OWN KIND!
YOUR KIND, YOU MEAN, RACCOON! I AM JUDSON JAKES--I AM BEYOND THE MERE ANIMAL EXISTENCE WHICH YOU SO ARDENTLY PROTECT!
YEAH? SO FAR BEYOND IT THAT YOU'LL THREATEN IT ALL WITH WHATEVER SECRETS YOU FIND IN GIDEON'S BIBLE, HUH?
THE BOOK, MOLE! I WANT IT NOW--OR ELSE YOU'RE GONNA BECOME SEVERELY DECOMPRESSED!
NO! DON'T DAMAGE SPACEWHEEL!
I'LL SUMMON PYKO!

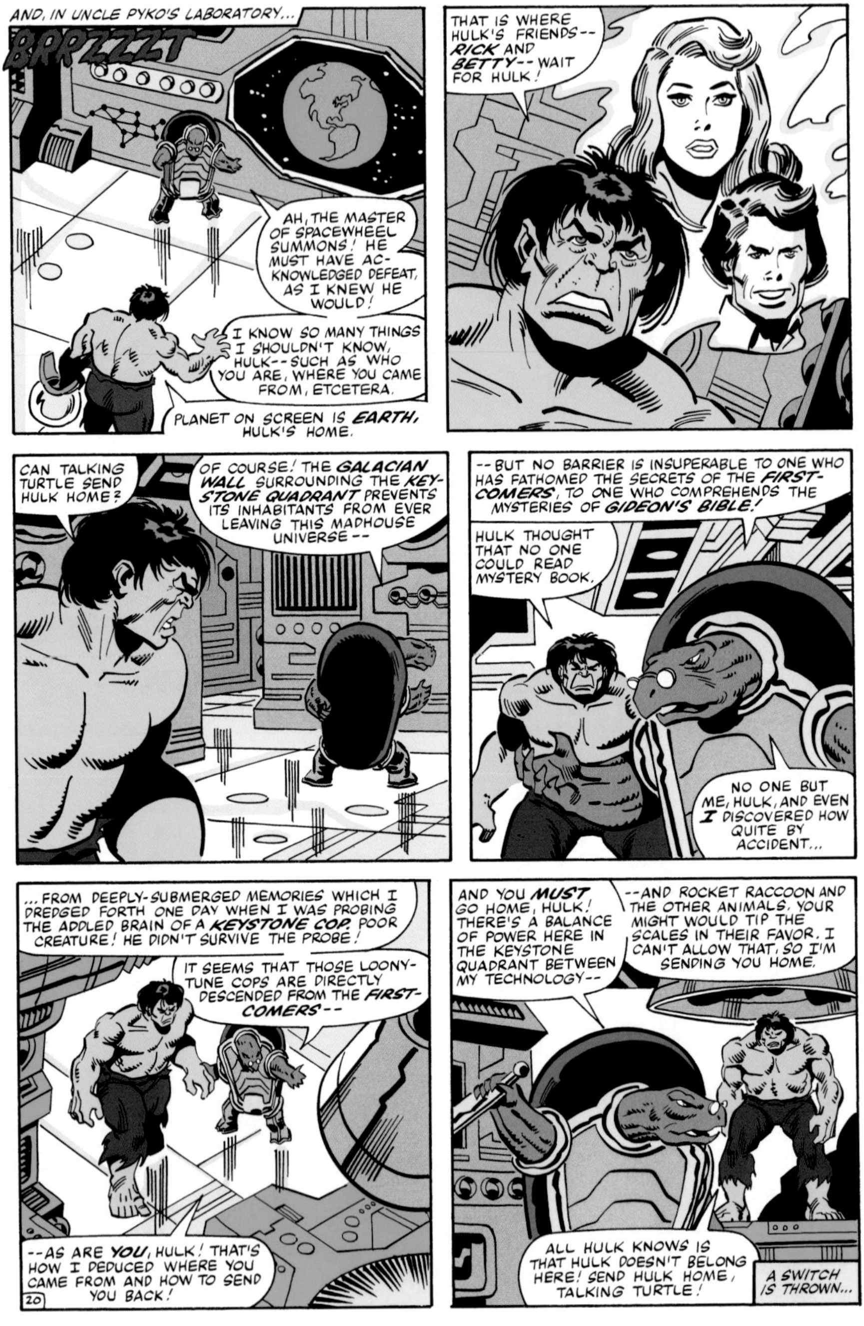
AND, IN UNCLE PYKO'S LABORATORY...
BRRZZZT
AH, THE MASTER OF SPACEWHEEL SUMMONS! HE MUST HAVE ACKNOWLEDGED DEFEAT, AS I KNEW HE WOULD!
I KNOW SO MANY THINGS I SHOULDN'T KNOW, HULK--SUCH AS WHO YOU ARE, WHERE YOU CAME FROM, ETCETERA.
PLANET ON SCREEN IS EARTH, HULK'S HOME.
THAT IS WHERE HULK'S FRIENDS--RICK AND BETTY--WAIT FOR HULK!
CAN TALKING TURTLE SEND HULK HOME?
OF COURSE! THE GALACIAN WALL SURROUNDING THE KEYSTONE QUADRANT PREVENTS ITS INHABITANTS FROM EVER LEAVING THIS MADHOUSE UNIVERSE--
--BUT NO BARRIER IS INSUPERABLE TO ONE WHO HAS FATHOMED THE SECRETS OF THE FIRST-COMERS, TO ONE WHO COMPREHENDS THE MYSTERIES OF GIDEON'S BIBLE!
HULK THOUGHT THAT NO ONE COULD READ MYSTERY BOOK.
NO ONE BUT ME, HULK, AND EVEN I DISCOVERED HOW QUITE BY ACCIDENT...
...FROM DEEPLY-SUBMERGED MEMORIES WHICH I DREDGED FORTH ONE DAY WHEN I WAS PROBING THE ADDLED BRAIN OF A KEYSTONE COP. POOR CREATURE! HE DIDN'T SURVIVE THE PROBE!
IT SEEMS THAT THOSE LOONY-TUNE COPS ARE DIRECTLY DESCENDED FROM THE FIRST-COMERS--
--AS ARE YOU, HULK! THAT'S HOW I DEDUCED WHERE YOU CAME FROM AND HOW TO SEND YOU BACK!
AND YOU MUST GO HOME, HULK! THERE'S A BALANCE OF POWER HERE IN THE KEYSTONE QUADRANT BETWEEN MY TECHNOLOGY--
--AND ROCKET RACCOON AND THE OTHER ANIMALS. YOUR MIGHT WOULD TIP THE SCALES IN THEIR FAVOR. I CAN'T ALLOW THAT, SO I'M SENDING YOU HOME.
ALL HULK KNOWS IS THAT HULK DOESN'T BELONG HERE! SEND HULK HOME, TALKING TURTLE!
A SWITCH IS THROWN...

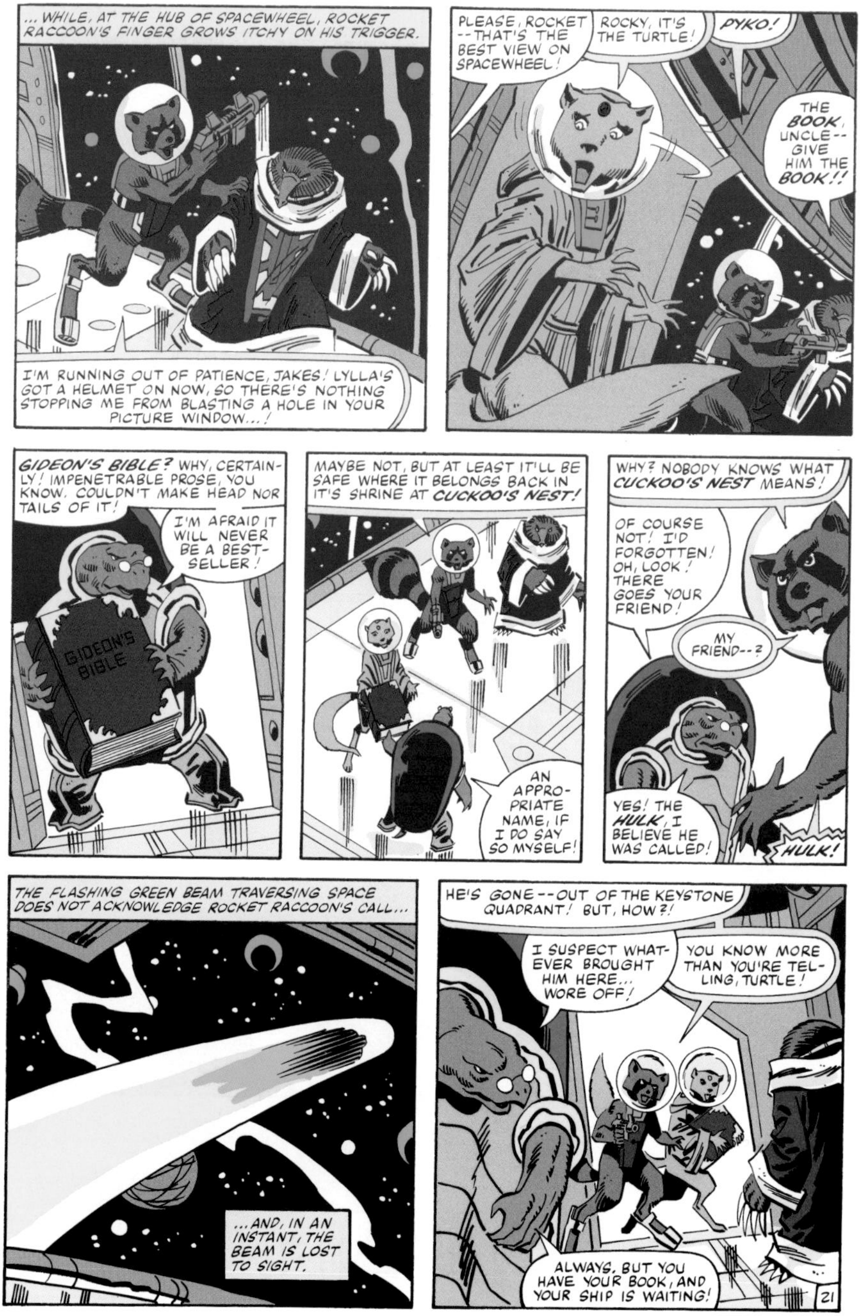

...WHILE, AT THE HUB OF SPACEWHEEL, ROCKET RACCOON'S FINGER GROWS ITCHY ON HIS TRIGGER.
I'M RUNNING OUT OF PATIENCE, JAKES! LYLLA'S GOT A HELMET ON NOW, SO THERE'S NOTHING STOPPING ME FROM BLASTING A HOLE IN YOUR PICTURE WINDOW...!
PLEASE, ROCKET --THAT'S THE BEST VIEW ON SPACEWHEEL!
ROCKY, IT'S THE TURTLE!
PYKO!
THE BOOK, UNCLE-- GIVE HIM THE BOOK!!
GIDEON'S BIBLE? WHY, CERTAINLY! IMPENETRABLE PROSE, YOU KNOW. COULDN'T MAKE HEAD NOR TAILS OF IT!
I'M AFRAID IT WILL NEVER BE A BEST-SELLER!
GIDEON'S BIBLE
MAYBE NOT, BUT AT LEAST IT'LL BE SAFE WHERE IT BELONGS BACK IN IT'S SHRINE AT CUCKOO'S NEST!
AN APPROPRIATE NAME, IF I DO SAY SO MYSELF!
WHY? NOBODY KNOWS WHAT CUCKOO'S NEST MEANS!
OF COURSE NOT! I'D FORGOTTEN! OH, LOOK! THERE GOES YOUR FRIEND!
MY FRIEND--?
YES! THE HULK, I BELIEVE HE WAS CALLED!
HULK!
THE FLASHING GREEN BEAM TRAVERSING SPACE DOES NOT ACKNOWLEDGE ROCKET RACCOON'S CALL...
...AND, IN AN INSTANT, THE BEAM IS LOST TO SIGHT.
HE'S GONE--OUT OF THE KEYSTONE QUADRANT! BUT, HOW?!
I SUSPECT WHATEVER BROUGHT HIM HERE... WORE OFF!
YOU KNOW MORE THAN YOU'RE TELLING, TURTLE!
ALWAYS, BUT YOU HAVE YOUR BOOK, AND YOUR SHIP IS WAITING!
21

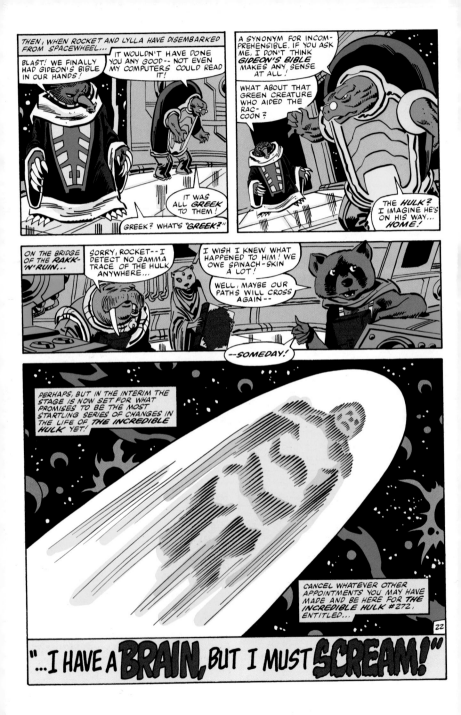

THEN, WHEN ROCKET AND LYLLA HAVE DISEMBARKED FROM SPACEWHEEL...

BLAST! WE FINALLY HAD GIDEON'S BIBLE IN OUR HANDS!

IT WOULDN'T HAVE DONE YOU ANY GOOD-- NOT EVEN MY COMPUTERS COULD READ IT!

IT WAS ALL *GREEK* TO THEM!

GREEK? WHAT'S *"GREEK?"*

A SYNONYM FOR INCOMPREHENSIBLE. IF YOU ASK ME, I DON'T THINK *GIDEON'S BIBLE* MAKES ANY SENSE AT ALL!

WHAT ABOUT THAT GREEN CREATURE WHO AIDED THE RACCOON?

THE *HULK?* I IMAGINE HE'S ON HIS WAY... *HOME!*

ON THE BRIDGE OF THE *RAKK-'N'RUIN...*

SORRY, ROCKET-- I DETECT NO GAMMA TRACE OF THE HULK ANYWHERE...

I WISH I KNEW WHAT HAPPENED TO HIM! WE OWE SPINACH-SKIN A LOT!

WELL, MAYBE OUR PATHS WILL CROSS AGAIN--

--SOMEDAY!

PERHAPS, BUT IN THE INTERIM THE STAGE IS NOW SET FOR WHAT PROMISES TO BE THE MOST STARTLING SERIES OF CHANGES IN THE LIFE OF *THE INCREDIBLE HULK* YET!

CANCEL WHATEVER OTHER APPOINTMENTS YOU MAY HAVE MADE AND BE HERE FOR *THE INCREDIBLE HULK #272,* ENTITLED...

22

"...I HAVE A **BRAIN,** BUT I MUST **SCREAM!**"

GUARDIANS OF THE GALAXY

BONUS PINUPS

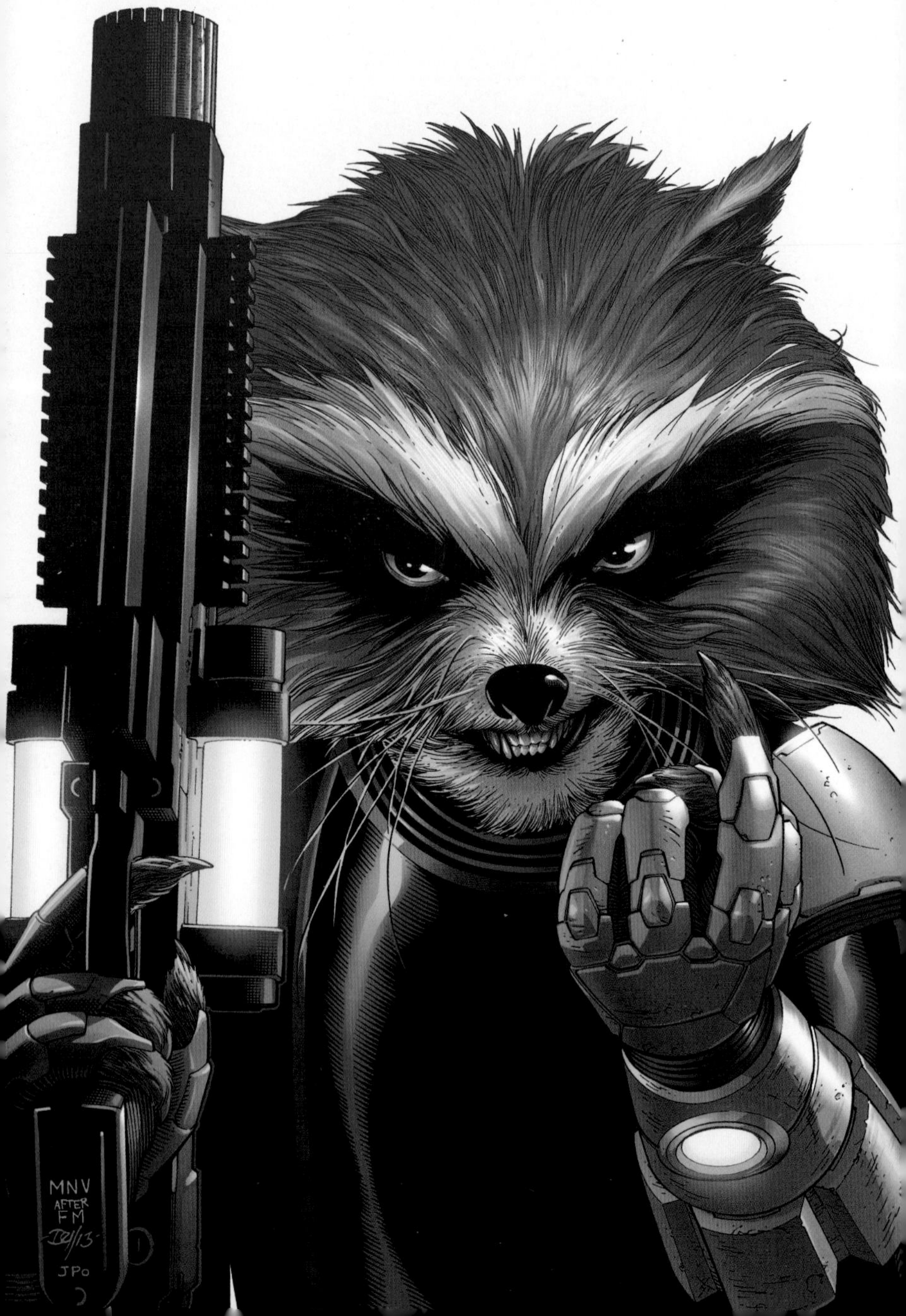
MNV
AFTER
FM
JPo

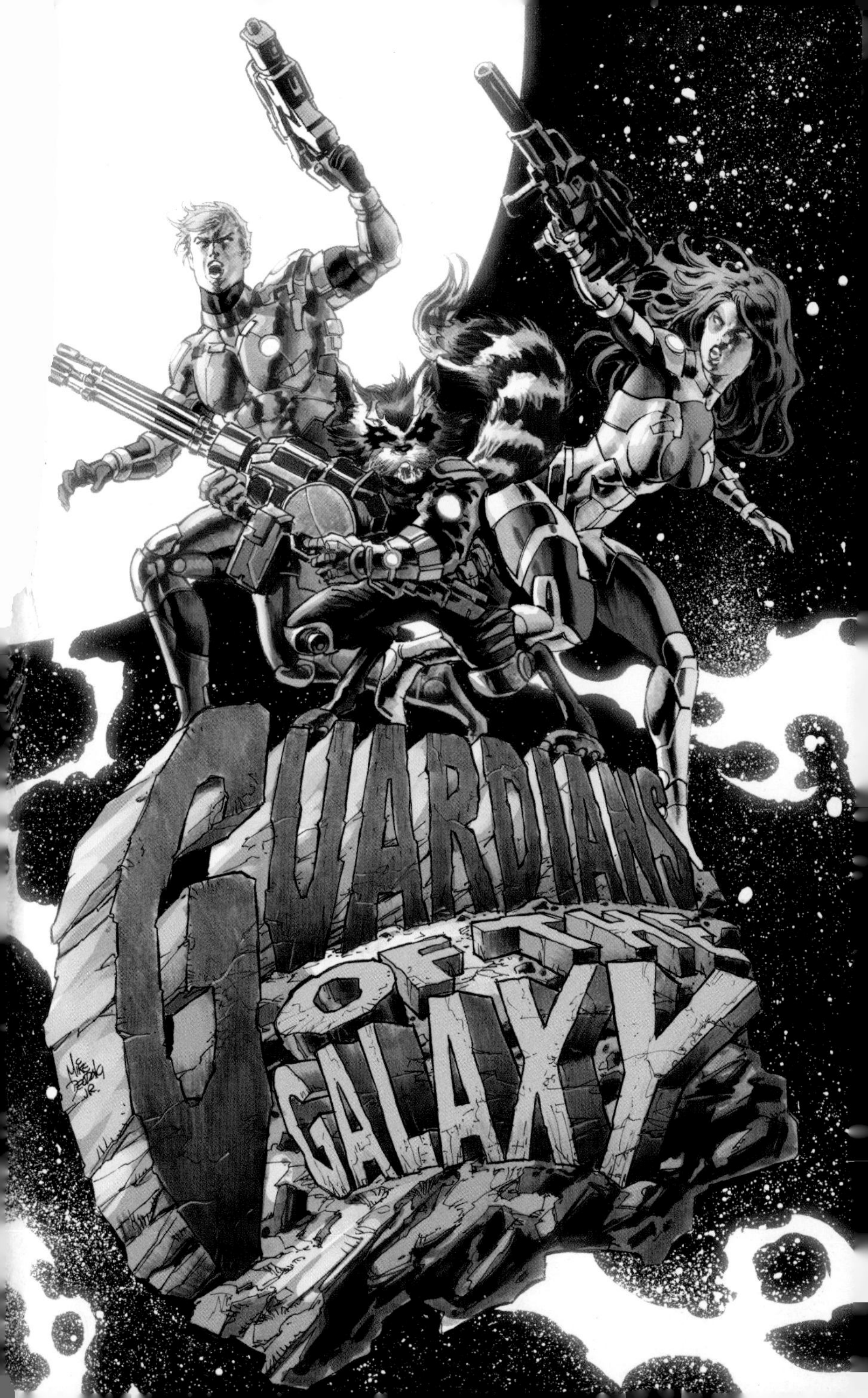
GUARDIANS
OF THE
GALAXY

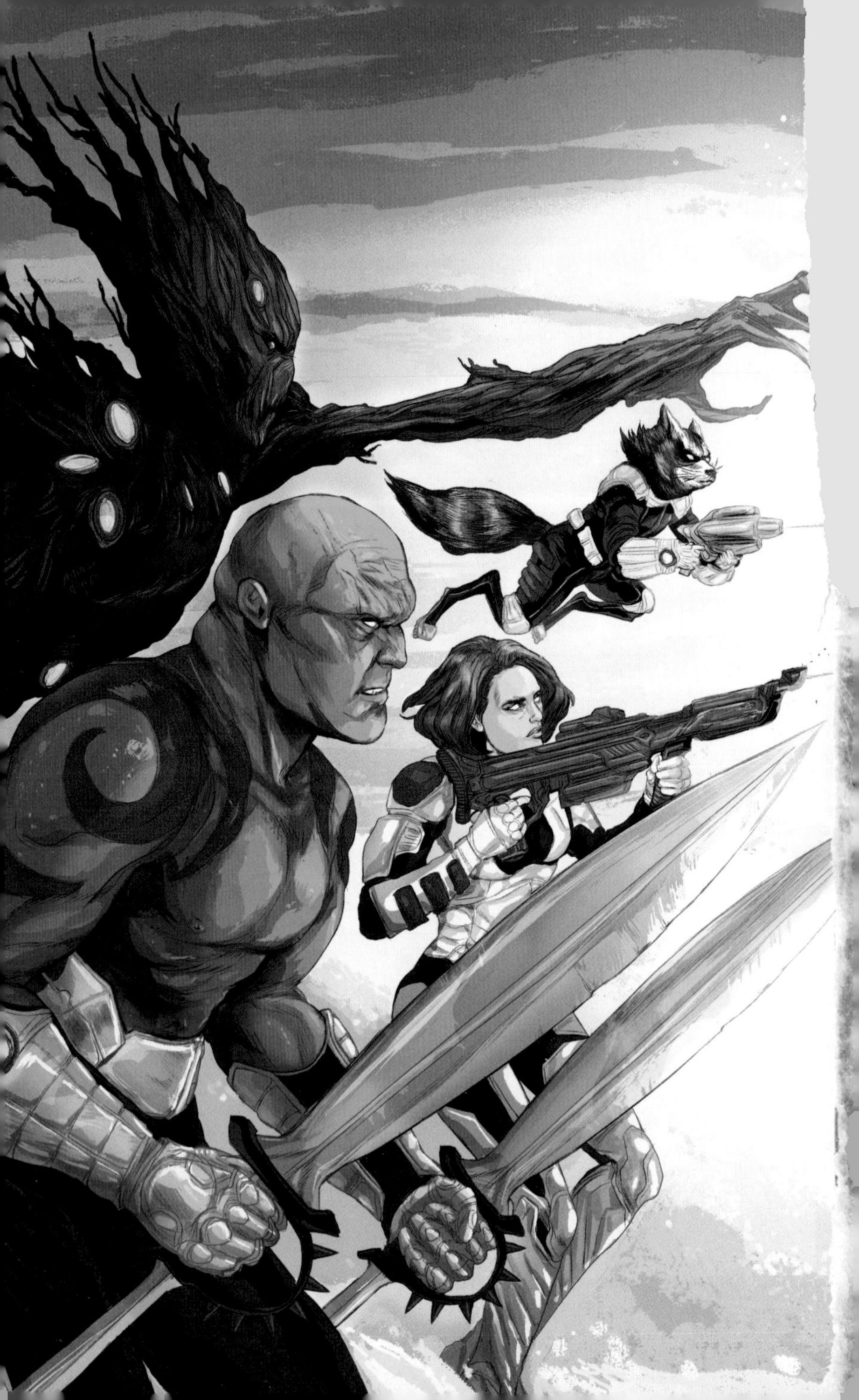